Does Company Ownership Matter?

Cournot Centre for Economic Studies

Series Editor: Robert M. Solow, *Emeritus Professor of Economics, Massachusetts Institute of Technology; President of the Cournot Centre for Economic Studies, Paris, France*

Conference Editor: Jean-Philippe Touffut, *Director of the Cournot Centre for Economic Studies, Paris, France*

Does Company Ownership Matter?

Edited by

Jean-Philippe Touffut

Director of the Cournot Centre for Economic Studies, Paris, France

THE COURNOT CENTRE FOR ECONOMIC STUDIES SERIES

Edward Elgar

Cheltenham, UK • Northampton, MA, USA

Published by
Edward Elgar Publishing Limited
The Lypiatts
15 Lansdown Road
Cheltenham
Glos GL50 2JA
UK

Edward Elgar Publishing, Inc.
William Pratt House
9 Dewey Court
Northampton
Massachusetts 01060
USA

A catalogue record for this book
is available from the British Library

Library of Congress Control Number: 2009936235

Mixed Sources
Product group from well-managed
forests and other controlled sources
www.fsc.org Cert no. SA-COC-1565
© 1996 Forest Stewardship Council

ISBN 978 1 84844 796 7 (cased)
ISBN 978 1 84844 797 4 (paperback)

Printed and bound by MPG Books Group, UK

Contents

Figures and tables

FIGURES

TABLES

Contributors

Jean-Louis Beffa is Chairman of the Board of Directors of Compagnie de Saint-Gobain and Co-President of the Cournot Centre for Economic Studies.

Margaret Blair is Professor of Law at Vanderbilt University Law School in Nashville, Tennessee. Her latest research focuses on team production and the legal structure of business organizations, legal issues in the governance of supply chains, and the role of private sector governance arrangements in contract enforcement.

Wendy Carlin is Professor of Economics at University College London and a Research Fellow at the Centre for Economic Policy Research (CEPR). Her research focuses on transition economies, macroeconomics and institutions.

Christophe Clerc is a Partner at Marccus Partners in Paris, France. He practises corporate and securities law for major international groups, with a focus on cross-border mergers and acquisitions, capital markets and corporate governance issues. He also teaches corporate governance at the Institut d'Études Politiques de Paris.

Simon Deakin is Professor of Law at the University of Cambridge, a Programme Director at the Cambridge Centre for Business Research (CBR) and an Associate Faculty Member of the Judge Business School. His research focuses on labour law, private law, company law, law and economics and EU law.

Jean-Paul Fitoussi is Professor of Economics at the Institut d'Études Politiques de Paris and President of the Scientific Council and of the Observatoire Français des Conjonctures Économiques (OFCE, the economic research centre of the Institut d'Études Politiques). He is General Secretary of the International Economic Association and serves as an expert at the European Parliament, Commission of Monetary and Economic Affairs. His main research interests include theories of inflation, unemployment, foreign trade and the role of macroeconomic policies.

Donatella Gatti is Professor of Economics at the University of Paris XIII and Director of the CEPN (Centre d'Économie de l'Université Paris Nord). Her research interests are institutional and labour economics and structural reforms and policies within European Monetary Union.

Gregory Jackson is Professor of Business and Society at the University of Bath. His research focuses on cross-national comparisons of corporate governance, particularly in Germany, Japan, the UK and the USA.

Xavier Ragot is a CNRS Researcher in Economics. His main research interests include monetary economics, incomplete markets, theory and computation of equilibria and macroeconomics.

Antoine Rebérioux is Associate Professor of Economics at the University of Paris X–Nanterre and a Researcher at the EconomiX research unit (University of Paris X–CNRS). His main research fields are corporate governance, theory of the firm and human resource management.

Lorenzo Sacconi is Professor of Economics at the University of Trento and Director of EconomEtica, an inter-university centre of research at the Milano Bicocca University. His research focuses on the foundations and application of game theory, the economic theory of institutions, contracts and the firm, as well as ethics and economics.

Robert M. Solow is Institute Professor Emeritus at the Massachusetts Institute of Technology. In 1987, he was awarded the Nobel Memorial Prize in Economics for his contributions to economic growth theory. He is a Visiting Scholar at the Russell Sage Foundation, New York, where he is a member of the advisory committee for the Foundation's project on the incidence and quality of low-wage employment in Europe and the United States. Professor Solow is President of the Cournot Centre for Economic Studies.

Jean-Philippe Touffut is Co-Founder and Director of the Cournot Centre for Economic Studies.

Preface

This volume is one of a series arising from the conferences organized by the Cournot Centre for Economic Studies, Paris. These conferences explore contemporary issues in economics, with particular focus on Europe. Speakers, along with other participants and members of the audience, are drawn from backgrounds in academia, business, finance, labour unions, the media and national or multinational governmental and non-governmental agencies.

The contributions of this book originated from the tenth conference of the Cournot Centre for Economic Studies held on 29 and 30 November 2007.

Acknowledgements

I would like to thank all the participants of the Cournot Centre conference on company ownership for their contribution to this volume, and, in particular, Robert Solow for his continued support and guidance of the Centre and its activities.

My heartfelt thanks go to Therrese Goodlett and Anna Kaiser. From the organization of the conference to the preparation of the manuscript, they have enabled this work to see the light of day under the best possible conditions. A very special thanks also goes to Richard Crabtree for translations and transcription work. A film of the whole conference is available on the Cournot Centre's website: www.centrecournot.org.

About the series

Professor Robert M. Solow

The Cournot Centre for Economic Studies is an independent, French-based research institute. It takes its name from the pioneering economist, mathematician and philosopher Antoine Augustin Cournot (1801–77).

Neither a think-tank nor a research bureau, the Centre enjoys the special independence of a catalyst. My old student dictionary (dated 1936) says that catalysis is the 'acceleration of a reaction produced by a substance, called the *catalyst*, which may be recovered practically unchanged at the end of the reaction'. The reaction we have in mind results from bringing together (a) an issue of economic policy that is currently being discussed and debated in Europe and (b) the relevant theoretical and empirical findings of serious economic research in universities, think-tanks and research bureaux. Acceleration is desirable because it is better that reaction occurs before minds are made up and decisions taken, not after. We hope that the Cournot Centre can be recovered practically unchanged and used again and again.

Notice that 'policy debate' is not exactly what we are trying to promote. To have a policy debate, you need not only knowledge and understanding, but also preferences, desires, values and goals. The trouble is that, in practice, the debaters often have only those things, and they invent or adopt only those 'findings' that are convenient. The Cournot Centre hopes to inject the findings of serious research at an early stage.

It is important to realize that this is not easy or straightforward. The analytical issues that underlie economic policy choices are usually complex. Economics is not an experimental science. The available data are scarce, and may not be exactly the relevant ones. Interpretations are therefore uncertain. Different studies, by uncommitted economists, may give different results. When those controversies exist, it is our hope that the Centre's conferences will discuss them. Live debate at that fundamental level is exactly what we are after.

There is also a problem of timing. Conferences have to be planned well in advance, so that authors can prepare careful and up-to-date texts. Then a publication lag is inevitable. The implication is that the Cournot Centre's conferences cannot take up very short-term issues of policy. Instead, a balancing act is required: we need issues that are short-term enough so that they are directly concerned with current policy, but long-term enough so that they remain directly relevant for a few years.

I used the words 'serious research' a moment ago. That sort of phrase is sometimes used to exclude unwelcome ideas, especially unfashionable ones. The Cournot Centre does not intend to impose narrow requirements of orthodoxy, but it does hope to impose high standards of attention to logic and respect for facts. It is because those standards are not always observed in debates about policy that an institution like the Cournot Centre has a role to play.

OTHER BOOKS IN THE COURNOT CENTRE SERIES

Introduction

Jean-Philippe Touffut

Do modes of management depend on company ownership? Does macro-economic performance rely on shareholder value? The contributions collected in this book explore these question from economic, historical and legal perspectives. Property rights are considered by most economists to be as fundamental as the concepts of scarcity or rationality; however, the expression of property, as a social construct, differs so much from one legal structure to another that its utilitarian justification only has common meaning in political discourse.

The nature of ownership is revealed in decision-making processes, which bring to light the interests that are protected by property. *Les Lumières* established the idea that all men enjoy the same *right to ownership* – whether inherited or acquired – whereas social distinction is merited rather than inherited. It does not matter if systems of inheritance lead to wide variations in the substance of goods owned by different individuals within society: the right to ownership provides an indisputable foundation to the inequality of distribution. In itself ownership cannot concern one isolated individual. It involves at least two persons: the one who owns and the one who does not.

From the perspective of classic civil law – as opposed to common law used notably by the UK and the USA – property rights are characterized by the right to use the property, to appropriate the returns from it and to dispose of it. It is an absolute right, in the sense that it is enforceable against everyone and bounded solely by the principle of the breach of law. The right to ownership is imprescriptible, meaning that failure to use the property does not annul the ownership. There is no doubt then that the shareholders are not the owners of the company's assets; they have no direct rights over them. Only the company, as a legal entity, can use them, appropriate their returns and dispose of them, according to the decisions made by the managers.

Independent of the contingencies, ownership is expressed differently according to whether the non-owners use, manage or build upon it. This observation appears to be self-evident, but the distinction does not neces-sarily appear in the vocabulary. In English, for example, the *share*holders are contrasted with *stake*holders. French proposes another dichotomy, between the category of *ayants droits* (literally, 'those having rights') – the stakeholders, including employees, managers and shareholders – and the category of shareholders alone. Thus, the inequality of distribution counterbalances the equality of the contracting parties, which is expressed in both discourse and contracts.

In the case of the company, the discretionary power of the legal holders of the interests attached to shares is limited to buying, keeping or selling the shares. The managers' power is expressed in issuing and acquiring, using and deploying assets. The shareholders have no more than *pro forma* control over the managers. The formal possession of shares may or may not, therefore, enable the holder to participate in decision making. The legal approach has been poorly adapted by the standard economic analysis, which adopts the utilitarian vision of the firm: the social link in the firm, as elsewhere, is reduced to a game of economic interests. This book challenges this economic axiom. A priori, the shareholders have the simplest utility function: maximizing their returns on investment. Employees, on the other hand, are concerned with job security and working conditions. It is thus not as simple as one might think to establish shareholders' role in the firm. How do they behave in relation to the management, who make the essential decisions in the company (hiring, firing, layoffs, financing modes, production quotas, prices) without having the right to residual payments or a priori to the interest made on the total value of the company? How does the management ensure the legitimacy of their decisions vis-à-vis the shareholders?

The question of shareholder legitimacy finds different answers in different eras. Since the 1930s, economic theory has been developing the idea that the nature of private ownership varies according to the system in which it finds expression. Adolf Berle and Gardiner Means (1932) showed how the birth of the modern corporation was accompanied by a fundamental change in the nature and locus of private ownership. The centrifugal dispersion of ownership rights occurred at the same time as the centripetal concentration of their control.

Up until the end of the 1970s, the control of company ownership differed widely on either side of the Atlantic, but in both cases it was based on the organized weakness of market mechanisms, especially in the financial markets (Aglietta and Rebérioux, 2005). In the United States, 'managerial capitalism', as Berle and Means called it, was characterized by the separation between ownership and control, resulting from the dispersion of ownership and giving managers autonomy in their choices of strategy. The absence of control blocks combined with the fragmentation of financial institutions initiated before the war rendered managers relatively impervious to the desires of shareholders. The increase in the number of conglomerates was a symptom of this particular configuration. The level of dividends, moreover, remained low throughout the first three post-war decades.

In continental Europe, it was the narrowness of the financial markets that saved companies from stock market control. Ownership concentration and shareholder stability made managers unreceptive to the logic of the capital markets: profits were massively reinvested to the detriment of dividend distributions, and hostile takeovers were very rare. The highly institutionalized nature of labour-relation compromises (such as collective agreements in France or co-determination in Germany) also gave companies more independence from the financial markets. The prevailing form of control was therefore internal, and very few companies were listed on the stock exchange.

The process of liberalization and integration of capital markets that started in the 1980s was accompanied by rising interest rates and tighter monetary policy. Creating a more favourable situation for creditors (shareholders and lenders), institutional reforms began to accumulate, aiming to improve the negotiability of securities and facilitate the transfer of risk. The supply-side dynamics picked up speed in the 1990s, as did the demand for financial securities. It was in this context that the analysis of 'shareholder value' quickly became established, as the contributors to this volume each point out. The relationship between those who supply and control credit to the company – seeking to defend the return on their assets – and those who manage it has come to be perceived as the foundation of the company. At the beginning of the 2000s, it was believed that the absence of resistance to these transformations would bring about convergence towards one best structure of control – that of shareholder value. The main problem remained the homogeneity of shareholders. Should all shareholders be favoured equally, whoever they might be, or should minority shareholders be protected against those owning control blocks? What role should the stakeholders who are not shareholders play when they appear in the standard analysis as externalities?

Another approach, competing with that of shareholder value, focuses on the relationship between the company, its owners, its activities and the institutions that frame it, arguing that there are at least as many forms of ownership as there are activities. This approach studies the complementarities between institutions and analyses the co-evolution of specialization and forms of ownership. The first contribution, by Wendy Carlin (Chapter 1), presents a statistical and econometric test of the two theories of the company that have become firmly established in economics. She finds that the mode of control does, indeed, only have a second-order influence on economic performance. There was no convergence in ownership structures between 1995 and 2005; what was striking was the increasing divergence. Ownership structures in France, for example, continued to move further away from those of the Organization for Economic Cooperation and Development (OECD). There were a few convergences, notably related to bond appreciation in the Eurozone or the correlation between foreign shareholdings and greater financial transparency, but not in the raising of obstacles against takeover bids. The persistence of control blocks helped to maintain the variety in management structures and, in return, in forms of ownership. In any case, the macroeconomic situation dominated all these transformations.

In Chapter 2, Donatella Gatti extends Carlin's analysis by studying the macroeconomic impact of each corporate capital structure: how does a company's capital structure and forms of employment affect the economic performance of a country? Her analysis does not stop with the consequences of market deregulation, supposed to accelerate growth and sustain employment, because the capital structure of a given company is partly dependent on the structure of the markets (for labour and for goods and services), and vice versa. From this point of view, the regulation of markets and the structure of capital are interdependent institutional characteristics. The problem is then to determine the influence of these different factors on economic performance according to their interdependences and their development over time. It remains for us to understand the endogenous evolution of these institutional arrangements, which tends to be overlooked in the broad consensus about the decisive role of institutions in determining the relative economic performance of different countries.

In Chapter 3, Jean-Louis Beffa and Xavier Ragot study the different types of shareholders, with particular focus on company ownership in France. Their typology of shareholders in large companies confirms the interdependence between the factors responsible for changes in French shareholding: French regulations, the European framework, position in the division of labour, and national and international financial markets. The authors note that the shareholding structure can equally well contribute to improving the management of companies as it can hinder their medium-term development. Their analysis concludes with the presentation of measures that could favour the long-term development of companies. Whatever the economic climate, they show that state action can facilitate the emergence of strategies that are in line with the long-term interests of the company and its stakeholders.

Christophe Clerc challenges the question of the legal foundations of the shareholder. He opens Chapter 4 with the commonsensical statement that shareholders – as owners – have a legitimate say in the running of the company. This is a central argument used by its proponents to have shareholders' power in listed companies constantly increased. Clerc thus investigates the foundations of this 'shareholder primacy' movement. What gives the shareholder the right to occupy a pre-eminent position in the institutional architecture of the company? He shows that the theoretical foundations of shareholder primacy are shaky, and empirical proof of its benefits is inconclusive. How, then, can we find the appropriate means to safeguard the interests of the other stakeholders while protecting the company from the consequences of the moral hazard resulting from the non-liability of the shareholder?

In their comparative analysis of the British and French cases (Chapter 5), Simon Deakin and Antoine Rebérioux illustrate in their own way the arguments put forward in the preceding contributions. The convergence between the two systems is only partial, at least in terms of law and formal regulations. France has adopted a legal regime that is more favourable to shareholders over the last decade, and the structure of French shareholdings has been subject to the growing influence of foreign investors as stock market activity intensifies. Nevertheless, the dynamics of French shareholdings remain far removed from the British trajectory, sustained by dispersed shareholdings in a highly liquid stock market. The determining factor in these two countries is labour law. In the UK, labour legislation is weak, although it is moving closer to the continental European model as far as information and consultation rights are concerned. In France, labour legislation acts as a 'beneficial constraint' on company management, so that the dominant model is that of negotiated shareholder value, based on the sharing of the economic rent between shareholders and stable employees.

Taking the abstraction of labour relations in the company as his point of departure, in Chapter 6 Lorenzo Sacconi presents an original study of the coordination between the different stakeholders. The aim is to make a case for corporate social responsibility within the framework of game theory. His approach is based on a revision of the classic objective function of the firm in terms of profit maximization, to bring it into line with the social contract of the firm, in which managers and directors cannot dictate actions arbitrarily. His study leads him to a model of social responsibility that gives meaning to the institutional nature of the company, operating to the mutual advantage of its stakeholders.

The round table discussion (Chapter 7) that concludes this work brought together Robert Solow, Margaret Blair, Jean-Paul Fitoussi and Gregory Jackson to discuss the reasons for the changes that have affected listed companies. Around the table, theoretical hypotheses – largely advanced by the contributors of the conference and this volume – were put to the test of experience. In the case of shareholder primacy, for example, there is no proof that the intervention of shareholder activists creates any value for the shareholders themselves, let alone anything in the way of *social* value. The attempt to align the interests of directors and managers with those of the shareholders by means of a practice that is widespread in the United States and is beginning to spread abroad – consisting in paying managers stock options – does not appear to have prevented managerial delinquency. On the contrary, a mechanism has appeared by which managers appropriate a larger share of the rents and succeed in substantially increasing their total pay. A strongly supported argument in favour of shareholder primacy is that the share price constitutes a practical, constantly available instrument for evaluating the performance of the managerial team and beyond that, of the company itself. The statistical results, however, are univocal: increasing shareholder rights appears to have little, if any, positive impact on growth, markets – through mergers and acquisitions, for example – or employment.

REFERENCES

Aglietta, Michel and Antoine Rebérioux (2005), *Corporate Governance Adrift: A Critique of Shareholder Value*, Cheltenham, UK and Northampton, MA, USA: Edward Elgar.
Berle, Adolf and Gardiner Means (1932), *The Modern Corporation and Private Property*, New York: Macmillan.

1. Ownership, corporate governance, specialization and performance: interpreting recent evidence for OECD countries[1]

Wendy Carlin

INTRODUCTION

> Firms, and societies, organized along the standard shareholder-oriented model
> seem[ed] to be outcompeting those that were organized differently.
>
> (Hansmann, 2006, p. 747)

There has been a great deal of activity in introducing shareholder-oriented changes to corporate governance codes and regulation across OECD economies over the past two decades (Goergen et al., 2005; Enriques and Volpin, 2007). The surrounding debate has been based on the standard definition of corporate governance as the system by which companies are controlled in order that suppliers of finance can be assured of getting a return on their investments (see, for example, Shleifer and Vishny, 1997; see also Tirole, 2005, Chapter 1). The motivation for the reforms is nicely summarized in Henry Hansmann and Reinier Kraakman's well-known paper, 'The end of history for corporate law', published in 2001.[2] The first claim is that the ideological or normative battle is over and that there is near universal agreement across the world that the best form of organization for large firms is the standard shareholder-oriented model with earnings and control rights allocated using a single class of shares. The second claim is that this form of organization is the most efficient one, and the third is that practice and law are converging on this model. In short, it is claimed that publicly traded firms of the standard type will continue to be 'society's dominant producers of goods and services' (Hansmann, 2006, p. 750). Hansmann's position captures well one view about the role played by ownership in economic performance.

According to this view, access to finance is the major problem to be solved by the firm through a system of corporate governance, and ownership is of interest because of how it affects the financing problem and the governance solution. Corporate governance reforms therefore impinge on ownership structures, and if successful, produce improved economic performance. The implementation of similar corporate governance codes across countries would be expected to promote convergence in ownership structures, eliciting the greatest transformations and improving performance most in countries that were initially characterized by regimes furthest from the standard shareholder-oriented model of best practice.

An alternative view is that ownership structures are related to the different activities in which firms and economies specialize. If there is persistence in activities, then countries would be expected to display different ownership structures and the adoption of similar corporate governance codes and regulations would not produce convergence in ownership across countries. Rather, one would predict variation in responses across countries dependent on the specific role played by the ownership structure in that country's economic activities, which in an open economy would be related to trade specialization. In this alternative view, the corporate finance problem is not the only problem to be solved by the structure of ownership and control. The firm faces multiple incentive problems, only one of which is access to finance. Set in this broader context, ownership structures can play a role not only in relation to the problem of corporate finance, but also in relation to other problems that cannot be solved contractually. Accordingly, firms in different countries evolve and emerge in ways that are influenced not only by changes in regulation and the forces of global competition in product and capital markets, but also by the activities in which they specialize and their national institutional environment including labour market regulation and education and training institutions. The impact of moves towards more uniform corporate governance codes and regulation would therefore be expressed differently in different countries.

According to the first hypothesis, which I shall summarize as 'ownership is all about finance', the failure of ownership patterns to converge in the wake of the introduction of more uniform legal and corporate governance frameworks is a reflection of the power of vested interests, who are able to find ways of protecting themselves from the changes. Failure to adapt, or adaptation to evade the regulatory changes, is evidence of inefficiency. According to the second hypothesis, which I shall summarize as 'ownership is related to the activities of firms, which vary across countries', although failure to converge may indeed reflect inefficient resistance by incumbents, it may also reflect the persistence of activities and represent an efficient adaptation given the other institutional inputs to firms' activities.

The first objective of this chapter is to provide an explanation of the two hypotheses by reference to the relevant literature. Whereas the first hypothesis is extensively developed within the corporate finance and law literature, the second spills over traditional disciplinary boundaries. In the third section, an examination of existing studies shows that although direct tests are difficult to design, econometric analysis may nevertheless shed some light on the two hypotheses. The fourth section draws together recent descriptive evidence from a range of sources and perspectives on patterns of ownership in a number of advanced economies. The aim is to see whether convergence appears to be emerging as predicted by the first hypothesis or whether there are signs of persistent national differences consistent with the predictions of the second. The chapter ends by attempting to identify the key empirical questions on which future research should concentrate.

TWO HYPOTHESES ON CORPORATE GOVERNANCE REFORMS AND OWNERSHIP CONVERGENCE

A simplified version of Luigi Zingales's (2000) typology of models of the firm helps to pin down the origins of the two different views about the role that ownership structures play. The 'ownership is all about finance' view arises from the corporate finance literature based on the conception of the firm as a nexus of explicit contracts. In the first variant – associated with Alchian and Demsetz (1972) and Jensen and Meckling (1976) – contracts are complete, whereas in the second variant – associated with Grossman and Hart (1986) and Hart and Moore (1990) – they are incomplete. I shall briefly summarize the assumptions that are made in each variant that lead to the common implication that securing the rights of (minority) shareholders is the pre-eminent public policy objective.

Zingales pointed to an alternative model of the firm as a nexus of explicit and implicit contracts, where the corporate finance problem ceases to be pre-eminent. As a consequence, the implications for performance and for welfare of corporate governance reforms are different. A key issue that I shall highlight is that characteristics of ownership and governance that are welfare-diminishing from the shareholder supremacy perspective may be consistent with efficiency if the correct model is of a firm characterized by implicit as well as explicit contracts.

'Ownership is all about finance'

Hypothesis 1: Unless inefficient resistance intervenes, shareholder-oriented corporate governance reforms lead to convergence in ownership structures and improved performance.

In the 'nexus of explicit contracts' model of the firm, the firm is simply the sum of the individual contracts. Since all other parties are fully protected by explicit contracts, the only residual claimant is the equity holder. The consequences for corporate governance then follow directly: as the shareholders are the only ones to bear the cost of decisions, the firm should be managed to maximize shareholder value.

The property rights view focuses on the incompleteness of contracts in the firm. From this perspective, the firm is a collection of assets that are jointly owned. Contracts are necessarily incomplete and the problem that has to be solved in the firm is how to allocate the right to make decisions when circumstances arise that cannot be specified in the initial contract. The ability to withdraw assets is associated with the residual right of control. Zingales argued that although other interpretations were possible, the typical way this approach was used in the ownership and governance literature was to assume that because insiders can withdraw their assets, they have more bargaining power, and therefore outside (minority) investors must be protected if they are to provide financing to the firm. This leads to the definition of private benefits of control as the amount of the surplus generated by the firm that is appropriated by insiders (that is, those with control) in excess of what they are entitled to by virtue of their equity stake.

These two models of the firm produce the same implications in terms of shareholder orientation and have formed the basis for the 'efficiency' versus 'entrenchment' interpretation of ownership and governance patterns and the large amount of empirical work that has sought to test these effects (see, for example, Shleifer and Vishny, 1997, and Stulz, 2001). Attention has centred on two agency problems: the first is between owners and managers, and the second is between blockholders and minority owners. In the classic 'Berle and Means' firm, the problem is between the shareholders and the manager. The firm is fixed-asset intensive, vertically integrated, and management has strong control over employees who have limited bargaining power, because either they are unskilled or their skills are predominantly firm specific and easily replicated. External finance is therefore the core problem faced by the firm. To secure finance from outsiders, corporate law and its enforcement provide some protection for shareholders (as well as debt-holders), but the double-edged problem of incentivizing managers and preventing them from extracting private benefits remains.

As the collective action problem of dispersed shareholders is eased by more concentrated ownership so that blockholders have both the incentive and the means to implement their objectives, we move away from the Berle–Means norm. Although the centrality of raising external finance remains, the agency problem associated with this model shifts to that between blockholders and minority owners. Rather than entrenched managers being the problem, it is entrenched blockholders who are able to extract private benefits to the detriment of the minority shareholders. The usual interpretation of the presence of concentrated ownership in some countries – including both the smaller share of the business sector listed on public stock markets and the more concentrated ownership of those that are listed – is that national corporate law and governance institutions provide inadequate protection for minority shareholders. The extent of concentrated ownership is viewed as being higher than optimal (that is, for the purpose of ensuring adequate monitoring of managers).

John Coffee's work (2005, 2006) helped to show how these two agency problems were manifested in characteristic pathologies as exemplified by those of Enron in the USA in 2001 and Parmalat in Italy in 2004. Coffee (2005) showed that in each case, the nature of the fraud was intimately related to the structure of ownership and the associated agency problem, which in turn appeared to be related to the underlying national contracting institutions in place. In the case of Enron, the fraud centred on the incentives for managers to manipulate company earnings so as to influence the share price. Such incentives are strong in a dispersed ownership system, where high-powered incentive contracts for managers that link their compensation to the share price have become an important mechanism for aligning the interests of owners and managers. By contrast, in the blockholder ownership system, fraud, as in the case of Parmalat, took the form of appropriation of resources by the blockholder (sometimes referred to as 'tunnelling') and was reflected in the manipulation by the perpetrator of the balance sheet rather than of the earnings statement.

Irrespective of whether the agency conflict is between managers and dispersed shareholders or between blockholders and minority owners, the common characteristic is that the ownership relationship creates the corporate governance, and hence the external financing problem. Policy is therefore directed towards measures that will enhance the access of firms to external finance by improving corporate governance. Corporate governance reforms focus on measures to improve the functioning of boards of directors, the accountability of managers and boards to shareholders, the disclosure of financial and governance information and the transfer of control by reducing takeover defences, such as mechanisms that provide blockholders with control disproportionate to their equity stake. The thrust of this literature is that governance problems are easier to deal with when the ownership structure is dispersed. The reason is that when there are powerful blockholders, such as family owners, mechanisms to contain their power and allow efficient transfers of control are by definition limited

Table 1.1   Hypothesis 1. 'Ownership is all about finance': two variants

	Variant 1	Variant 2
Conception of the firm	A complete nexus of explicit contracts	A collection of assets that are jointly owned and incomplete contracts
Consequences for shareholders	They bear the cost of decisions. Hence firms should maximize shareholder value	Insiders have more bargaining power. Hence outsider (minority) investors should be protected
Common implication: shareholder orientation of governance		
Main agency problem	Between owners and managers	Between blockholders and minority owners
Pathology	Manipulation of earnings by managers ENRON	Appropriation of resources by the blockholders PARMALAT

(ibid.). Blockholders wield control legally whereas poorly monitored managers do not. This lies behind the body of corporate governance reform directed at lubricating control transfers and removing mechanisms that permit disproportionate ownership structures to persist. Hence the prediction from this literature is that successful corporate governance reform will lead to a convergence of ownership structures towards the dispersed ownership model (Table 1.1).

'Ownership is related to the activities of firms, which vary across countries'

Hypothesis 2: Shareholder-oriented corporate governance reforms lead to country-specific responses.

An alternative to the 'law and finance' approach to modelling the firm introduces implicit contracts and reputation. There is no canonical model in this tradition and both formal analysis and systematic empirical testing are less developed than is the case for the shareholder-oriented approaches. Important theoretical contributions include those of Franklin Allen and Douglas Gale (see, for example, 2000, Chapter 12) and Masahiko Aoki (see 1990, 2001). Referring to the model in George Baker et al. (2002), Zingales used the concept of organizational capital to capture the idea that the economic definition of the firm is not the same as the legal definition, which is at the core of the first hypothesis. The firm as a legal entity undertakes financing, whereas the firm as an economic entity comprises the set of relationships and assets including organizational capital that are affected by (and in turn, affect) financing decisions.

Zingales's motivation for opening up the debate about models of the firm stemmed not from a cross-country analysis, but from the fact that 'new economy' firms in the USA appeared to fit the shareholder-oriented paradigm poorly. His example of the advertising agency Saatchi and Saatchi emphasized the importance of human capital to the essence of the firm: a shareholder revolt against the chairman's proposal to award himself a generous compensation scheme resulted in the departure from the firm of the top talents including the chairman, and led to the decline of the firm. The key employees/managers took much of the original firm's business with them. More broadly, increased access to finance, new technology and new suppliers created new kinds of firms that were less physical-asset and more human-capital intensive, less vertically integrated and that operated in more competitive labour and product markets than was the case in the past. Zingales argued that these pressures changed the landscape of firms in the United States, introducing reputational factors and associated implicit contracts for an important tranche of firms engaged in activities that were very human-capital intensive. Although disproportionate ownership structures have long been prevalent for media firms in the USA (Coates, 2003, p.14), the emergence of new economy activities was the catalyst for seeking a model with normative predictions for ownership structures different from the traditional shareholder-oriented one.

The introduction of a third party, namely workers with human capital, into the core problem of the firm alongside shareholders and managers links the new economy firm, which stimulated Zingales to search for new foundations for corporate finance, with the relationship- or stakeholder-oriented firm characteristic of some continental European and East Asian economies.

In his recent textbook, *The Theory of Corporate Finance*, Jean Tirole (2005) has a discussion of 'shareholder value or stakeholder society?', in which he contrasts the debates about corporate governance framed in terms of the primacy of shareholder value with an alternative where firms take account of broader stakeholder interests. Tirole lists a number of objections to a 'stakeholder-society governance structure'. The first is that if control rights are given to stakeholders (that is, non-investors), then this may reduce the availability of external finance. The second is that if control is shared between stakeholders and investors, this may lead to inefficiencies in decision making, and the third is that giving the manager the objective of maximizing stakeholder value may be ill-defined and hard to verify.

Behind Tirole's account is the notion that the justification for including stakeholder objectives is the failure of the firm to internalize its external effects (for example, on employees or the local community if a plant is shut down). This leads directly to the remedies he suggests, which allow shareholder supremacy to be retained as the objective of the firm and for the externalities to be dealt with in other ways, such as through the contractual and legal apparatus. Olivier Blanchard and Jean Tirole (2004) provide illustrations of this approach to internalizing externalities from layoffs via the introduction of a layoff tax. The second approach is for policy to aim to make employees as insensitive as possible to 'biased decision-making' (p. 60) through, for example, raising the level of general training of workers and improving the flexibility of the labour market, thereby enhancing their exit option. But does the concept of externalities really capture what Zingales was looking for in his search for new foundations?

The hint from Zingales's example of Saatchi and Saatchi, that ownership structures may be related to the activities in which firms engage, can be illustrated in another context. Let us suppose that the activities in which firms specialize require transferable human capital, that is, skills that are valuable to some, but not all employers. To continue to thrive, such firms must solve difficult incentive problems, such as how the acquisition of such skills can be financed, how to retain these skilled workers given the incentives for other firms to poach them, and how to prevent them – once trained – from using their 'insider' bargaining power to extract resources from the firm. Can we follow Tirole's suggestion and consider these problems as an externality that could be solved either contractually (presumably if the stakeholders possessed some *ex ante* bargaining power) or by appropriate government policy (if their protection is viewed as being socially valuable)?

The externality interpretation does not seem appropriate since the specific incentive problems associated with skilled labour do not arise as an unintended byproduct of the firm's value maximization. Moreover if some activities require workers with industry- and firm-specific skills for whom there is inherently a thin outside labour market, encouraging general skills acquisition and a more flexible labour market will not provide a solution. An efficient method of solving the problem of production with heavy reliance on workers with transferable skills may entail non-standard ownership arrangements, such as constraints on the transfer of ownership in order to preserve the value of sunk investments in human capital. The firm is organized differently from the standard model because handling stakeholder interests is intrinsic to the firm's success.

This example introduces the possible complementarity between different institutions in the economy in relation to the activities pursued. As argued, for example, by Peter Hall and David Soskice (2001), there is clear differentiation in the clusters of institutions that are observed across advanced economies with access to the same global product and financial markets. The clusters relate to ownership structures, training and education institutions, the relationships between firms (for example, for the transfer of technology) and the regulation of labour, including unions and works councils. Their claim is that these clusters may be efficient because they allow the problems faced by firms involved in particular kinds of activities to be solved. Similar arguments about ownership structures and activities are made by Allen and Gale and by Aoki in the references cited above.

The above example can be extended to describe the cluster of institutions referred to as a 'coordinated market economy'. Blockholders play a role both in allowing long-run relationships between workers and the firm to be sustained and in facilitating the monitoring of performance within the firm. Neither worker nor manager performance in these activities is easily evaluated in external markets, and as noted above, external markets are thin. Technology and workers' skills are developed together within the firm or in related firms. Under such circumstances, skilled workers potentially have the power to hold up the firm (that is, extract rents), and from the perspective of workers, they need mechanisms to ensure that their investments in acquiring new competences will not be undermined by radical changes in asset use. Union wage agreements play a role in containing the power of skilled insiders, and works councils facilitate cooperation between employees and managers. Economies with this cluster of institutions have a comparative advantage in activities that require long-term cooperative relationships between firms and their suppliers and customers, and between managers and employees, in order to develop and improve internationally competitive products and deliver an adequate long-run return to the blockholders.

The other cluster that has been explored extensively in the 'varieties of capitalism' literature is associated with a so-called 'liberal market economy'. The liberal market economy is characterized by flexible labour markets without significant unions or employment protection legislation, by workers having general skills (or easily acquired firm-specific skills) and relatively short job tenure, and where they have access to a well-developed external labour market. In turn, managers have the incentive to take risks and be rewarded in the open managerial labour market. Information about workers, managers and companies is revealed in markets, and the possibility of being richly rewarded for taking risks that pay off encourages managers to engage in such activities (accounting also for the relatively small pool of successful CEOs, and hence the high individual rewards they receive). A diversified ownership structure facilitates managers' engagement in risky ventures. An active market for control allows potential owners, who believe they can achieve a higher expected return from using the assets in a different way, to gain control. Crucial to this synergy between institutions and activities is the authority of managers within the firm – to enter and leave markets, introduce and scrap products, acquire and sell off assets and subsidiaries. Economies with these structures, including diversified ownership, have a comparative advantage in high-risk activities.

Summing Up

We can now draw together the implications of the two hypotheses for thinking about corporate governance reforms, ownership and economic performance. From the perspective of the first hypothesis, the policy implications are clear. The objective is to improve corporate governance and encourage ownership structures that minimize the private benefits accruing either to managers or to blockholders. The policy implications of the second hypothesis are more complicated, because private benefits can be good as well as bad.[3] For economies where activities are captured by the 'liberal market economy' type, the second hypothesis emphasizes the positive role of manager autonomy, friendly boards and high manager compensation to encourage and reward risk-taking. Similarly, the second hypothesis allows blockholder structures to be efficient in coordinated market economies, which greatly complicates performance evaluation and policy advice. As suggested in Zingales's paper, for some activities, non-standard ownership structures may also be efficient in economies where listed companies have mainly been of the traditional shareholder-oriented type (Table 1.2). The impact of new technology and new forms of financing and organization afforded by globally integrated production arrangements has raised more questions about the simple relationship between governance reforms, ownership types and performance proposed by the first hypothesis. It has also highlighted the pitfalls of trying to classify countries into different types as proposed by the second.

WHAT DOES THE EXISTING EVIDENCE SAY ABOUT THE EFFICIENCY OF THE SHAREHOLDER-ORIENTED MODEL AND ABOUT THE RELATIONSHIP BETWEEN OWNERSHIP AND ACTIVITIES?

The first hypothesis – that ownership is all about finance – suggests that shareholder-oriented economies will have better governance and

Table 1.2   Comparison of Hypotheses 1 and 2

	Hypothesis 1	Hypothesis 2
Conception of the firm	Nexus of explicit contracts, some of which may be incomplete	Allows for implicit contracts: some activities require them; others do not
Implications for ownership & governance	Shareholder orientation; dispersed ownership	Activities requiring long-term relationships between managers & skilled workers → blockholders are valued Activities requiring risk-taking → dispersed ownership is valued
Evolution of ownership	International convergence, whatever the sector, towards dispersed ownership	Related to specific activities, especially human capital intensity, hence diversity (e.g., Saatchi and Saatchi, new economy) even within economies
	Implicitly assumes workers with standardized or publicly verifiable skills with no say in management	Stakeholder presence implies non-standard ownership arrangements

performance than countries where firms are organized differently. The second hypothesis points towards an association between ownership and types of activities, suggesting that it is comparative rather than absolute advantage that is at stake. Hence countries competing in open international markets would be expected to specialize, displaying different activities and different institutional arrangements. What evidence is there from existing empirical studies to support or refute these conjectures?

The characterization of an economy as shareholder oriented is usually related to either the dominance of widely held firms or the size of the stock market (relative to GDP). Figure 1.1 shows this relationship for the sample of countries analysed by La Porta et al. (1999). Hong Kong and Singapore are clear outliers, but nevertheless there is a strong positive relationship (significant at the 1 per cent level) between a measure of widely held ownership and stock market capitalization. I shall refer to both financial and ownership structures in the following discussion to capture the orientation of the financial system and the extent to which concentrated ownership dominates the economy.

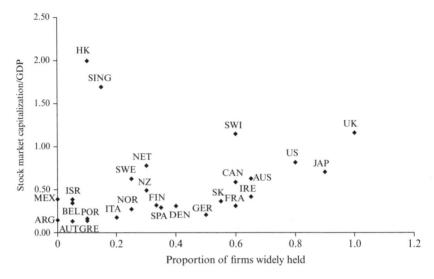

Notes:
HK – Hong Kong; SNG – Singapore; ISR – Israel; Mex – Mexico; ARG – Argentina; AUT
– Australia; BEL – Belgium; POR – Portugal; GRE – Greece; SWE – Sweden; ITA – Italy;
NOR – Norway; NET – Netherlands; NZ – New Zealand; FIN – Finland; SPA – Spain;
DEN – Denmark; GER – Germany; SK – South Korea; FRA – France; IRE – Ireland;
CAN – Canada; AUS – Australia; US – United States; SWI – Switzerland; JAP – Japan;
UK – United Kingdom.

Sources: 'Widely held' corresponds to La Porta et al. (1999, Table II Panel A). 'Stock
market capitalization' is from the World Bank Database (as described in Table 1.4 below).
Data are for 1995 apart from Ireland where stock market capitalization is for 1996.

*Figure 1.1   Stock market capitalization and the La Porta et al. ownership
concentration data, mid-to-late 1990s*

Cross-Country Evidence

It is very difficult to test the hypothesis that one kind of financial and
ownership system and associated form of corporate governance is better
for national economic performance than another. An interesting attempt
to do so was made by Daron Acemoglu and Simon Johnson (2005). They
sought to distinguish between the roles of property rights institutions on
the one hand (that is, those regulating the relationship between the state
and private agents) and of contracting institutions on the other (that is,
those regulating the relationship between private sector lenders and borrowers) as determinants of economic growth, financial development and

financial structure. This is relevant to our question since it is contracting institutions rather than property rights institutions that appear to be most closely related to financial and ownership structures. A finding that the type of contracting institutions that are associated with the shareholder-oriented model caused better long-run economic performance would provide evidence supportive of the view of the superior efficiency of that model.

The key to establishing causality is to find satisfactory instrumental variables that are causal for the particular institution, but have no direct effect on the outcome variable of interest such as long-run growth. For a set of ex-colonies, Acemoglu and Johnson extended the analysis of Acemoglu et al. (2001) and proposed the use of potential settler mortality over 200 years ago as an instrumental variable for property rights institutions. Mortality was an important determinant of whether a settler colony was established (rather than a purely extractive one), and hence whether European property rights institutions were replicated in the colony. The legal code associated with the colonizing nation was the chosen instrumental variable for contracting institutions on the grounds that different legal codes affected the relationships between private-sector agents, and in particular, between lenders and borrowers.

The aim was to test whether different institutions matter for different economic outcomes, and indeed they found that for a group of ex-colonies, property rights institutions were causal for both long-run growth and broad financial development, but not for the structure of the financial system as measured by the size of the stock market. On the other hand, they found that contracting institutions were causal for financial structure, but not for economic or financial development. Their work therefore failed to find evidence that 'societies organized along the standard shareholder-oriented model' were outcompeting those organized differently: economies with better contracting institutions (defined by lower transaction costs) had larger stock markets but not higher living standards. Their results also indicated that although legal origin was causal for contracting institutions, it had no direct effect on financial structure (if it did, it would have been an invalid instrumental variable) and had neither a direct nor an indirect effect on long-run growth. These results run counter to a 'law and finance' view that places weight on the impact of legal origin itself on growth.

Given the persistence of institutions and the difficulty in finding satisfactory instrumental variables, there is little convincing evidence about a causal link from financial structure to economic performance available from cross-country studies.[4] René Stulz (2001, pp. 175–180) summarized the earlier evidence. He highlighted the difficulties of the law and finance view in accounting for the large swings in the role of market finance and in attitudes towards the stock market *within* individual advanced countries over the course of the twentieth century as a whole when, by definition, legal origin had remained constant.[5] He looked for evidence that the organization of financial activities affected the ability of firms to raise capital, including the terms on which they could do so, and the efficiency with which firms were managed. What he found was inconclusive: 'The country studies must therefore be viewed more as evidence that financial structure matters than as evidence that one type of financial structure dominates other types of financial structure' (p. 180).

Industry–Country Evidence (the Rajan–Zingales 1998 Methodology)

Given the inherent difficulties in making progress in testing empirically how financial and ownership structure affect country growth, indirect methods have emerged. One methodology that has generated new insights was pioneered by Raghuram Rajan and Luigi Zingales in a paper in the *American Economic Review* in 1998. Instead of trying to explain country performance directly, their idea was to see whether specific aspects of financial development and structure at the country level promoted growth more in industries with particular financing needs. The country measures used by Rajan and Zingales included measures both of broad financial development (bank credit to GDP) and of financial structure (stock market turnover to GDP; stock market value traded to GDP) and a measure of the quality of accounting standards. The industry measure was constructed from US data on the assumption that US firms operated in the most frictionless financial markets and therefore provided a 'country free' indicator of the dependence of industries on external finance around the world. The evidence from 45 countries and 38 industries for the 1980–90 period reported by Rajan and Zingales was that there was a statistically and economically significant second-order effect of each of these measures of financial development/structure on industry growth according to the industry's dependence on external finance. As emphasized, this was not a direct test of the role of the country financial factors in growth, but only of 'abnormal' growth relative to country and industry average growth.

Subsequent studies using variations of the Rajan–Zingales (RZ) methodology produced additional results. Closely related to the concerns of this paper was Wendy Carlin and Colin Mayer (2003), which took a step towards extending the testing of the relationship between financial/ownership structure and growth beyond the boundaries defined by corporate law and finance. They sought to test whether aspects of financial and ownership structure had a second-order effect on growth in industries characterized by skill and bank-finance dependence as well as equity dependence. The focus on external finance as the sole causal channel of interest from financial institutions to performance was therefore supplemented with others.

Tests were conducted using a sample of 28 industries in 14 OECD countries over the period from 1970 to 1995, and evidence was found that higher accounting standards (although not measures of the size or turnover of the stock exchange) interacted with industry equity dependence to boost both research and development (R&D) as a percentage of GDP and output growth relative to industry and country averages. The most important new results related to the interaction between ownership concentration at the country level and the dependence of industries on skilled labour. Parallel with the RZ procedure described above for external financial dependence, the dependence of industries on skilled labour was measured in the country where skill acquisition was least constrained, namely, Germany.[6] The results showed that both R&D and growth were abnormally high in skill-intensive industries in countries in which company ownership was more concentrated and in countries with higher accounting standards. This exercise showed that concentrated ownership and greater transparency could be important in boosting performance in industries with specific characteristics, namely those heavily dependent on the use of skilled labour.

A recent paper by Claudio Michelacci and Fabiano Schivardi (2007) used the RZ methodology to investigate a different role of ownership patterns. Using a sample of 36 industries in 20 OECD economies, they tested the hypothesis that greater dominance of family ownership of companies in the economy would depress growth in those industries characterized by high volatility. Industry volatility was measured in the United States on the assumption that financial frictions were least there, and hence underlying volatility was likely to be most accurately observed. The logic of the argument was that family firms are typically undiversified in terms of idiosyncratic risk, and this would make them reluctant to engage in industries that were especially volatile or risky. The outcome would be abnormally low growth in such industries in family-ownership-dominated countries. They found considerable support for this hypothesis in the data.

Although the papers of Rajan and Zingales and Michelacci and Schivardi were motivated by the first-order question of the impact of finance on growth, the evidence they uncovered was of the second-order effects, that is, the effect on growth relative to country (and industry) averages. One interpretation of these results is that they reveal mechanisms through which financial or ownership structures have their effects on growth. The tests themselves, however, allow for an alternative interpretation along the lines proposed by the second hypothesis: that there may be an effect of ownership or financial structure on comparative rather than absolute advantage. For example, countries with dominant family ownership may be less well placed to succeed in high volatility industries, but better suited to industries where high levels of skills are required, for instance.

IS THERE EVIDENCE OF CONVERGENCE IN OWNERSHIP PATTERNS?

Both the theoretical literature and the econometric studies discussed in the previous two sections suggest that it may be misleading to expect that the shareholder-oriented corporate governance reforms that have been introduced would be reflected in some combination of convergence of ownership structures and inefficient resistance to such reforms. This section explores what has happened to patterns of ownership by asking the following questions. Is there evidence of convergence/resistance? Are there signs that responses to the wave of corporate governance reforms have produced differentiated responses by firms across countries? Are such changes consistent with the second hypothesis, which highlights the importance for ownership and governance patterns of the nature of the activities undertaken?

Ownership and Control: Cross-Country Differences and Trends

Stock market capitalization and financial structure
Table 1.3 documents the changes in the weight of companies from different countries in global stock market capitalization. US firms now account for a minority of world market capitalization, down from nearly 60 per cent in 1999 to 40 per cent in 2007. The share of the EU15 countries remained stable over this period at just under one-third. As Table 1.3 shows, the emergence of large quoted companies in Brazil, Russia, India and China – the so-called BRIC countries – accounted for 45 per cent of the fall in US share. Within Europe, the UK's dominance declined and France moved clearly away from Germany and towards the UK over this period, with France and the UK between them accounting for half of the EU15's share of global stock market capitalization in 2007.

The third column of Table 1.3 provides information on the turnover of companies in the FT Global 500: it shows the number of companies present in 2007 that were also present in the list in 1999. In most countries, two-thirds of 2007-listed companies were in the list in 1999. The exceptions were the UK and Italy, where turnover of companies was lower than this

Table 1.3 *Country shares of world stock market capitalization (FT Global 500), 1999 and 2007 (%)*

Country	Country shares of world stock market capitalization (%)		Company turnover in Global 500: per cent of companies present in 2007 that were also present in 1999
	1999[a]	2007[b]	
US	57.5	40.4	69 (127/184)
Japan	6.8	8.0	57 (28/49)
Europe (EU15)	31.9	32.8	67 (100/150)
Of which,			
UK	11.9[c]	9.5	80 (33/41)
Ireland	0.2	0.3	67 (2/3)
Germany	5.2	3.9	65 (13/20)
France	3.9[d]	6.7	69 (22/32)
Italy	2.0	2.1	88 (7/8)
Spain	1.3	2.3	58 (7/12)
Sweden	1.1[e]	1.1	44 (4/9)
China	–	3.3	0
Russia	–	2.5	0
India	0.1	0.9	0
Brazil	0.2	1.3	14 (1/7)

Notes and sources:
a. Data refer to information accessed 29 June 2007 at, http://specials.ft.com/ln/ftsurveys/q3666.htm
b. Data refer to information accessed 29 June 2007 at, http://www.ft.com/cms/s/0/ad53b3b2-2586-11dc-b338-000b5df10621,dwp_uuid=95d63dfa-257b-11dc-b338-000b5df10621.html
c. Includes companies jointly owned with Netherlands (2.0%), Switzerland (0.3%) and Australia (0.2%).
d. Includes companies jointly owned with Belgium (0.1%).
e. Includes companies jointly owned with Switzerland (0.1%) and Finland (0.1%).

(more than 80 per cent of the 2007 firms were in the Global 500 in 1999) and, at the other end of the spectrum, Japan and Sweden, where turnover was much higher than typical of this group of countries.

Table 1.4 shows the widely used indicators of financial development and structure: private credit by deposit banks and other financial institutions, stock market capitalization, and private bond market capitalization (all as a percentage of GDP). Broad financial development as measured by the size of the banking system increased most in the three countries where it was

Table 1.4   Standard measures of financial development and financial structure (ratios to GDP)

Country	Private credit by deposit banks & other financial institutions[a]		Stock market capitalization[b]		Private bond market capitalization[c]	
	1994/6	2003/5	1994/6	2003/5	1994/6	2003/5
USA	1.28	1.81	0.85	1.28	0.81	1.12
Japan	1.80	1.00	0.72	0.76	0.43	0.44
UK	1.10	1.46	1.21	1.26	0.14	0.16
Ireland	0.67	1.24	0.41[d]	0.53	0.04	0.22
Germany	0.99	1.13	0.23	0.41	0.51	0.39
France	0.86	0.88	0.33	0.76	0.48	0.41
Italy	0.56	0.83	0.17	0.41	0.31	0.46
Spain	0.72	1.17	0.31	0.78	0.14	0.33
Sweden	1.11	1.03	0.65	0.94	0.52	0.41

Notes:
a.   Raw data are from the electronic version of the IMF's International Financial Statistics, October 2005. Private credit by deposit money banks and other financial institutions.
b.   Value of listed shares.
c.   Private domestic debt securities issued by financial institutions and corporations.
d.   Refers to 1996 only.

Source: World Bank Financial Structure Data Sheet A (updated October 2007).

initially relatively small (Ireland, Italy and Spain). Substantial increases were also recorded, however, in the USA and the UK (with already large levels of bank credit to GDP) where household consumption booms persisted through this period. Expansion was less in France and Germany, and minor and major contractions were recorded, respectively, in Sweden and Japan.

Stock market capitalization went up across all countries, but least in those where it was initially highest. Convergence was not uniform, however. France and Spain showed large increases, which left them at the end of the period with stock markets of about the same size (relative to GDP) as had characterized the USA a decade earlier. Germany and Italy remained at the bottom of the table throughout the period. The persistent differences in the size of the stock market across these countries underline the differential importance of the unlisted firm sector.

The private bond market played a completely different role in the UK as compared with the USA in 1995, and this difference persisted over the period.[7] The other notable feature of the table is that there appears to have

Table 1.5   Breakdown of market capitalization by type of shareholder

Country	Year	Foreign	Domestic, of which				
			Financial institution		Non-financial company	Individual/ family	Public sector
				Of which banks			
UK	1997	24.0	56.3	0.1	3.1	16.5	0.1
	2004	32.6	51.5	2.7	1.7	14.1	0.1
Germany	1996	15.3	20.6	9.5	37.5	15.7	10.9
	2004	21.0	15.0	6.6	42.9	14.5	6.6
France	1996	24.9	27.6	8.7	29.3	12.4	2.6
	2004	39.6	31.4	9.9	16.3	6.3	6.3
Italy	1996	15.0	21.2	3.6	11.3	22.8	29.8
	2004	16.3	19.5	4.5	28.4	25.2	10.6
Spain	1996	37.4	21.3	14.1	6.9	23.6	10.9
	2004	35.2	17.3	8.7	23.1	24.1	0.3
Sweden	1996	31.6	30.3	1.6	10.8	19.1	8.3
	2004	33.9	28.5	3.4	10.5	17.8	9.5

Source: FESE (2007) share ownership data of companies listed on European stock exchanges. The main information sources are: registers of significant shareholdings and of the entities regulating the market; central banks; national statistical offices; official registries of international transactions; central registry entities.

been convergence in the size of the bond market in the eurozone countries – in the range of 30 to 50 per cent of GDP in 2005.

Ownership of shares and control of companies
Table 1.5 presents data on the structure of shareholdings of listed firms by type of owner over the last decade. Changes in the structure of French shareholdings are the most notable feature of these data. Foreign owner-ship of shares in German and Italian companies was lower in 2004 than it was in French companies almost a decade earlier. In terms of trends, France also looked different from Spain and Sweden, where like Italy there was relatively little change in foreign ownership over this period. In Germany and Italy, the holdings of domestic banks and non-bank financial institutions remained modest and, if anything, they were declin-ing while they were larger and rising in France. These contrasting trends between Germany and Italy on the one hand and France on the other in foreign and financial institutional holdings were reflected in the larger and rising shares of equity held by 'inside' owners (private non-financial com-panies) in Germany and Italy and their clear decline in France. In Italy

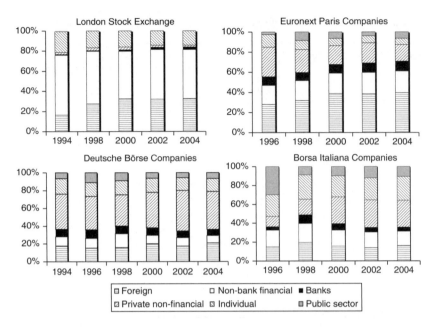

Source: FESE (2007) share ownership data of companies listed on European stock exchanges. The main information sources are: registers of significant shareholdings and of the entities regulating the market; central banks; national statistical offices; official registries of international transactions; central registry entities.

Figure 1.2 Share ownership by type of owner, 1994–2004

and Spain, the big increases in the holdings of non-financial companies were mirrored by the fall in shares held by the state.

By 2004, the French pattern of share ownership looked distinct from that of its two large continental neighbours (see Figure 1.2). It still did not resemble, however, the ownership structure of shares in the UK, where foreign ownership was lower (30 per cent in the UK, 40 per cent in France) and half of shares were in the hands of financial institutions as compared with 30 per cent in France.

Deeper investigation is required to reveal the control structures that lie behind share ownership patterns. Detailed cross-country analysis is available for a large cross-section of countries in the late 1990s, but there is no consistent time-series evidence on a comparable basis across countries.[8] Rather than looking at the identity of those holding shares as in Table 1.5, the question here is to take each company and ask where ultimate ownership and control lie. A comprehensive analysis of firms in Western European countries was provided by Mara Faccio and Larry Lang (2002):

they tracked down the ultimate owner in a sample of over 5000 Western European firms in the mid-to-late 1990s, which provides complete coverage of listed firms. Ultimate owners were identified at the control threshold of 20 per cent – that is, when control of at least 20 per cent of the voting rights is held by a family (or by an unlisted firm, the owners of which could not be identified), the state, a widely held financial institution or a widely held non-financial institution. There was also a category of miscellaneous owners (for example, charities, employees, cooperatives). Firms for which such a controlling owner did not exist were classified as 'widely held'.

Columns (2) and (3) of Table 1.6 show the share of widely held firms reported in the La Porta et al. (1999) study, where data were gathered on a relatively small number of firms in a larger sample of countries than covered by Faccio and Lang. Column (4) reports a different measurement of control: for each of the 10 largest domestically owned (non-state-owned) corporate groups, Kathy Fogel (2005) identified the extent to which it was collectively controlled by a single family. In column (1) three groups of countries can be identified: the UK and Ireland with a substantial majority of listed firms that were widely held; Germany, France and Italy with only a small fraction (10 to 14 per cent); and Spain and Sweden with between 25 and 40 per cent. Column (2) shows that when attention is confined to the very largest (20) firms in the economy, Germany and France looked more similar to the Anglo-American countries, and the contrast was between them on the one hand and Italy, Spain and Sweden on the other, where widely held firms were still rare. Column (3) samples further down the size structure, looking at 10 'mid-cap' companies – at this level, the only countries with a majority of widely held firms were the Anglo-American ones.

Column (4) is illuminating, because there the focus is on identifying the 10 largest domestically owned groups and then selecting those that were controlled (20 per cent of the votes) *and* managed by members of a single family. In each of France, Italy, Spain and Sweden between four and six of the groups were classified as family controlled. Interestingly, in Japan there was no group controlled by a family and in the USA and Germany only one. In the UK and Ireland, there were two. In a study of medium-sized firms (with median employment of 675) in manufacturing, John Van Reenen and Nicholas Bloom also found that the USA and Germany were similar in having a much lower proportion of family owned *and* managed firms than was the case in the UK and France (2007, Table IV).[9]

While the data shown in Table 1.6 have the merit of the application of a common methodology across the set of countries (both in terms of sample selection and in the method of calculating ultimate ownership), this brings with it disadvantages. In particular, this approach ignores

Table 1.6   Ultimate ownership of publicly listed companies, mid-to-late 1990s

	(1)	(2)	(3)	(4)
Source	Faccio & Lang (2002)	La Porta et al. (1999)	La Porta et al. (1999)	Fogel (2005)
Definition	Per cent of listed firms widely held[a]	Per cent of top 20 firms widely held[a]	Per cent of 10 smaller listed firms widely held[a]	Per cent of 10 largest groups in family control[b]
Complete sample (selected countries shown below)	13 European countries; 5232 firms virtually complete coverage of listed firms	27 countries worldwide – top 20 firms ranked by market capitalization of common equity at the end of 1995	27 countries worldwide – smallest 10 firms with market capitalization of at least $500 million at the end of 1995	41 countries – 10 largest domestically owned, non-government corporate groups, by employee numbers
Sample average	36.9	36.5	23.7	
USA	N/A	80	90	10
Japan	N/A	90	30	0
UK	63.1	100	60	20
Ireland	62.3	65	63	20
Germany	10.4	50	10	10
France	14.0	60	0	40
Italy	13.0	20	0	50
Spain	26.4	35	0	50
Sweden	39.2	25	10	60
Source table	Table 3	Table II panel A	Table III panel A	Table 1 column 2

Notes:
a. No shareholder controlling 20% of the votes.
b. Members of a single family collectively control more than 20% of the votes, control a greater stake than any other shareholders, and occupy multiple top executive positions in group member firms.

the country-specific variation in regulation that affects the ways in which blockholders can exert influence. These problems are examined in detail in Becht and Mayer (2001). Country studies (Barca and Becht, 2001) demonstrated the variety of mechanisms through which private (blockholder)

Table 1.7   Listed non-financial firms: voting blocks by blockholder type

	No. of listed firms in sample	Size of largest ultimate voting block (median), %	Identity of owners of voting blocks % total no. of blocks; mean size of blocks, %	
			1st ranked owner type	2nd ranked owner type
UK, 1992	207	9.9	Financial institutions **62**; *6*	Directors **24**; *5*
Germany, 1996	372	57	Individuals & families **32**; *27*	Companies: Domestic **28**; *62*
Italy, 1996	214	54.5	Individuals & families **30**; *20*	Companies: Domestic **20**; *20* Foreign **15**; *9*
Spain, 1996	193	34.5	Companies: Domestic **32**; *24* Foreign **20**; *21*	Individuals & families **26**; *16*

Source: Becht and Mayer (2001 from Tables 1.1, 1.2).

control was exerted across a range of continental European economies. They also highlighted the contrast in control transfer mechanisms between the UK and the USA, where widely held firms dominate. In the USA, many devices ensure manager control by defending them from takeovers. In the UK, there are fewer anti-takeover devices, but managers gain protection due to the extent of 'arm's-length' regulation that prevents blockholders from exerting influence on boards. Another striking characteristic of the British structure is the extent to which both executive and non-executive directors hold voting blocks (Table 1.7). In the UK, therefore, the hostile takeover remains as a last resort control transfer mechanism. From this perspective, Marco Becht and Colin Mayer identify continental European economies as privately controlled (by large blockholders), the USA as manager controlled and the UK as more market controlled. Table 1.7 highlights the small size of voting blocks in the UK consistent with the dominance of widely held firms presented in the other data sources. The comparison between Germany, Italy and Spain brings out patterns that are not evident in the previous tables and figures.[10] The very large size of the blocks held by other domestic non-financial companies in Germany stands out. In the Spanish case, the prominence of foreign owners is striking, as is the fact that the average size of block held by foreign companies was similar to that of domestic company blockholders.

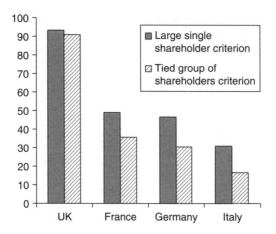

Source and notes: See Figure 1.3b.

*Figure 1.3a   Percentage of the top 100 widely held companies in four
countries, 2002*

Given the relative stability in the identity of owners of shares in Table
1.5 in Germany and Italy and the more dramatic changes in France over
the past decade, it is possible that control patterns in Germany and Italy
have changed less than in France. There is consistent cross-country data
on ownership and control for these four countries for a more recent year,
2002. Jeremy Grant and Tom Kirchmaier (2004) present ownership data
for about the top 100 firms in each country (Figures 1.3a and 1.3b). Their
study highlights that in spite of the changes in share ownership in France
shown in Table 1.5, the control pattern for the top 100 companies was
much more similar to that of Germany and Italy than to that of the UK,
just as displayed in the earlier data by, for example, Faccio and Lang.

Country studies for Germany and Italy provide additional insights on
changes in control structures. A study of German listed firms (Clark and
Wojcik, 2007) provides information on changes in the size of ultimate
voting blocks over the past decade. Companies are required to register the
direct and indirect control blocks (voting rights) at a series of thresholds
from 5 to 75 per cent. Gordon Clark and Dariusz Wojcik added these
blocks together for each company to create a measure they referred to as
the 'sum of voting blocks', showing the share of the company that was
not widely held.[11] Two data points were available: 1997 and 2003. The
coverage of firms was narrower than the German sample in Faccio and
Lang (415 firms in 1997 compared with 704 in 1996 in Faccio and Lang),
although it increased sharply in the later year (to 750).[12] When comparing

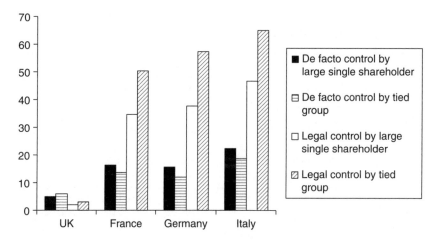

Notes: From the initial group of the top 110 companies in each country, the following were excluded: firms without reliable ownership data, investment trusts, asset managers, insurance companies, real estate investment companies and listed foreign subsidiaries. The following remained: UK 100, France 93, Germany 97, Italy 97.

Widely held – no single shareholder or tied group of shareholders own a percentage of capital above the mandatory bid threshold (UK 30%, France 33.3%, Germany and Italy 30%).

De facto control – controlling the national mandatory bid threshold, the level at which local regulators have concluded that a shareholder will have significant influence on the annual meeting but with less than 50% of votes.

Legal control – more than 50% of votes.

Source: Data from Grant and Kirchmaier (2004).

*Figure 1.3b   Percentage of companies controlled either by a single
shareholder or by a tied group of shareholders*

the control structure in 1997 with that in 2003, there was a fall in the mean sum of voting blocks in sample firms from 74 to 65 per cent; similarly, the mean stake of the largest blockholder fell from 62 to 54 per cent. This, however, conflates changes taking place within the set of core firms (that is, the 262 firms present in both years) and the composition effect of firms dropping out of the sample and those entering. A striking finding was that when looking at the core set of firms, the size of control blocks rose (see Table 1.7). The composition effect is clear: firms dropping out of the sample had substantially higher than average blockholder stakes and newcomers, much lower ones. Thus the overall fall in blockholder stakes was entirely due to the difference in concentration between drop-outs and newcomers.

The sectoral pattern is also interesting. Table 1.8 shows changes

Does company ownership matter?

Table 1.8 *Ownership concentration in German listed companies by industry, 1997 and 2003*

	Sum of voting blocks (mean)						
	Total		Core		Dropouts 1997	Newcomers 2003	
	1997	2003	1997	2003			
Sum of voting blocks	74.5	65.4	69.5	72.1	82.9	57.2	
Largest voting block	61.9	54.0	55.2	60.1	73.3	44.6	

Distribution of firms by industry	Total		Core	Dropouts 1997	Newcomers 2003	Sum of voting blocks, total	
	1997	2003	1997 and 2003			1997	2003
Consumer goods	9.9	11.9	16.0	9.8	6.9	74.0	74.3
Industrials	17.8	16.9	18.3	17.0	16.5	67.7	61.5
Software	0.5	12.3	0.8	0	20.6	92.8	49.1
Financial services	9.9	11.9	10.7	8.5	12.4	79.1	74.3
4 industry total	38.1	53.0	45.8	35.3	56.4		

Note: The distribution of core companies by sector in 1997 and 2003 is the same.

Source: Clark and Wojcik (2007, Tables 2 and 3).

in control for firms in the four largest sectors of the economy, which accounted for just over half the total number of firms in the sample in 2003. In the lower part of Table 1.8 the percentage of firms in the sample that are in each industry is shown. The ownership structure was fairly stable in the traditional sectors of 'consumer goods' and 'industrials' and in 'financial services'. Software firms were hardly represented at all in the sample in 1997, but made up over 12 per cent in 2003. These newcomers were characterized by mean voting blocks of just below 50 per cent – considerably smaller than was characteristic of firms in the other sectors. Foreign holdings of shares were about 20 to 25 per cent for consumer goods, industrials, and financial services in 1997. By 2003, foreign stakes in software firms were also at this level. The only noteworthy change was the reduction in foreign holdings of financial services firms to 11 per cent. Overall, the picture was one of stability in the core companies and core sectors of the economy, with a modest move towards somewhat smaller blockholder stakes in the firms present in the listed firm sample in 2003, but not in 1997.

A detailed recent study of Italian firms (Bianchi and Bianco, 2006) demonstrated the changes in the group structure of Italian companies in response to major reforms to the legal and economic framework of financial markets. The ownership changes led to the dismantling of pyramidal control patterns. These were, however, largely replaced by the creation of formal and informal shareholder agreements. In 2005, these so-called 'shareholder coalitions' controlled one-third of listed companies and almost one-half of market capitalization in Italy (up from, respectively, 11 and 20 per cent in 1990). In unlisted companies, 56 per cent of firms were controlled by a pyramidal group in 1993; by 2005, this had fallen to 46 per cent, but 10 per cent of firms were controlled by shareholders' agreements, leaving unchanged the coverage of firms by one or other of these mechanisms. The dismantling of the pyramids is indicated by the fact that in 1990 only 4 per cent of the capitalization of the 10 largest non-financial listed groups was in the top level of the pyramid, whereas in 2005 over 60 per cent was in the top level. This analysis confirmed that Italian firms continued to be controlled by blockholders, and indicated that active measures were taken to maintain this structure over the last decade. As the authors pointed out, the fundamental unanswered question is the extent to which this adaptation to the regulatory changes was the result of inefficient manoeuvring by entrenched owners or whether there was an efficiency rationale.

Institutional investors

From Table 1.5, we can see that domestic financial institutions owned 50 per cent of shares in the UK and between 15 and 30 per cent in the European countries in the table. Since foreign owners will also include financial institutions, the substantial increases in foreign and financial institutional ownership in France are especially notable. This points to the wider question of whether the role of financial institutions as owners of firms has changed over the last decade.

Data assembled by the OECD (2004) compared the portfolio composition of the assets of institutional investors themselves over a period from 1993 to 2001, showing the distribution of holdings between shares, bonds, loans and other assets such as cash (Figure 1.4). At the beginning of the period, UK institutional investors held mainly shares, and this had changed very little by 2001. By contrast, the portfolios of institutions on the continent were dominated by bonds in 1997, with one-fifth or less in the form of shares. The balance between shares and bonds changed by 2001. This change was most marked in the case of France. France began

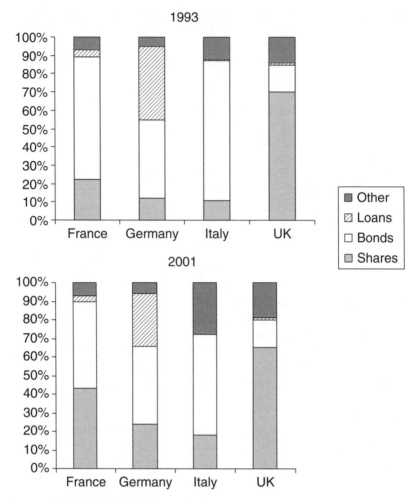

Source: OECD (2004, Table S.11, pp. 32–4).

Figure 1.4 Portfolio composition of institutional investors in four European countries, 1993 and 2001

the period looking fairly similar to Germany and Italy, but ended it closer to the UK: in 2001, shares comprised 43 per cent of the portfolio of institutional investors compared to 65 per cent in the UK and 24 per cent in Germany.

Looking next at the distribution of assets of institutional investors by type (insurance companies, pension funds, investment companies)[13] and

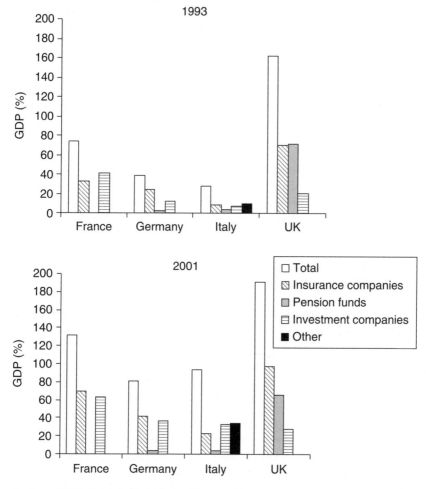

Source: OECD (2004, Table S.9, pp. 26–30).

Figure 1.5   Composition of assets by type of institutional investor (% GDP) in four European countries, 1993 and 2001

size relative to GDP, Figure 1.5 shows that the weight of institutional investors as asset holders was already much higher in France than in Germany and Italy in 1993, but still less than one-half that in the UK (shown by the 'total' bars in Figure 1.5). Over the period to 2001, the asset holdings of these institutions grew in all three countries faster than in the UK. The other interesting feature shown in Figure 1.5 is that although insurance and pension funds held far more assets (relative to GDP) in the UK than in the continental economies throughout the period, investment companies grew more rapidly in France, Germany and Italy than in the UK, and in each country had a larger asset base relative to GDP by 2001 than was the case in the UK.

Different types of institutional investor are different kinds of owners. Marcel Kahan and Edward Rock (2006) distinguished between the traditional institutional investors (insurance, pension, mutual funds) on the one hand and hedge funds on the other. They argued that both types may play a role as activist owners. The active role of traditional institutional investors is largely through effecting small *systemic* changes (for example, pressure for improved corporate governance practices, such as greater transparency). At a company level, hedge funds are active in relation to specific companies in a strategic and *ex ante* fashion, whereas traditional institutional investors intervene intermittently and *ex post*, for example, through sales of their stake.

A recent survey of US evidence on the effects of institutional shareholder activism (Gillan and Starks, 2007) concluded:

> The empirical evidence on the influence of shareholder activism has shown mixed results. Although studies have found some short-term market reaction to the announcement of certain types of activism, there is little evidence of improvement in long-term stock market performance or operating performance resulting from the activism. Studies have found some change in the real activities of the firm subsequent to the shareholder pressure, but it has been difficult to establish a causal relationship between shareholder activism and these changes. (p. 69)

There is fragmentary evidence available on the presence of different types of institutional investors in different economies. The most systematic comparison appears to be between the presence of different US institutional investors in Germany and France (Goyer, 2006, 2007). Michel Goyer contrasted the incentives of pension, mutual and hedge funds. Pension funds are long-term investors who purchase equity stakes as part of their diversification strategy. The incentives of pension fund managers are given by the need to generate a flow of revenue to meet the commitments to pension recipients. Mutual funds face a shorter-term horizon and greater liquidity orientation, because investors can withdraw funds at will. Hedge funds have even shorter-term horizons as they seek to deliver higher returns than index funds. Unlike pension and mutual funds, which make portfolio choices based on diversification motives and intervene in governance, if at all, *ex post*, hedge funds decide whether a firm would benefit from activism and then acquire a stake and become active (Kahan and Rock, 2006).

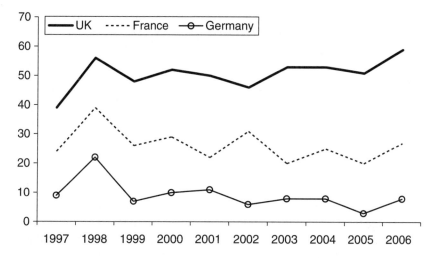

Source: Data from Goyer (2007).

Figure 1.6   *US mutual funds with foreign holdings: top three destination countries*

Goyer (2006, 2007) argued that foreign pension funds acquired small stakes in large firms in both France and Germany as part of their diversification strategies. He provided some evidence to suggest that it is not pension funds, but mutual and hedge funds where a clear difference in preference for stakes in French versus German firms can be observed.[14] The argument is that these shorter-term and, in the case of hedge funds, *ex ante* more interventionist strategies favoured investment in France over Germany because of the greater unilateral control by top management in French firms. In German firms, decision making is more consensual as reflected, for example, by the involvement of works councils. As argued earlier, ownership patterns in Germany prevent radical changes in asset use because of the costs of undermining long-term investments by related parties. Another reflection of this is the weaker autonomy of managers and hence the lower attractiveness of participation by more activist investors such as mutual and hedge funds. Figure 1.6 shows the evolution over time of the exposure of US mutual funds to firms in the UK, France and Germany. The UK's presence in the top three destinations remains steady at about 50 (in the approximately 75 US mutual funds with foreign equity holdings); there is a gentle downward trend for both France and Germany, but the German presence is at a much lower level throughout.

Table 1.9   *Presence of equity stakes above 5% by Anglo-American mutual*
             and hedge funds in French and German companies, 1997–2005

Sample: Top 1000 European companies by market capitalization	Top 20		Top 60		Top 1000 minus Top 60	
	Firms	Instances	Firms	Instances	Firms	Instances
France	10	27	41	122	207	370
Germany	6	16	27	52	114	149

Source: Goyer (2007, p. 32 and Annex 1).

Table 1.9 illustrates the greater preference of US- and UK-based mutual and hedge funds for investment in French rather than German companies. The data refer to the top 1000 European companies by market capitalization. Looking first at the top 20 companies, there were almost twice as many French as German firms with Anglo-American mutual and hedge funds holding stakes of above 5 per cent. A stake of 5 per cent or more is interpreted as an indication of an interest of the institution in 'activism'. The pattern of greater engagement in French than in German firms held across the top 60 firms, and more generally in the top 1000 firms. The columns headed 'instances' capture the fact that there were frequently multiple purchases of a stake of at least 5 per cent in the same company, and this measure underlines the preference for French firms.

Private equity
The last few years have seen a second bout of leveraged buyouts (LBOs: 'private equity' deals) in the USA and Europe. As compared with the first wave in the late 1980s, the size of deals this time has been substantially larger. In the UK and the EU, these accounted for 5 to 7 per cent of GDP as compared with less than 2 per cent in the late 1980s, and amounted to 25 to 30 per cent of all mergers and acquisitions against 15 to 20 per cent in the earlier LBO boom (Blundell-Wignall, 2007). Private equity investment by US firms in Europe rose from €7 billion in 2001 to €26 billion in 2005. Of the top 14 deals in 2005, the UK was in 2nd, 8th, 10th and 13th places; France was in 1st, 6th and 9th places, whereas there was only one deal in Germany, in 14th place. British private equity investors were also active in foreign acquisitions – although on a much smaller scale than US buyout deals. While the number of cross-border deals by UK investors peaked at the end of the 1990s, the average value of the transactions rose more than tenfold from €38 million in 1991 to €421 million in 2005 (Wright et al., 2006, p. 29). The engagement of British private equity in Europe was

concentrated in France and Germany, with 34 per cent of cumulative deals in France and 20 per cent in Germany (10 per cent in Italy).

The rise of private equity deals resulted from the confluence of global macroeconomic conditions that produced excessive liquidity and very low interest rates, along with increased corporate governance pressures and curbs on opportunities to provide executive compensation via stock options in listed companies (as a consequence of post-Enron regulatory and governance code changes). Both of these made debt-driven deals that take firms off the public markets highly attractive. In contrast to the very short-term-oriented activist strategies of some hedge funds, a typical private equity deal might involve a four-year time horizon from de-listing to the exit of the private equity firm through an initial public offering (IPO) or a trade sale to a strategic listed or unlisted buyer.[15] In addition to favourable global macroeconomic conditions, the required industry and company characteristics favouring private equity deals[16] means that its ultimate significance as a force for ownership change and corporate restructuring is limited.

Corporate governance ratings

Given the breadth of reform in corporate governance codes and regulation, it is useful to report changes in corporate governance standards across companies in different countries. Data are now collected by commercial firms on the quality of corporate governance at the firm level across countries in order to provide information to institutional investors. Table 1.10 shows the scores for a number of European countries across four dimensions of corporate governance in 2004, along with the change in the scores since 2000. Unsurprisingly, the results showed that British and Irish firms had higher standards on these governance indicators than the continental firms. The difference was least in the dimension of 'disclosure' and greatest in the dimension of 'takeover defences'. Disclosure refers to the availability and quality of information to shareholders about the firm's finances and governance characteristics. Takeover defences are the structures and mechanisms in place to protect the firm from hostile takeovers. It was also in disclosure that the greatest improvements were recorded since 2000. French and German companies looked similar, with the higher overall French rating due to a better score on 'board structure and functioning' – the dimension on which German firms scored worst across all the countries in the sample. Board structure and functioning captures the composition of the board of directors including the independence of board members from managers *and* major shareholders, its diversity, the frequency of meetings, the committee structure and the link between executive directors' remuneration and financial results.

Table 1.10   Corporate governance ratings, 2004; in parentheses, the change in the median value of the index, 2000–2004

	No. firms	Total	Shareholder rights, duties	Takeover defences	Disclosure	Board structure & functioning
	(1)	(2)	(3)	(4)	(5)	(6)
UK	81	32.1 (4.5)	8.0 (1.1)	9.0 (1.0)	8.1 (1.5)	7.3 (1.1)
Ireland	7	30.4 (2.2)	7.8 (0.7)	9.0 (−1.0)	7.6 (1.5)	7.0 (1.0)
Germany	32	19.6 (3.0)	6.9 (−0.2)	1.0 (−1.6)	6.7 (3.1)	4.5 (1.7)
France	42	21.3 (4.3)	6.5 (0.1)	1.0 (1.0)	6.9 (2.3)	6.0 (1.4)
Italy	25	18.6 (3.9)	5.7 (−0.6)	1.0 (1.0)	6.6 (1.9)	5.1 (1.5)
Spain	17	19.8 (6.7)	6.8 (1.2)	1.0 (1.0)	6.5 (3.4)	5.1 (1.1)
Sweden	16	23.8 (3.7)	6.2 (0.8)	5.1 (−1.4)	6.8 (3.3)	5.2 (1.8)

Source: From Clark and Wojcik (2007, Tables 2.1 and 2.2). Data were collected from the firm Deminor, now part of Institutional Investor Services. The maximum score in each category was 10.

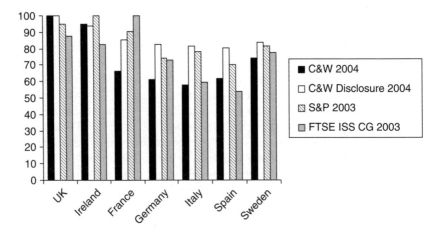

Sources and notes: In each case the original index was rebased so that the highest score among the countries is 100. C&W 2004 refers to the four-component measure reported in Column 2 and C&W Disclosure of Column 5 of Table 1.10 above.

   S&P 2003 refers to an index comprising three elements: transparency and disclosure; board structure and management process; ownership structure and investor relations (Doidge et al., 2007, Table 1).

   FTSE 2003 refers to ratings on an eight-category basis: board, audit, charter/bylaws, anti-takeover provisions, executive and director compensation, qualitative factors, ownership and director education (Doidge et al., 2007, Table 1).

Figure 1.7   Measures of corporate governance

Figure 1.7 displays the overall score and the disclosure subscore from Table 1.10 along with two other indices from 2003: the Standard and Poor's index and the FTSE rating. There is greater variation in the scores across countries in the two broader-based measures: the C&W 2004 and the FTSE ISS 2003. In the indices where most weight was placed on disclosure (C&W Disclosure and S&P), the scores were more similar. The results for France stand out in the sense that it scored very differently on the two broader-based measures – very high on the FTSE ISS index in line with the Anglo-American countries and much lower and close to the continental countries on the C&W measure. One interpretation of these results is that higher standards of disclosure are compatible with improved functioning of companies in blockholder as well as shareholder systems, whereas other features such as board structure and anti-takeover provisions are not. Better disclosure encourages investment by passive institutional (minority) shareholders without threatening the co-specific investments of the related parties that are essential to the core business of companies. Studies by Martin Höpner (2001, 2003) provide some evidence that the adoption of shareholder value orientation by large German companies, 'does not make companies opt out of central collective agreements or endanger the existence of employees' codetermination, but it does lead to more market-driven industrial relations' (2001, p. 2). Company works councils appear to play a larger role in cooperating with management in more shareholder value-oriented firms, especially those exposed to international competition.

Summary

The data presented in this section showed that the recent period of corporate governance reform and increased international financial integration produced a combination of common trends and persistent national differences. The common trends related to:

- increased foreign ownership; and
- improved corporate governance, especially concerning disclosure, but not in respect of takeover defences.

Persistent national differences took the following forms.

- Global stock market capitalization became less dominated by the standard shareholder-oriented model as the share of Anglo-American companies fell.
- 'Insider' blockholders strengthened their position in core German companies and in Italy.

- Developments in France meant that it increasingly differentiated itself from the other continental economies, and particularly from Germany. This applied to the following characteristics:

  - higher stock market capitalization;
  - higher foreign and institutional ownership of shares, and lower insider ownership;
  - stronger engagement by mutual, hedge and private equity funds; and
  - higher scores on some measures of corporate governance.

  Nevertheless, data on control structures for 2002 continued to show that for the top 100 French companies, blockholders remained highly significant. Better data are required to clarify these developments.

In spite of common regulatory changes, the international forces of greater competition and increased liquidity appear to have prompted differentiated responses both to and from firms in different countries. Whereas in France foreign investors, including institutions, played an important role in introducing increased shareholder value orientation, this was less evident elsewhere. In Italy, blockholder control via pyramids was replaced by informal and formal shareholder coalitions. In Germany, *activist* institutional investors from abroad showed limited interest in taking stakes in companies.

CONCLUSIONS

How do the reported empirical patterns relate to our two hypotheses? The first hypothesis predicted a convergence of both ownership structures and the behaviour of firms in response to corporate governance reforms and increased internationalization of world financial markets. The absence or weakness of moves in the direction of shareholder orientation would, according to the first hypothesis, be due to effective resistance by incumbent stakeholders and would be detrimental to performance. The second hypothesis emphasized a diversity of responses to common corporate governance reforms ranging from inefficient resistance to efficient adaptation. A major impediment to the evaluation of these hypotheses is the absence to date of detailed descriptive data on how ownership and control patterns have changed over the past decade. The fragmentary evidence on ownership changes and on the engagement of different institutional investors assembled in this chapter suggests that the second hypothesis cannot be ruled out.

Italy, Germany and France present three very different pictures. Italy represents a promising *prima facie* case for the 'inefficient resistance' interpretation. As documented, control structures in Italy have adapted to far-reaching changes in regulation so as to reproduce the pre-existing control patterns: pyramids have been replaced by shareholder coalitions to ensure blockholder control. Moreover, using the test of competition in international markets, Italy appears to have performed relatively poorly over the last decade.[17] Nevertheless, serious empirical testing of the productivity effects of the changes in control structures remains to be done. The deeper investigation of the second hypothesis would focus on uncovering whether exogenous shocks such as the emergence of new competitors in the sectors of Italy's specialization prompted resistance to necessary restructuring. The first hypothesis would seek evidence of the inherent tendency of the ownership structure – in its old and new variants – to produce high levels of (negative) private benefits (see, for example, Dyck and Zingales, 2004). Such an approach would place more stress on why institutions, such as vigilant media, for containing these abuses are absent in Italy.

Germany, on the other hand, is a candidate for interpretation in terms of efficient adaptation within a stable institutional cluster in line with the second hypothesis. It seems that changes in governance standards towards greater transparency encouraged the participation of institutional investors (including those from abroad) seeking portfolio diversification. Yet in the core export-oriented activities of the German economy, key changes resulted from cooperation between company managers and their employees, through the medium of works councils. A major restructuring in organization, training and in employment conditions was negotiated within a broadly unchanged structure of control. The engagement by institutional investors appears to have been of the more passive kind: investors who were content with existing management and control arrangements sought to take advantage of opportunities for portfolio diversification. The introduction of greater transparency and disclosure by firms is consistent with this interpretation. The result was a strong performance of German companies in international markets based on improved price and non-price competitiveness. The profitability of German firms improved and this is reflected in national accounts measures, where the net profit share in both manufacturing and non-manufacturing business staged a very impressive recovery, returning by 2005 to levels of the early 1970s (Carlin and Soskice, 2009).

France is an interesting case because the data presented appear to suggest that France may be in transition towards a different institutional cluster. The first hypothesis would propose an explanation of developments in France in terms of the narrow view of corporate governance:

changes in regulation prompted the replacement of inefficient blockholder arrangements by greater engagement of activist institutional investors, including those from abroad. Support for the second hypothesis would come from a more detailed examination of the kinds of activities in which ownership changes have occurred and evidence on whether performance has been enhanced most where the greater authority of the CEO (released from the constraints imposed by blockholders) could make the most difference by taking on riskier projects. By contrast, the first hypothesis would emphasize the reduction of malfeasance of managers and blockholders through the intervention of active investors.

The final contribution of this chapter is to suggest how future research could help to reveal more clearly the role of ownership patterns and the implications for public policy of the past decade. In terms of research strategies, the recent work by Claudio Michelacci and Fabiano Schivardi suggests that more can be learnt from using the Rajan–Zingales methodology to identify complementarities between country and industry (activity) characteristics. The data requirements for such work are nevertheless challenging. Better measures of ownership across a large number of countries (for example, the 20 'old' OECD countries) and of industry characteristics are required to take this work further.

Single-country studies could exploit variations in product market competition to investigate whether inefficient resistance has characterized company responses to regulatory changes in corporate governance. Persistence of inefficient activities and ownership structures is less likely where firms are operating in competitive product markets. Hypothesis 1 would suggest that performance and ownership structure would have improved more (in surviving firms) in exposed sectors of the economy than in sheltered ones. By contrast, the second hypothesis would predict efficient adaptation even in sheltered sectors, according to whether investment in co-specific assets was important for the activity. In testing these hypotheses, it is important that measures of performance should include productivity rather than only the traditional measures of shareholder value, such as Tobin's Q or accounting rates of returns on capital invested. Finally, there is probably no alternative to detailed comparative country case studies to complement the econometric approaches discussed above if the question of how ownership relates to specialization and performance is to be convincingly answered.

NOTES

1. Elaine Kelly has provided excellent research assistance for this project. I am very grateful to Colin Mayer and David Soskice for comments and for useful discussions about

these issues and especially to Robert Boyer for his insightful suggestions, which have influenced the revised version of this chapter.

2. An even more concise statement can be found in Hansmann's 2006 piece, 'How close is the end of history?'.

3. Coates (2003) provides an interesting discussion of 'bad', 'good' and 'inherent' private benefits.

4. As noted above, Acemoglu and Johnson (2005) found evidence that the quality of property rights institutions affected both broad financial development as measured by the size of the banking sector relative to GDP and the level of development itself. The independent causal role of financial development in affecting long-run living standards remains contentious. A much-cited paper arguing in favour is Levine (1997); for a more sceptical view, see Manning (2003).

5. For further evidence along these lines, for Germany, see Franks et al. (2006), and for the UK, Franks et al. (2007).

6. In line with the procedure adopted by Rajan and Zingales, the countries supplying the data for the industry characteristic in question, for example, the US for external financial dependence or Germany for skill dependence, were dropped from the regression sample.

7. Private sector bond-issuing activity in the City of London relates predominantly to foreign rather than domestic companies (Allen et al., 2005).

8. This important gap in the literature will be filled in the near future when research by Julian Franks, Colin Mayer and co-authors on the ownership and control of the largest 1,000 (listed and unlisted) firms in the UK, France, Germany and Italy for 1996 and 2006 becomes available.

9. Note that in Van Reenen and Bloom's sample, 30 per cent of firms had a family as the largest shareholder in the UK, France and Germany, but only 10 per cent in the USA.

10. Unfortunately comparable information for France was not published in the French country study in Barca and Becht (2001).

11. It is not clear from the description of their methodology that Clark and Wojcik take fully into account the complexities of the means through which voting power is concentrated in Germany (see, for example, Becht and Böhmer, 2001, and Becht and Mayer, 2001).

12. Data for 1997 included all listed companies at the end of 1997; data for 2003 included all companies listed both on the 'official' and on the 'regulated' markets, which reflected the reorganization of the German stock market, the Deutsche Börse, in this period (Clark and Wojcik, 2007).

13. Investment companies are constituted differently in different countries but cover, for example, mutual funds, unit trusts, and in France, undertakings for collective investment in transferable securities (OPCVMs). Full details for each country are provided in OECD (2004).

14. The percentage of the international portfolio of the largest US pension funds invested in French firms is 60 per cent higher than in German firms in the 2003–05 period (Goyer, 2007, Table 4, p. 17). This is, however, a much smaller discrepancy between the two countries than is shown by the mutual and hedge fund data.

15. According to one estimate, only 5 per cent of hedge fund assets are available for shareholder activism – some funds do not hold equity and some use quantitative strategies and do not engage in activism (Kahan and Rock, 2006). Note that the 'long-term' time horizon of a private equity investor is far shorter than the 'long-term' engagement of blockholders and other stakeholders in continental economies.

16. Attractive industries are those with stable cash flows over the cycle (non-durable consumer goods), stable industries with monopoly-like markets. Attractive firms are those with undergeared balance sheets, margins and valuations below their peers and with high free cash flow (Blundell-Wignall, 2007, p. 69).

17. Using the OECD's measure of export market competitiveness (the annual change in the ratio of export volumes of goods and services to export markets), Italy's performance

declined at an annual average rate of 5.3 per cent, France's by 1.6 per cent and the UK's by 2.1 per cent over the 1997–2007 period. Germany's performance increased by 1.1 per cent per year over the same period (OECD 2007, Annex, Table 44).

REFERENCES

Acemoglu, D. and S. Johnson (2005), 'Unbundling institutions', *Journal of Political Economy*, **113** (5), pp. 949–95.

Acemoglu, D., S. Johnson and J.A. Robinson (2001), 'The colonial origins of comparative development: an empirical investigation', *American Economic Review*, **91** (5), pp. 1369–401.

Alchian, A. and H. Demsetz (1972), 'Production, information costs and economic organization', *American Economic Review*, **62** (5), pp. 777–95.

Allen, F. and D. Gale (2000), *Comparing Financial Systems*, Cambridge, MA: MIT Press.

Allen, F., L. Bartiloro and O. Kowalewski (2005), 'The financial system of the EU 25', mimeo, Wharton School, University of Pennsylvania.

Aoki, M. (1990), 'Toward an economic model of the Japanese firm', *Journal of Economic Literature*, **28**, pp. 1–27.

Aoki, M. (2001), *Toward a Comparative Institutional Analysis*, Cambridge, MA: MIT Press.

Baker, G., R. Gibbons and K.J. Murphy (2002), 'Relational contracts and the theory of the firm', *Quarterly Journal of Economics*, **117** (1), pp. 39–84.

Barca, F. and M. Becht (eds) (2001), *The Control of Corporate Europe*, Oxford: Oxford University Press.

Becht, M. and E. Böhmer (2001), 'Ownership and voting power in Germany', in Barca and Becht (eds), pp. 128–53.

Becht, M. and C. Mayer (2001), 'Introduction', in Barca and Becht (eds), pp. 1–45.

Bianchi, M. and M. Bianco (2006), 'Italian corporate governance in the last 15 years: from pyramids to coalitions?', ECGI Finance Working Paper 144/2006, European Corporate Governance Institute, Brussels, available at SSRN: http://ssrn.com/abstract=952147 (accessed 10 July 2007).

Blanchard, O. and J. Tirole, (2004), 'The optimal design of unemployment insurance and employment protection', NBER Working Paper 10443, National Economic Research, Cambridge, MA, available at: http://www.nber.org/papers/w10443.

Blundell-Wignall, A. (2007), 'The private equity boom: causes and policy issues', *OECD Financial Market Trends*, **92** (1), pp. 59–86.

Carlin, W. and C. Mayer (2003), 'Finance, investment and growth', *Journal of Financial Economics*, **69** (1), pp. 191–226.

Carlin, W. and D. Soskice (2009), 'German economic performance: disentangling the role of supply-side reforms, macroeconomic policy and coordinated economic institutions', *Socio-Economic Review* 2009, **7** (1), pp. 67–99

Clark, G.L. and D. Wojcik (2007), *The Geography of Finance: Corporate Governance in the Global Marketplace*, Oxford: Oxford University Press.

Coates, J.C. (2003), 'Ownership, takeovers and EU law: how contestable should EU corporations be?', Discussion Paper 450, John Olin Center for Law, Economics and Business, Harvard Law School, Cambridge, MA.

Coffee, J.C. (2005), 'A theory of corporate scandals: why the USA and Europe differ', *Oxford Review of Economic Policy*, **21** (2), pp. 198–211.

Coffee, J.C. (2006), *Gatekeepers: The Role of the Professions in Corporate Governance*, Oxford: Oxford University Press.

Doidge, C., G.A Karolyi and R.M. Stulz (2007), 'Why do countries matter so much for corporate governance?', *Journal of Financial Economics*, **86**, pp. 1–39.

Dyck, A. and L. Zingales (2004), 'Private benefits of control: an international comparison', *Journal of Finance*, **59** (2), pp. 537–600.

Enriques, L. and P. Volpin (2007), 'Corporate governance reforms in Continental Europe', *Journal of Economic Perspectives*, **21** (1), pp. 117–40.

Faccio, M. and L.H.P. Lang (2002), 'The ultimate ownership of Western European corporations', *Journal of Financial Economics*, **65**, pp. 365–95.

FESE (Federation of European Securities Exchanges) (2007), *Share Ownership Structure in Europe*, Brussels: FESE.

Fogel, K. (2005), 'Oligarchic family control, social economic outcomes and the quality of government', *Journal of International Business Studies*, **37**, pp. 603–22.

Franks, J., C. Mayer and H.F. Wagner (2006), 'The origins of the German corporation – finance, ownership and control', *Review of Finance*, **10** (4), pp. 537–85.

Franks, J., C. Mayer and S. Rossi (2007), 'Ownership: evolution and regulation', mimeo, London Business School.

Gillan, S. and L.T. Starks (2007), 'The evolution of shareholder activism in the United States', *Journal of Applied Corporate Finance*, **19**, pp. 55–73.

Goergen, M., M. Martynova and L. Renneboog (2005), 'Corporate governance convergence: evidence from takeover regulation reforms in Europe', *Oxford Review of Economic Policy*, **21** (2), pp. 243–68.

Goyer, M. (2006), 'Varieties of institutional investors and national models of capitalism: the transformation of corporate governance in France and Germany', *Politics and Society*, **34** (3), pp. 399–430.

Goyer, M. (2007), 'Institutional investors in French and German corporate governance: the transformation of corporate governance and the stability of coordination', Working Paper 07.2, Center for European Studies, Harvard University, Cambridge, MA.

Grant, J. and T. Kirchmaier (2004), 'Who governs? Corporate ownership and control structures in Europe', mimeo, London School of Economics and Political Science.

Grossman, S. and O. Hart (1986), 'The costs and benefits of ownership: a theory of vertical and lateral integration', *Journal of Political Economy*, **94**, pp. 691–719.

Hall, P. and D. Soskice (2001), 'An introduction to varieties of capitalism', in Hall and Soskice (eds), *Varieties of Capitalism: The Institutional Foundations of Comparative Advantage*, Oxford: Oxford University Press, pp. 1–68.

Hansmann, H. (2006), 'How close is the end of history?', *Journal of Corporate Law*, 2005–2006, pp. 745–51.

Hansmann, H. and R. Kraakman (2001), 'The end of history for corporate law', *Georgetown Law Journal*, **89**, pp. 439–68.

Hart, O. and J. Moore (1990), 'Property rights and the nature of the firm', *Journal of Political Economy*, **98**, pp. 1119–58.

Höpner, M. (2001), 'Corporate governance in transition: ten empirical findings on shareholder value and industrial relations in Germany', MPIfG Discussion Paper 01/5, Max Planck Institute for the Study of Societies, Cologne.

Höpner, M. (2003), *Wer beherrscht die Unternehmen? Shareholder Value, Managerherrschaft und Mitbestimmung in Deutschland*, Frankfurt am Main: Campus.

Jensen, M.C. and W. Meckling (1976), 'Theory of the firm: managerial behaviour, agency costs and capital structure', *Journal of Financial Economics*, **3**, pp. 305–60.

Kahan, M. and E.B. Rock (2006), 'Hedge funds in corporate governance and corporate control', Institute for Law & Economy Research Paper 06–16, University of Pennsylvania, available at SSRN: http://ssrn.com/abstract=919881 (accessed 14 July 2007).

La Porta, R., F. López-de-Silanes and A. Shleifer (1999), 'Corporate ownership around the world', *Journal of Finance*, **54**, pp. 471–518.

Levine, R. (1997), 'Financial development and economic growth: views and agenda', *Journal of Economic Literature*, **35** (June), pp. 688–726.

Manning, M.J. (2003), 'Finance causes growth: can we be so sure?', *Contributions to Macroeconomics*, **3** (1), Article 12, available at: http://www.bepress.com/bejm/contributions/vol3/iss1/art12 (accessed 10 July 2007).

Michelacci, C. and F. Schivardi (2007), 'Does idiosyncratic risk matter for growth?', CEPR Discussion Paper 6910, available at: http://www.cemfi.es/~michela/IdiosyncraticMS.pdf.

OECD (2004), *Institutional Investors Yearbook* (final issue), Paris: OECD.

OECD (2007), *Economic Outlook*, **81**, Paris: OECD.

Rajan, R. and L. Zingales (1998), 'Financial dependence and growth', *American Economic Review*, **88**, pp. 559–86.

Shleifer, A. and R. Vishny (1997), 'A survey of corporate governance', *Journal of Finance*, **52**, pp. 737–83.

Stulz, R. (2001), 'Does financial structure matter for economic growth? A corporate finance perspective', in A. Demirguc-Kunt and R. Levine (eds), *Financial Structure and Economic Growth: A Cross-Country Comparison of Banks, Markets and Development*, Cambridge, MA: MIT Press, pp. 143–88.

Tirole, J. (2005), *The Theory of Corporate Finance*, Princeton, NJ: Princeton University Press.

Van Reenen, J. and N. Bloom (2007), 'Measuring and explaining management across firms and countries', *Quarterly Journal of Economics*, **127** (4), pp. 1351–408.

Wright, M., A. Burrows, R. Ball, L. Scholes, M. Meuleman and K. Amess (2006), *The Implications of Alternative Investment Vehicles for Corporate Governance: A Survey of Empirical Research*, Paris: OECD.

Zingales, L. (2000), 'In search of new foundations', *Journal of Finance*, **55** (4), pp. 1623–53.

2. Ownership concentration, employment protection and macroeconomic performance: making a case for interdependent time-evolving institutions

Donatella Gatti

INTRODUCTION

This chapter aims at analysing the macroeconomic impact of owner-ship structure and employment protection by taking into account their interdependencies and changes over time. Two streams of literature deal separately with these issues. On the one hand, there is a wide consensus in economics about the crucial role of institutions in determining cross-country economic performances. On the other hand, a large body of literature within political economy and political science shows that the roots of institutional diversity are to be found in political, institutional and economic factors. Approaches from these two streams of literature rarely come together. At the cross-border of economics, political economy and political science, two frontier issues are emerging: first, the question of interdependencies across existing institutional devices, and second the endogenous evolution of those institutional arrangements.

A multidisciplinary approach – bringing together separate fields, such as economics, political economy and political science – is needed to account for interdependent time-evolving institutional arrangements. In order to take interdependencies seriously, a framework is needed, where the economic impact of institutions depends not only on history, but also on context(s). The issue of time-evolving institutions raises the question of feedbacks from economic performance onto pre-existing institutional arrangements, and their subsequent transformations. This calls for moving away from static approaches based on assessing the economic impact of (almost) fixed exogenous institutions. In this chapter, I shall address empirically the question of measuring interdependencies and accounting for endogeneity. I shall rely on advances in the econometric treatment of slowly changing variables as well as on the literature on systems of endogenous equations.

The structure of ownership, and in particular ownership concentration, is a crucial topic within the literature on law and economic performance. Recent contributions (following La Porta et al., 1998 and 1999) suggest that investor protection fosters financial market development and ownership dispersion. Some authors report negative effects of ownership concentration on growth and institutional development (see, for instance, Morck et al., 2005). This literature focuses primarily on the process of development. This chapter, on the contrary, aims at investigating the macroeconomic effects of ownership concentration in developed countries.

Important insights on the effects of ownership structure can be grasped from the literature on corporate governance models (Shleifer and Vishny, 1997; Becht and Mayer, 2001; Faccio and Lang, 2002; Gugler et al., 2004). The separation between ownership, control and finance creates serious agency problems to which investor protection and/or ownership concentration are possible solutions. Nevertheless, they also raise new issues. Although legal protection may help to secure owners' returns on investments, legal protection differs widely across countries: not only, or not so much, the degree, but the nature of investor protection legislation is crucial in determining corporate performance and macroeconomic consequences. Ownership concentration may help to improve control by owners, but large investors may also introduce new distortions in the redistribution of wealth, or act as powerful 'elites' to maintain inefficient governance systems.

The literature makes a distinction between two models of governance: the 'insider' model (based on concentrated ownership) and the 'outsider' model (based on dispersed ownership). The crucial question is to know if there exists one best corporate governance model that yields better economic performance. Part of the existing literature gives a positive answer to this question and identifies the Anglo-American (outsider) corporate governance model as the best-performing one, in particular during the last decade. Some authors, however, insist on the fact that each model of corporate governance has its own strengths and weaknesses (Shleifer and Vishny, 1997).

Does that mean that there is no one best way? The literature on 'varieties of capitalism' suggests that corporate governance models are embedded in larger institutional frameworks, and interdependencies exist across corporate governance, labour, product and financial market structures, as well as legislative frameworks (see, for instance, Aguilera and Jackson, 2003). More specifically, some recent literature focuses on the role of cooperation among several actors within the corporation (shareholders as well as stakeholders). Cooperation makes it possible to achieve better economic performance by favouring specific investments by/on stakeholders, as well as long-term projects by corporate managers (Hall and Soskice, 2001; Deakin et al., 2002).

How can one assess the macroeconomic impact of specific corporate governance features, such as ownership structure? Recent literature on aggregate performance points to the need for market deregulation in order to speed up employment and growth, particularly when a country is approaching the technological frontier (Nicoletti and Scarpetta, 2003; Aghion, 2006; Conway et al., 2006; Acemoglu et al., 2007). These analyses focus, however, on the macroeconomic impact of deregulation alone. Now, contributions such as Deakin et al. (2002) and Blair (2003) clearly make the point that the consequences of a given ownership structure partially depend on the structure of (labour and product) markets, and vice versa. In this sense, market regulation and ownership structure should be seen as interdependent institutional features.

MACROECONOMIC CONSEQUENCES OF OWNERSHIP CONCENTRATION: MAIN THEORETICAL CHANNELS

Ownership concentration is traditionally seen as one possible way to improve control by owners in the absence of sufficient legal protection of (dispersed) shareholders. The theoretical literature on the (macro)economic effects of ownership concentration delivers contrasting results, however.

Ownership and the Logic of Financial Discipline

The theoretical literature on corporate governance focuses on one 'best solution' to the agency problem between managers and owners, based on a system of dispersed ownership coupled with strong legal protection for shareholders. Within this system, owners are prevented from exerting strong direct control, because they own small shares of public companies. Managers are exposed to financial market discipline via exit or takeover threats. On the one hand, market discipline ensures that managers 'do the right thing' to maximize the company's value. On the other hand, dispersed ownership prevents owners from becoming too powerful and thus diverting wealth according to their own private interests. This leads to an efficient allocation of investments, yielding positive effects on growth.

Building on similar arguments, Randall Morck et al. (2005) analyse thoroughly the negative impact of ownership concentration by focusing in particular on specific structures such as wealthy family control and pyramids. They review the existing literature on the topic and focus on the fact that pyramids create distortions in the allocation of wealth, thus yielding a negative impact on investment and growth. Moreover, the authors underline the possible emergence of perverse political economy mechanisms leading powerful owners (frequently one single wealthy family) to save their interest by countering (at the political level) the financial development of a country. Hence, concentrated ownership can lead to underdevelopment traps with immature financial markets and weak growth.

Ownership and the Labour Market: The Logic of Interdependence

It follows that the effects of concentrated ownership are probably very different according to a country's level of development (Carlin and Mayer, 2003). Focusing on developed countries, it is indeed possible to identify important drawbacks of financial market discipline and a few positive consequences of concentrated/connected ownership. The issue was first raised by Morck et al. (2005). In one of their contributions, they ask if the rich guys are really that 'greedy' and self-centred, or if their utility has other people's well-being or general economic growth as an argument?

I shall raise a similar question here, though I am not concerned about the wealth of owners. I aim rather to highlight a few channels through which ownership concentration may contribute to improving owners' perspective with respect to the externalities stemming from their investment decisions, as well as their propensity to establish stable partnerships with employees and other crucial actors (unions, competitors, suppliers and so on).

Following a seminal work by Peter Hall and David Soskice (2001), one can characterize developed countries according to the degree of coordination among relevant economic actors. Coordination is achieved through several devices, including workers' and employers' associations, connected ownership, networks and cross-participations. Hence, concentrated ownership, as well as market regulations, appears to be an institutional device that makes it possible to strengthen the positive effects of coordination. Strong coordination allows businesses to engage credibly in long-term partnerships with competitors, employees, unions and suppliers. Moreover, because coordinated businesses are embedded in a larger set of connected relationships, individual actors have a better perception of the external effects of their economic actions. This improves the allocation of investments in domains where externalities are important, such as in research, education and innovation. Nevertheless, ownership structure alone cannot sustain the emergence of such coordinated and stable economic relations.

In fact, concentrated ownership and market regulations can be seen as the double-sided result of a political economy equilibrium supporting a 'corporatist' type of society. Marco Pagano and Paolo Volpin (2005) suggest that such an equilibrium can emerge out of a political compromise between employees and managers, achieved by exchanging greater independence for managers against stronger employment protection (see also Amable and Gatti, 2004). Roger Barker and David Rueda (2007, p. 21) describe 'the situation prevailing in the "golden age of social democracy"' as the result of a de facto coalition between 'insider capital' and 'insider labor': this coalition would allow insider actors to extract rents from outsider actors and redistribute the benefits from these rents among insiders. This literature suggests that interdependencies exist between the structure of ownership and the regulation of relevant markets.

Coordination and externalities in innovation

Concentrated ownership is associated with the emergence of economic and/or political 'elites'. In the presence of externalities and market failures, such elites can improve the coordination across economic actors and favour industrial modernization (see, for France, Amable and Hancké, 2001). A well-known argument by Lars Calmfors and John Driffill (1988) suggests that connected owners can contribute to coordination in wage setting, and beyond, by negotiating with trade unions and other social partners. Hence, elites can take into account external effects in wage setting, as well as in technological investments, thus achieving an allocation of resources at least as satisfactory as more atomized owners would be.

This mechanism has important consequences for innovation and growth as well. Donatella Gatti (2000) presents a theoretical model where business coordination (through connected ownership and networks) allows firms to better account for externalities stemming from radical innovations. In fact, radical innovations yield a stronger labour turnover and affect the stability of employment relations. In the presence of incentive constraints, a stronger labour turnover leads to higher incentive, compatible wages or weaker productive effort. To avoid such a perverse macroeconomic effect, connected businesses tend to invest more in research in order to favour a more incremental innovation trajectory. Hence, the models suggest that corporations embedded in more coordinated environments are more likely to engage in research investments, while deregulated markets favour more fundamental research carried out by external laboratories.

Market imperfections and regulations

Market imperfections can actually be good for macroeconomic performance and growth. This theoretical argument is made by Bruno Amable and Donatella Gatti (2004, 2006). These papers show that labour and product market regulation are complementary policies in contexts where wages are set according to an incentive compatible mechanism (that is, an efficiency wage mechanism). Better job security, stemming from increased regulation in labour and product markets, lowers the wage premium and/ or increases productive effort. In some cases, this makes it possible to improve aggregate employment.

A connected argument is explored by Enisse Kharroubi (2008). The author studies the effects of labour and financial market imperfections on technology and growth. The model developed in the paper shows that stable employment relations coupled with liquidity constraints push firms to invest in more productive technologies. In fact, firms face a twofold incentive for improving their technologies: first, this allows firms to make 'almost-fixed labour' more efficient through up-to-date equipment; second, whenever technological investment is successful, this generates higher cash flows, easing liquidity constraints.

In all three papers (labour, product and financial) market regulations promote more stable labour relations and generate positive macroeconomic effects in terms of employment and growth.

Stability and commitment to long-term investments

One important consequence of financial market discipline is that it might favour a bias in strategic investments towards short-term maximization of the firm's market value. According to Margaret Blair (2003), the short-term bias is one major weakness of the 'shareholder model' of corporate governance.

The literature has focused on possible alternatives to the 'shareholder model', namely the 'stakeholder model'. Stakeholders, and in particular employees, are seen as actors who make specific investments, and thus contribute to improving their company's capital stock and value. Simon Deakin et al. (2002) focus on the role of partnerships with employees: ownership structure and market regulations are preconditions to long-term partnerships. In fact, stable partnerships are more likely to emerge if ownership is concentrated, and if firms are not exposed to tight market conditions: large shareholders ensure more stable ownership and are straightforward partners in bilateral relationships with employees. Moreover, stable partnerships can only emerge if market conditions do not yield high turnover in business and labour relations. Hence, concentrated ownership, together with regulation (in product and labour markets), contributes to sustaining long-term partnerships.

Stable partnerships can actually be crucial to sustaining long-term specific investments. This argument is made in a model proposed by

Amable et al. (2005): the authors show that financial market imperfections favour the emergence of long-term cooperative strategies by firms and unions.

ASSESSING THE MACROECONOMIC IMPACT OF OWNERSHIP CONCENTRATION AND EMPLOYMENT PROTECTION

The theoretical arguments reviewed above suggest that concentrated ownership and market regulations can improve coordination across economic actors and favour the emergence of credible commitments and long-term partnerships with employees (in particular). This can improve economic performance by favouring firm-specific investments, more-efficient technologies, as well as greater efforts in research activities characterized by strong externalities. Finally, ownership structure and market regulation appear as interdependent institutional features.

Hence, one crucial aspect in my argument relies on the role of stability in labour, financial and ownership relations. The relevant question to be asked is, thus: do stable economic relations favour better macroeconomic performance?

To answer this question, I shall explore the interplay between ownership concentration and market regulation by addressing two important aspects that are generally neglected in the existing literature. First, I aim at 'being fair' with respect to the role of regulation and concentration. That means accounting for all channels through which increased regulation/concentration yield a deterioration as well as an improvement in macroeconomic performance. Second, I shall extend the analysis of interdependency across institutions to account for the existence of both institutional complements and institutional substitutes. Through this approach, I shall challenge the common complementarity argument recommending decreasing market regulation while increasing ownership dispersion in order to improve macroeconomic performance. In fact, increasing market regulation may actually be a good policy in some contexts, and a decrease in ownership dispersion could also be beneficial. A complementarity effect might even exist across different institutional arrangements: regulation and concentration might reinforce each other, making their respective positive impact more effective. Moreover, situations may exist where joint deregulation policies have conflicting effects on aggregate performance, that is, where a substitution effect emerges across institutional reforms.

Employment

The debate about the persistence of high unemployment in some European countries generally focuses on the structure of labour relations: employment protection legislation (EPL), replacement rates, wage taxes and union density are considered to lead to real wage pressure and lower equilibrium employment (see, for instance, Nickell, 1997; Siebert, 1997; Blau and Kahn, 1999, and Bertola et al., 2002). The same argument applies to the structure of product and financial markets: stronger regulation of those markets would hinder competition and prevent the creation of jobs and firms (Nickell, 1999; Acemoglu, 2001; Wasmer and Weil, 2004). One notable exception, however, in the standard view concerns the role of coordination in wage bargaining. In fact, since the seminal work by Calmfors and Driffill (1988), coordination has always been acknowledged as enhancing employment performance by allowing for wage moderation. A debatable aspect of the standard view concerns the issue of employment protection and job precariousness. Guiseppe Bertola (1990) (and more recently Giulio Fella, 2000) argues that labour market regulation (that is, job protection) may yield a positive effect on employment by fostering long-term labour relations. Amable and Gatti (2006) show that firing costs dampen the effects of product market deregulation on labour turnover, and thus help limit real wage pressure. Hence, the effects of product and labour market deregulation stand in opposition to one another: they could indeed be substitute (rather than complementary) policies.

My aim is to evaluate the effect of ownership concentration, market regulations and coordination on aggregated employment performance. I shall rely on the empirical strategy proposed by Amable et al. (2007a). The framework is inspired by Stephen Nickell et al. (2005), and has been enriched in various directions. I include a measure of ownership concentration and estimate (using OECD data on 18 developed countries over the 1980–2004 period, maximum time length) a lagged dependent variable model with (country and years) dummies, which has the following form:

$$u_{i,t} = \alpha_i + \phi \cdot u_{i,t-1} + \beta_1 \cdot X_{i,t} + \beta_2 \cdot Z_{i,t} + \eta \cdot Y_{i,t} + \gamma_1 \cdot pmr_{i,t}$$

$$+ \gamma_2 \cdot epl_{i,t} + \gamma_3 \cdot oc_{i,t} + \gamma_4 \cdot pmr_{i,t} \times epl_{i,t} + \varepsilon_{i,t}, \qquad (2.1)$$

where $u_{i,t}$ = rate of joblessness, $Y_{i,t}$ = vector of macroeconomic controls, $Z_{i,t}$ = vector of time-invariant institutional variables, $X_{i,t}$ = vector of time-varying institutional variables, $pmr_{i,t}$ = product market regulation, $epl_{i,t}$ = employment protection legislation, $oc_{i,t}$ = ownership concentration.

This specification makes it possible to capture the interdependence across labour and product market structure through a specific interaction term. Moreover, the role of ownership concentration as a 'coordination device' can be tested against other standard measures of coordination.

Productivity and Growth

The debate concerning the consequences of market regulation on innovation and growth focuses on the role of competition and the well-known Schumpeterian effect. According to Joseph Schumpeter (1934), increased competition across firms decreases rents stemming from investments (such as research and development). Therefore, incentives to innovate may be harmed. On the other hand, competition can also favour innovation. For instance, Philippe Aghion et al. (2005) consider a situation where firms innovate to decrease their production costs 'step by step'. When firms have comparable productivity levels ('neck-and-neck' competition), increased competition pushes them to increase their innovative effort in order to have a chance to become the leader. On the contrary, in industries/countries where the leader is far ahead of its competitors, increased competition is a much less effective policy (and could harm innovation).

Along the same lines, recent empirical contributions (Nicoletti and Scarpetta, 2003; Aghion, 2006; Conway et al., 2006; Acemoglu et al., 2007) propose an approach in terms of countries' distance from the technological frontier: the effect of market regulation on productivity and growth would vary in response to a change in country distance to the technological frontier. The main argument is that the costs of market regulation would increase as the economy gets closer to the technological frontier. For instance, Daron Acemoglu et al. (2007) suggest that increased regulation is more 'effective' in reducing incentives to innovate in countries/sectors close to the technological frontier. A few recent contributions cast some doubt on the robustness of this result (Amable et al., 2007b), however.

In fact, the standard view neglects the importance of coordination effects and the role of stable economic relations favoured by the *joint presence* of (sufficiently strong) market regulation and ownership concentration. As already mentioned above, one can theoretically expect these effects to be sizeable. Moreover, the size of the effects may vary in response to changes in the countries' distance from the technological frontier. Countries that are closer to the technological frontier may benefit more than laggards from improved coordination and more stable labour relations. Stronger incentives to invest in up-to-date technologies, greater productive effort and investment by workers, and a better perception of externalities linked to innovation could all be crucial advantages to gaining a leadership position.

To tackle this issue, I have stuck to a standard estimation strategy including externalities from leader countries as well as individual countries' distance from the technological frontier (see, in particular, Nicoletti and Scarpetta, 2003). I tested the joint effects of market regulation and ownership concentration on growth by using OECD data on 18 developed countries over the 1980–2004 period (maximum time length). The estimated model has the following form (M–PR):

$$\Delta \ln y_{i,t} = \alpha_i + \phi_1 \cdot \Delta \ln y_{Ft} + \phi_2 \cdot df_{i,t} + \beta_1 \cdot X_{i,t} + \beta_2 \cdot Z_{i,t}$$

$$+ \eta \cdot Y_{i,t} + \zeta_1 \cdot oc_{i,t} + \zeta_2 \cdot epl_{i,t} + \zeta_3 \cdot oc_{i,t} \cdot epl_{i,t}$$

$$+ \zeta_4 \cdot df_{i,t} \cdot oc_{i,t} + \zeta_5 \cdot df_{i,t} \cdot epl_{i,t} + \varepsilon_{i,t} \tag{2.2}$$

where $y_{i,t}$ = GDP per employee, $\Delta \ln y_{i,t}$ = difference between logGDP at the end and at the beginning of the period, $Y_{i,t}$ = vector of macroeconomic controls, $Z_{i,t}$ = vector of time-invariant institutional variables, $X_{i,t}$ = vector of time-varying institutional variables, $epl_{i,t}$ = employment protection legislation, $oc_{i,t}$ = ownership concentration, $df_{i,t} = -\ln(y_{i,t} / y_{F,t})$ = distance of country i at time t with respect to the frontier: the smaller the distance (and the closer the country is to the frontier), the smaller the value of $df_{i,t}$. The frontier country is the country that has the highest GDP per employee level at period t.

This specification accounts for several interdependences across and between institutional features, as well as country distance from the frontier. In particular, it allows me to test the idea that ownership concentration might contribute to increasing GDP per employee growth, conditional to the presence of highly regulated (labour) markets, in countries that are not necessarily laggards.

The next section gives more details about the data and the estimation procedure adopted here.

DATA AND METHODOLOGY

Data

My sample includes 18 countries (Australia, Austria, Belgium, Canada, Denmark, Finland, France, Germany, Ireland, Italy, Japan, the Netherlands, Norway, Portugal, Spain, Sweden, the United Kingdom and the United States) over the period from 1980 to 2004.

Macroeconomic data are provided by OECD annual sets (credit to the economy, real effective exchange rate, trade balance). GDP per employee data come from the OECD and the Penn World Table. Education is measured as the proportion of enrolled students to the corresponding age–class population (OECD data).

Population data, such as the share of the population aged 65 years and older (elderly population), were obtained from the OECD. The indicator of central bank dependence (CBdep) is commented by Amable et al. (2007a). It is a composite index constructed out of four other indicators. It ranges from 1 to 3, where '1' stands for a maximum of central bank independence. Concerning the institutional features of market regulation, I have relied on standard OECD indicators, such as union density and tax wedge. Wage coordination data are provided by Nickell et al. (2005). Time-series data for unemployment benefit net replacement rates are available from Lyle Scruggs (2004). The OECD also provides indicators of product market regulation (PMR and REGREFF): PMR is the standard global regulation indicators (two points in time), while REGREFF is a time-series indicator that assesses the extent of regulation in key service sectors (such as gas, electricity, transport and so on). The OECD has also provided a decomposition of PMR according to fields of regulation: state intervention, barriers to firms' creation and trade barriers. I expect that the extent of state intervention might be a potentially crucial variable in my analysis: state intervention is indeed an important aspect of companies' ownership structures.

As for employment protection legislation, I have exploited an updated annual indicator provided by Amable et al. (2007a). The indicator is built by relying on the FRDB Social Reforms Database, which has been developed by the Fondazione Rodolfo Debenedetti (http://www.frdb.org). This database collects, on an annual basis, information about social reforms in European countries over the 1985–2005 period in the areas of employment protection legislation. The exact procedure for constructing my EPL series is described in Appendix 2A.

There exist a few possible indicators for the structure of ownership. In particular, one can proxy effective ownership concentration or alternatively rely on indirect measures of the legal environment (shareholder protection, for instance). Unlike other institutional indicators, no common standard (similar to OECD or World Bank standards) has been set in this area. Therefore, I have chosen to rely on data about effective ownership concentration, provided by well-known and influential contributions to the field (La Porta et al., 1998, 1999; Djankov et al., 2006). Effective concentration links up more directly to the stability of ownership – that is the main focus of this chapter.

La Porta et al. provide one single observation in time concerning effective ownership concentration (OC): concentration is measured as the average percentage of common shares owned by the top three sharehold-ers in the ten largest non-financial, privately owned domestic firms in a given country. A firm is considered privately owned if the 'state is not a known shareholder in it' (1999). More details are given in Appendix 2A.

Turning to political data, I have relied on several indicators from the Comparative Political Data Set (Armingeon et al., 2005): the Rae index of fractionalization of the political party system, the share of 'protest' votes (defined as the sum of votes for radical parties and abstentions), and a dummy for corporatist countries. Moreover, some data were obtained from Marco Pagano's online data (www.csef.it/people/pagano_data.htm), namely a dummy for proportional voting systems, as well as dummies for countries' legal origins (German, common law and Scandinavian). Finally, I have considered an annual indicator of left/right ideological positioning of governments (left/right) elaborated and proposed by Amable et al. (2006).

Methodology

Dealing with slowly changing variables
Several institutional variables (such as ownership concentration and overall PMR) are either invariant or change slowly. These variables refer to features that characterize more particularly a single country, or a given subset of countries. They are thus close to individual country effects. As noted in Amable et al. (2007a), the inclusion of country fixed effects in time-series cross-section (TSCS) models precludes the inclusion of time-invariant or slowly changing variables as independent variables. This feature has made many comparative analysts uncomfortable with the use of such models since no explanation of what fixed effects stand for can be given. If, however, one does not include fixed effects in the model, the time-invariant variables will carry the weight of all the country-specific factors determining macroeconomic performance.

Thomas Plümper and Vera Tröger (2007) propose a new estimator for analysing the effect of time-invariant variables in a model including fixed effects: the FEVD (Fixed Effects Vector Decomposition) estimator. The procedure has three steps: (i) estimate a fixed-effects model, (ii) regress the unit effects on the time-invariant variables, and (iii) re-estimate the first stage including the error term of the second stage (FEVD procedure). The procedure involves extracting from the fixed effect the part of it that is explained by slowly changing variables. This gives more meaning to fixed effects by explicitly modelling their institutional components.

The procedure is particularly helpful in the present study, given the absence of a time profile for variables such as OC and PMR and its components.

Accounting for interdependencies

To investigate more deeply the interdependency between ownership concentration and market regulation, I include in the model interaction terms between institutional variables. The inclusion of an interaction term means that the marginal effect of one variable – say ownership concentration – varies with the level of the variable with which it interacts (Braumoeller, 2004).

A specific procedure presented by Amable et al. (2007a) makes it possible to evaluate the effects of each relevant variable for different levels of interaction. In particular, I would like to know if these two features are complementary or substitutes. Following a standard definition of complementarity, two institutional devices are complementary if each of them is more effective in improving performance when the other one is also implemented. By contrast, two institutions are substitutable if implementing one of them decreases the effectiveness of the other.

Analysing the marginal effects of ownership concentration and market regulation allows me to answer a set of related questions. First, is concentrated ownership (market regulation) more effective for growth in the presence of stricter market regulation (more concentrated ownership)? If the answer is yes, then one would conclude that there exists a positive interdependence between ownership structure and market structure. Second, does the impact of ownership concentration and market regulation depend on the country's distance from the frontier? In other words, do concentrated ownership and regulated markets prevent countries from getting closer to the frontier? Or, on the contrary, do these features favour mostly advanced rather than lagging-behind countries? Interpreting the results makes it possible to determine the nature of the interdependency between ownership structure and market regulation.

Coping with endogeneity

The recent theoretical and empirical literature suggests that institutional features change over time. Existing contributions show a strong divide between those authors who think that growth and internationalization of the economies will lead to institutional convergence, and those who believe that institutional diversity will nevertheless persist.

In particular, institutional devices such as ownership concentration and market regulation may well be endogenous and depend on several concurring processes: feedback from economic performance, political pressures, legal constraints and path dependence (Amable and Gatti, 2004; Pagano and Volpin, 2005; Gatti and Glyn, 2006; Cusack et al., 2007; Persson et al., 2007).

From an empirical point of view, the question is how to satisfactorily account for endogeneity. A few recent papers tackle the issue of endogeneity with longitudinal data for developed and developing countries (La Porta et al., 1998, 1999; Djankov et al., 2006). Amable et al. (2006) investigate the determinants of changes in replacement rates in a TSCS model. These contributions make use of an instrumental variable (IV) approach to tackle endogeneity. The IV approach can, however, be seen as an unsatisfactory procedure. In fact, one concentrates on a single equation model while the true model is composed of several endogenous variables (macroeconomic performance and institutions) that are simultaneously determined.

My approach in this chapter is to investigate the problem of endogeneity by using a simultaneous-equation model. The model includes one equation for economic performance (the growth equation presented above) and two equations for institutional variables: employment protection legislation and ownership concentration. The evolution of institutional devices is assumed to depend on a number of explanatory variables, among which economic pressure (country distance from the frontier/growth), political institutions and political ideology, social and demographic structure of the population, and so on.

This analysis allows me to study more precisely the feedbacks from economic performance onto ownership structure and market structure. In this respect, the central question is: does higher growth necessarily lead countries towards a more dispersed/less regulated model, or is the feedback mediated through the effects of political, social and demographic variables?

RESULTS

Employment

Results presented in this section rely on previous work done with Bruno Amable and Lilas Demmou (Amable et al., 2007a). This work is extended to account for the effects of ownership concentration. The dependent variable in the analysis is the rate of joblessness, that is, one minus the employment rate. This measure of non-employment makes it possible to take into account both unemployment and inactivity.

Table 2.1 provides results of regressions run by using the FEVD estimator. Invariant variables in regressions are: OC, PMR, CBdep, and

Table 2.1   Joblessness rate

Joblessness rate	(A)	(B)
Joblessness rate ($t-1$)	0.796***	0.796***
	(0.034)	(0.035)
EPL	−4.514***	−4.497***
	(1.248)	(1.234)
EPL*PMR	1.595**	1.584**
	(0.636)	(0.628)
PMR	2.356***	2.670***
	(0.154)	(0.179)
Coordination	−0.181**	−0.094
	(0.090)	(0.090)
OC		−2.205***
		(0.403)
CBdep	−0.690***	−0.818***
	(0.070)	(0.071)
Replacement rate	0.913	0.906
	(0.946)	(0.952)
Union density	0.078***	0.077***
	(0.023)	(0.023)
Lagged productivity	−0.100	−0.139
	(2.210)	(2.219)
Credit to economy	−0.072***	−0.072***
	(0.011)	(0.011)
Trade balance	−0.097**	−0.096**
	(0.045)	(0.046)
Real effective exchange rate	−1.931**	−1.932**
	(0.908)	(0.907)
Income tax	0.034	0.033
	(0.027)	(0.027)
eta	0.933***	0.928***
	(0.025)	(0.027)
Cons	2.431***	3.300***
	(0.334)	(0.303)
Time/country dummies	Yes	Yes
Number of obs	266	266
Final rho	0.227	0.227

Note: Standard errors in parentheses; ** $p < 0.05$, *** $p < 0.01$.

coordination. Two variants of the model are proposed, without and with the OC indicator. The results are fairly standard for all variables except EPL. Amable et al. (2007a) provide a thorough analysis of the effects of EPL on joblessness (and its components), conditional to the structure of product markets (proxied by PMR). The authors study the marginal effect of EPL and PMR (given their interaction term) and conclude that there exists a substitution effect across deregulation policies: increasing EPL appears to be a good policy reform in response to product market deregulation (that is, lowering PMR).

Concerning ownership concentration, the coefficient of OC appears to be highly significant and negative: more concentration reduces joblessness. This effect appears, as expected, to be working through improved coordination. In fact, the standard coordination measure (Nickell et al., 2005) proves significant and negative in regressions without OC. Nevertheless, the variable becomes non-significant as soon as I control for ownership concentration (see column B).

Productivity and Growth

I now turn to the analysis of GDP per employee growth. My baseline model was (2.2), which included institutional indicators, macroeconomic controls and a proxy for human capital (education). My main focus was on the effects of ownership concentration and employment protection legislation. I also included, however, institutional variables controlling for other characteristics of product market structure, such as state intervention (PMR-SI) and the extent of regulation in key-service sectors (REGREFF).

I ran regressions using two alternative estimators: the FEVD estimator, which yields more efficient estimations of slowly changing institutional variables, and IVREG2 (two-stage instrumental variable estimator), which makes it possible to control for a possible endogeneity of regressors. Invariant variables in FEVD regressions are: PMR, PMR-SI and OC.

For the IV regressions, I considered the following variables as endogenous: Distance to frontier, EPL*Distance to frontier, OC*Distance to frontier, EPL, OC, EPL*OC, PMR-SI and REGREFF. I used the following instruments: country-specific trends, lagged endogenous variables, age structure of the population (proportion of elderly), unions' bargaining power (union density rate), Rae's index of fractionalization of party system, and incidence of protest votes.

The results presented in Table 2.2 show similar coefficients for the two alternative estimation procedures. Coefficients obtained via instrumental variables are in some cases larger or more significant than FEVD

Table 2.2   DlogGDP per employee

DlogGDP per employee	FEVD	IVREG2
DlogFrontier	0.302***	0.328***
	(0.108)	(0.099)
Distance to frontier	0.119	0.230*
	(0.086)	(0.134)
Effective real exchange rate	−0.024*	−0.029**
	(0.014)	(0.013)
Education	0.061***	0.072***
	(0.015)	(0.018)
EPL*distance to frontier	0.114***	0.153***
	(0.032)	(0.042)
OC*distance to frontier	−0.409*	−0.785**
	(0.218)	(0.342)
EPL	−0.075***	−0.109***
	(0.026)	(0.042)
EPL*OC	0.154***	0.228***
	(0.053)	(0.087)
REGREFF	0.000	0.002
	(0.001)	(0.001)
OC	−0.039***	
	(0.007)	
PMR-SI	0.011***	−0.017
	(0.001)	(0.012)
eta	1.000***	
	(0.045)	
Time/country dummies	Yes	Yes
Number of obs	410	380

Note: Standard errors in parentheses; * $p < 0.10$, ** $p < 0.05$, *** $p < 0.01$.

estimations. Those changes are marginal, however. I consider this as a mark of robustness of my results.

One should note that the IV estimation presents a major drawback with respect to the FEVD procedure: it appears to be impossible to accurately estimate coefficients for time-invariant variables such as OC and PMR-SI. The OC variable automatically drops out of regressions (and does not show up in the results below), because it is confounded with the unit fixed effects in the first-stage regressions. The crucial advantage of the FEVD procedure is that it makes it possible to cope with this problem by extracting, from fixed effects, the component that is explained by time-invariant institutional features.

As expected, stronger growth in frontier countries and human capital contribute to increasing GDP per employee growth, while distance to the frontier appears to play mostly through the interaction terms. EPL, OC and PMR-SI all prove significant in FEVD regressions. This confirms that institutional features crucially shape the process of growth and convergence: state intervention appears to yield positive effects, which can easily be linked to the role of state-owned companies in fostering innovation in crucial sectors of the economy.

The direct effect of EPL and OC is negative, but their interaction term has a positive and significant coefficient, suggesting that a complementarity effect may be at work: stronger employment protection/ownership concentration would favour growth in contexts where EPL and OC levels are higher. One should be careful, however, in interpreting the estimated coefficients at this stage. In fact, the institutional variables have also been interacted with country distance to frontier. Hence, the overall impact of EPL and OC on growth depends on the country's progression towards the frontier. In particular, I want to know if stronger EPL and/or OC favour or prevent countries from getting closer to the frontier. I turn now to this crucial question.

I shall now rely on FEVD regression results, which provide more robust estimations for time-invariant institutional indicators. Since I have included several interaction terms (between ownership concentration, employment protection legislation and country distance to frontier), I shall assess the overall impact of OC and EPL by computing their marginal effect conditional on specific values of the interacted variables (see Braumoeller, 2004). From model (2.2) one gets:

$$\frac{\partial \Delta \ln y_{i,t}}{\partial oc_{i,t}} = \hat{\zeta}_1 + \hat{\zeta}_3 \cdot epl_{i,t} + \hat{\zeta}_4 \cdot df_{i,t}$$

$$\frac{\partial \Delta \ln y_{i,t}}{\partial epl_{i,t}} = \hat{\zeta}_2 + \hat{\zeta}_3 \cdot oc_{i,t} + \hat{\zeta}_5 \cdot df_{i,t} \qquad (2.3)$$

Note that the marginal effect of ownership concentration on GDP per employee growth depends not only on the institutional context (that is, the value of EPL), but also on the country's level of convergence (that is, the value of the distance to the frontier). The same reasoning applies to employment protection legislation. Given the signs of the estimated coefficients, one can see that the positive effect of EPL is magnified when a country's distance from the frontier is large, while the negative effect of OC is smaller when approaching the frontier.

In order to carefully assess the overall impact of EPL and OC, I shall now evaluate the above marginal effects and their significance conditional to five

Table 2.3   *Marginal effect of employment protection legislation and of ownership concentration according to the distance to frontier*

	Min distance to frontier	Short distance to frontier	Average distance to frontier	Long distance to frontier	Max distance to frontier
Marginal Effect of EPL					
Min OC	−0.045***	−0.042**	−0.024*	−0.006	0.040***
	(0.017)	(0.016)	(0.013)	(0.011)	(0.015)
Mean OC less 1sd	−0.031**	−0.028**	−0.010	0.007	0.054***
	(0.013)	(0.012)	(0.009)	(0.008)	(0.016)
Mean OC	−0.012	−0.009	0.009	0.026***	0.073***
	(0.008)	(0.008)	(0.006)	(0.008)	(0.020)
Mean OC plus 1sd	0.007	0.011	0.028***	0.046***	0.092***
	(0.008)	(0.008)	(0.009)	(0.013)	(0.025)
Max OC	0.017*	0.020**	0.038***	0.055***	0.102***
	(0.009)	(0.010)	(0.012)	(0.016)	(0.027)
Marginal Effect of OC					
Min EPL	−0.031***	−0.044***	−0.107**	−0.107**	−0.338**
	(0.010)	(0.014)	(0.045)	(0.078)	(0.167)
Mean EPL less 1sd	0.042	0.030	−0.033	−0.097	−0.264
	(0.032)	(0.033)	(0.052)	(0.081)	(0.166)
Mean EPL	0.128**	0.115*	0.052	−0.011	−0.179
	(0.061)	(0.061)	(0.071)	(0.093)	(0.171)
Mean EPL plus 1sd	0.213**	0.200**	0.137	0.074	−0.093
	(0.090)	(0.090)	(0.096)	(0.112)	(0.180)
Max EPL	0.267**	0.255**	0.191*	0.128	−0.039
	(0.109)	(0.109)	(0.113)	(0.126)	(0.188)

Note: Standard errors in parentheses; * $p < 0.10$, ** $p < 0.05$, *** $p < 0.01$.

alternative values of the relevant variables: minimum and maximum levels, mean value and mean plus/minus one standard deviation. In Table 2.3, the results are reported separately for the marginal effects of EPL and OC.

The marginal effect of EPL on GDP per employee growth appears to be significant and positive for lagging-behind countries; this positive effect becomes stronger, the higher the ownership concentration. For countries with an average-to-short distance from the frontier, EPL coefficients are negative at low levels of ownership concentration and become positive again at high levels of ownership concentration. This suggests that a positive interdependence across EPL and OC emerges as countries get closer to the frontier. When countries are very close to the frontier, however, the interdependence shows up only for maximum levels of concentration.

These results are strengthened by the analysis of the marginal effect of OC on GDP per employee growth. In fact, the coefficients for OC appear to be negative at low levels of EPL. For distances to the frontier ranging from average to very small, however, one observes positive coefficients for OC at average-to-high levels of EPL. Hence, ownership concentration appears to favour growth when countries get closer to the frontier, provided that those countries also show (at least) average levels of employment protection legislation. This effect becomes stronger the closer a country gets to the frontier. Hence, the analysis of marginal effects reveals that, far from being harmful to growth and convergence, specific institutional features can favour growth provided that they are combined in appropriate ways.

Simultaneous Equations

I now turn to the crucial issue of grasping the 'dynamic' feedbacks at work along the growth and convergence paths. In particular, I shall try to capture the existing pressures towards changing the institutional framework in response to the economic, social and political environment. My aim is not to present final results in this section, but rather to blaze a possible line of research that will (hopefully) be enriched by further contributions.

In order to be able to model, at the same time, the determinants of GDP per employee growth and the determinants of institutional change, I shall turn to simultaneous regression techniques and rely in particular on three-stage least squares estimations. This will allow me to run simultaneous equation estimations for growth, employment protection legislation and ownership concentration.[1] I shall model the growth equation exactly as in the previous section. Concerning institutional variables, I shall rely on a growing body of literature at the frontier of political economics and political economy, and model, one at a time, institutional features as determined by economic, social and political factors.

More specifically, I have assumed that economic feedbacks might stem from growth itself and/or from the convergence path (that is, distance to frontier). Political institutions are crucial in shaping an institutional framework. I have captured this effect by introducing a standard dummy for proportional electoral systems. The intuition is that proportional voting systems are more encompassing and might favour stronger institutional regulation. Political ideology of government can also shape one country's institutional trajectory, as was the case during the building phase of the welfare state in North European countries, for instance. I therefore have included an indicator of the position of governments along a standard left/right scale. Finally, population structure is also important as the debate on the effects of ageing populations in Europe has clearly shown. Hence, I consider a variable that

Table 2.4 Three-stage least squares estimations for growth, employment protection legislation and ownership concentration

DlogGDP per employee		EPL		OC	
DlogFrontier	0.121 (0.079)	Distance to frontier	0.954*** (0.148)	DlogGDP per employee	−4.297*** (0.643)
Distance to frontier	0.037 (0.025)	Proportional	0.089*** (0.013)	Proportional	0.076*** (0.005)
Effective real exchange rate	−0.019* (0.011)	Left/right	−0.002*** (0.001)	Left/right	0.000 (0.000)
EPL	−0.022*** (0.007)	Elderly population	0.053*** (0.007)	Elderly population	−0.012*** (0.003)
OC	−0.064*** (0.023)	German LO	−0.280*** (0.045)	German LO	−0.037** (0.015)
PMR-SI	0.007*** (0.002)	Scandinavian LO	−0.288*** (0.058)	Scandinavian LO	0.047** (0.021)
REGREFF	0.001 (0.001)	Common LO	−0.711*** (0.055)	Common LO	0.091*** (0.021)
EPL*OC	0.037*** (0.014)	Corporatist	0.361*** (0.054)	Corporatist	0.195*** (0.020)
EPL*distance to frontier	0.042** (0.018)	Time dummies	Yes	Time dummies	Yes
OC*distance to frontier	−0.131* (0.079)				
Education	0.072*** (0.011)				
German LO	0.013*** (0.003)				
Scandinavian LO	0.010*** (0.003)				
Common LO	−0.001 (0.004)				
Time dummies	Yes				

Note: Number of observations 322. Standard errors in parentheses; * $p < 0.10$, ** $p < 0.05$, *** $p < 0.01$.

captures the proportion of elderly people out of the total population. Results of three-stage estimations are presented in Table 2.4.

Simultaneous regressions deliver results for the growth equation that are remarkably consistent with previous results, although less robust, which is not surprising given that time-invariant variables cannot be treated properly. Regression coefficients in the EPL and OC equations show up significantly and with expected signs, except for the left/right variable in the OC equation whose coefficient is not significant.

Concerning the economic pressures on the institutional environment, I find that feedbacks do not work in the same way for EPL and OC: for ownership concentration, feedbacks work through the growth channel, while for employment protection legislation, convergence appears to be the driving economic force.[2] Hence, there does not seem to be a common economic force sustaining institutional change.

Turning to social and political variables, results suggest that some socio-political preconditions are common to regulation and concentration: proportional electoral systems appear to favour labour market regulation and ownership concentration, this being reinforced by the presence of a corporatist environment. Nevertheless, a few differences also appear between the two equations: the left/right ideological divide seems to apply to the field of regulation and not to ownership concentration; the structure of the population would play in opposite directions, with the ageing population sustaining stronger regulation and weaker concentration.

Taken together, these results suggest that institutional frameworks are shaped by common tendencies as well as contrasting pressures: political institutions (electoral systems and corporatist regulations) are unsurprisingly a crucial force setting the path for coherent institutional reforms. On the other hand, economic factors, as well as ideological and demographic pressures (ageing population), yield more contrasted effects that could be at the root of a weakening coherence in existing institutional configurations.

CONCLUSION

This chapter has analysed the macroeconomic impact of ownership structure and employment protection by taking into account their interdependencies and changes over time.

Econometric analysis has shown that ownership concentration might favour employment through improved coordination across agents. Ownership concentration also favours growth when countries get closer to the technological frontier, provided that those countries also show (at least) average levels of employment protection legislation.

To investigate the interdependence between OC and EPL across countries and over time, simultaneous three-equation estimations have been provided. Results for the growth equation are consistent with single equation results. Turning to the determinants of institutional variables (OC and EPL), I find that proportional electoral systems favour labour market regulation and ownership concentration, this being reinforced by the presence of a corporatist environment.

APPENDIX 2A

EPL Indicator

For countries that are documented in the FRDB Social Reforms Database, I estimated a model explaining the evolution of the EPL indicator by Nickell et al. (2005) using the indicators of employment protection given in the database, as well as country dummies and time trends as regressors. In particular, I ran ordinary least squares (OLS) estimations using the following regressors by the FRDB Database.

index_fepl: a measure indicating the precise number of reforms passed each year in each country, as well as the direction of their effect on labour market flexibility. Reforms are characterized as being directed towards more flexibility if they decrease restrictions in several domains, such as wage setting, firing restriction, working-time regulation and so on.

impact_fepl: a measure accounting for the number of reforms towards more flexible labour markets (per year, per country) as well as their more or less comprehensive nature: reforms are characterized as more comprehensive if they apply to all, or a large majority of, professional categories, contract typologies, and so on. Reforms are less comprehensive if they apply only to specific categories of workers, contracts, firms and so on.

The models that I estimated typically had the following specification:

$$y_{i,t} = \alpha_i + \beta \cdot x_{i,t} + t + \varepsilon_{i,t}, \qquad (2A.1)$$

with $y_{i,t}$ being the EPL indicator by Nickell et al. (2005); $x_{i,t}$ being equal to *index_fepl* and/or *impact_fepl*; t being a common and/or country-specific trend. On the basis of such regressions, I predicted annual EPL series over the 1980–2004 period for each country in my sample that was included in the FRDB Database. These series were then checked against reported values of the indicators by the OECD and by Nickell et al. The advantage of using my EPL series (with respect to previous existing ones) is that it embeds additional annual information about the evolution of employment protection legislation, provided by the FRBD Database.

OC Indicator

Ownership structure is proxied in existing studies by measures of ownership concentration, the size of voting blocks, the presence of specific

Table 2A.1   *Ownership concentration, voting rights and voting blocks*

Country	OwnerConc country	AvConStake country	VotBlock
Japan	18		10
UK	19 UK	24 UK	
US	20		
Australia	28		
Sweden	28 Sweden	27 Sweden	34
France	34 France	50 France CAC 40	20
Norway	36 Norway	42	
Finland	37 Finland	38	
Ireland	39 Ireland	31	
Netherlands	39	Netherlands	43
Canada	40		
Denmark	45		
Germany	48 Germany	51 Germany	57
Spain	51 Spain	40 Spain	34
Portugal	52 Portugal	51 Ireland	
Belgium	54 Belgium	45 Belgium	56
Austria	58 Australia	54 Austria	52
Italy	58 Italy	56 Italy	54

Notes and sources:
For Spain, see Alonso et al. (2005).
For Sweden, see Henrekson and Jacobson (2003).
OwnerConc = average % of common shares owned by 3 largest shareholders, Djankov et al. (2006).
AvConStake = % votes controlled by largest shareholders, Pagano and Volpin (2005).
VotBlock = size of largest median voting block for non-financial companies on official market, Becht and Mayer (2001).

structure (as pyramids), the incidence of insider capital, and so on. Only a few contributions make it possible to focus on relatively large-scale cross-country analyses: La Porta et al. (1998, 1999) and Djankov et al. (2006) are pre-eminent examples. These contributions provide one single observation in time concerning effective ownership concentration: concentration is measured by the 'average percentage of common shares owned by the top three shareholders in the ten largest non-financial, privately owned domestic firms in a given country. A firm is considered privately owned if the state is not a known shareholder in it'. This indicator has no time profile.

Bong-Chan Kho et al. (2006) propose an indicator of ownership concentration based on Worldscope data, available for two points in time (1994 and 2004). This indicator allows for developments in/the evolution of OC to be traced over time and suggests that there might be sizeable changes in OC over time. The authors themselves, however, highlight several weaknesses in their data, in particular the fact that Worldscope firms' population is very heterogeneous (in size and composition) across countries and not stable over time (it has actually been increasing over time). This is why I have decided to stick to the standard La Porta et al. (1999) measure. The only important difference between the La Porta et al. and the Kho et al. measures seems to concern Japan.

More focused contributions give additional information on specific subsets of countries. The main indicators are reproduced in Table 2A.1. The overall results are compatible with La Porta et al.'s analysis, minus a few exceptions. These exceptions concern countries where either the main shareholders are frequently observed but own shares in small firms (Sweden), or the main shareholders are concentrated in large companies where they own major shares (Spain).

NOTES

1. The exercise is extremely appealing. Nevertheless, when interpreting results, one should be aware of several caveats. First, to the best of my knowledge, there is no available three-stage regression estimator for panel data in STATA. I have therefore relied on existing time-series estimators. This would not be a matter of concern if I could properly treat individual country effects. I am prevented from doing so, however, by the presence of time-invariant variables in my regressions. To be able to model feedback onto ownership concentration, I have to work with 'loose' country dummies, such as legal origins and corporatism.
2. Growth is not significant in the EPL equation and has thus been removed. The same holds for distance to frontier in the OC equation.

REFERENCES

Acemoglu, Daron (2001), 'Credit market imperfections and persistent unemployment', *European Economic Review*, **45**, pp. 665–79.

Acemoglu, Daron, Philippe Aghion and Fabrizio Zilibotti (2007), 'Distance to frontier, selection and economic growth', *Journal of the European Economic Association*, **4** (1), pp. 37–74.

Aghion, Philippe (2006), 'A Primer on Innovation and Growth', BRUEGEL Policy Brief Issue 2006/06.

Aghion, Philippe, Nick Bloom, Richard Blundell, Rachel Griffith and Peter Howitt (2005), 'Competition and innovation: an inverted U relationship', *Quarterly Journal of Economics*, May, pp. 701–28.

Aguilera, Ruth and Gregory Jackson (2003), 'The cross-national diversity of corporate governance: dimensions and determinants', *Academy of Management Review*, **28**, pp. 447–65.

Alonso, Pablo de Andrès, Felix Iturriaga and Juan Rodriguez Sanz (2005), 'Financial decisions and growth opportunities: a Spanish firm's panel data analysis', *Applied Financial Economics*, **15**, pp. 391–407.

Amable, Bruno and Donatella Gatti (2006), 'Labour and product market reforms: questioning policy complementarity', *Industrial and Corporate Change*, **15** (1), pp. 101–22.

Amable, Bruno and Bob Hancké (2001), 'Innovation and industrial renewal in France in comparative perspective', *Industry and Innovation*, **8** (2), pp. 113–33.

Amable, Bruno and Donatella Gatti (2004), 'The political economy of job protection and income redistribution', IZA Discussion Paper 1404, Institute for the Study of Labour, Bonn.

Amable, Bruno, Lilas Demmou and Donatella Gatti (2007a), 'Employment performance and institutions: new answers to an old question', IZA Discussion Paper 2731, Institute for the Study of Labour, Bonn.

Amable, Bruno, Lilas Demmou and Ivan Ledezma (2007b), 'Competition, innovation and distance to frontier', mimeo, CEPREMAP, Paris.

Amable, Bruno, Ekkehard Ernst and Stefano Palombarini (2005), 'How do financial markets affect industrial relations: an institutional complementarity approach', *Socio-Economic Review*, **3** (2), pp. 311–30.

Amable, Bruno, Donatella Gatti and Jan Schumacher (2006), 'Welfare state retrenchment: the partisan effect revisited', *Oxford Review of Economic Policy*, **22** (3), pp. 426–44.

Armingeon, Klaus, Philipp Leimgruber, Michelle Beyeler and Sarah Menegale (2005), 'Comparative Political Data Set 1960–2003', Institute of Political Science, University of Berne.

Barker, Roger and David Rueda (2007), 'The labor market determinants of corporate governance reform', CLPE Research Paper 5/2007, Comparative Research in Law and Political Economy, York University, Toronto.

Becht, Marco and Colin Mayer (2001), 'Corporate control in Europe', in Becht and Mayer (eds), *The World's New Financial Landscape: Challenges for Economic Policy*, Tübingen: Mohr-Siebeck, pp. 1–45.

Bertola, Giuseppe (1990), 'Job security, employment and wages', *European Economic Review*, **34**, pp. 851–86.

Bertola, Giuseppe, Francine Blau and Lawrence Kahn (2002), 'Comparative analysis of employment outcomes: lessons for the United States from international labor market evidence', in A. Krueger and R. Solow (eds), *The Roaring Nineties: Can Full Employment Be Sustained?*, New York: Russell Sage and Century Foundations, pp. 159–218.

Blair, Margaret (2003), 'Shareholder value, corporate governance, and corporate performance', in P.K. Cornelius and B. Kogut (eds), *Corporate Governance and Capital Flows in a Global Economy*, Oxford: Oxford University Press, pp. 53–82.

Blau, Francine and Lawrence Kahn (1999), 'Institutions and laws in the labor market', in O. Ashenfelter and D. Card (eds), *Handbook of Labor Economics: Volume 3A*, Amsterdam: Elsevier Science, pp. 1399–461.

Braumoeller, Bear F. (2004), 'Hypothesis testing and multiplicative interaction terms', *International Organization*, **58** (4), pp. 807–20.

Calmfors, Lars and John Driffill (1988), 'Bargaining structure, corporatism and macroeconomic performance', *Economic Policy*, **6**, pp.13–61.

Carlin, Wendy and Colin Mayer (2003), 'Finance, investment and growth', *Journal of Financial Economics*, **69** (1), pp. 191–226.

Conway, Paul, Donato de Rosa, Guiseppe Nicoletti and Faye Steiner (2006), 'Regulation, competition, and productivity convergence', OECD Economics Department Working Papers 509, Paris.

Cusack, Thomas, Torben Iversen and David Soskice (2007), 'Economic interests and the origins of electoral systems', *American Political Science Review*, **101**, August, pp. 373–91.

Deakin, Simon, Richard Hobbs, Susanne Konzelmann and Frank Wilkinson (2002), 'Partnership, ownership and control: the impact of corporate governance on employment relations', *Employee Relations*, **24** (3), pp. 335–52.

Djankov, Simeon, Rafael La Porta, Florencio López-de-Silanes and Andrei Shleifer (2006), 'The law and economics of self-dealing', *Journal of Financial Economics*, November, pp. 306–60.

Faccio, Mara and Larry H.P. Lang (2002), 'The ultimate ownership in Western European corporations', *Journal of Financial Economics*, **65** (3), pp. 365–95.

Fella, Giulio (2000), 'Efficiency wage and efficient redundancy pay', *European Economic Review*, **44**, pp. 1473–91.

Gatti, Donatella (2000), 'Unemployment and innovation patterns: the critical role of coordination', *Industrial and Corporate Change*, **9** (3), pp. 521–44.

Gatti, Donatella and Andrew Glyn (2006), 'Welfare states in hard times', *Oxford Review of Economic Policy*, **22** (3), pp. 301–12.

Gugler, Klaus, Dennis C. Mueller and B. Burcin Yurtoglu (2004), 'Corporate governance and globalization', *Oxford Review of Economic Policy*, **20**, pp. 129–56.

Hall, Peter and David Soskice (2001), 'An introduction to varieties of capitalism', in P. Hall and D. Soskice (eds), *Varieties of Capitalism: The Institutional Foundations of Comparative Advantage*, Oxford: Oxford University Press, pp. 1–68.

Henrekson, Magnus and Ulf Jakobsson (2005), 'The Swedish model of corporate ownership and control in transition', in H. Huizinga and L. Jonung (eds), *Who Will Own Europe? The Internationalisation of Asset Ownership in Europe*, Cambridge: Cambridge University Press, pp. 207–46.

Kharroubi, Enisse (2008), 'Labor market flexibility in the presence of credit constraints', mimeo, Banque de France.

Kho, Bong-Chan, René M. Stulz and Francis E. Warnock (2006), 'Financial globalization, governance, and the evolution of the home bias', NBER Working Paper 12389, Cambridge, MA.

La Porta, Rafael, Florencio López-de-Silanes and Andrei Shleifer (1999), 'Corporate ownership around the world', *Journal of Finance*, **54** (2), pp. 471–518.

La Porta, Rafael, Florencio López-de-Silanes, Andrei Shleifer and Robert W. Vishny (1998), 'Law and finance', *Journal of Political Economy*, **106** (4), pp. 1113–55.

Morck, Randall, Daniel Wolfenzon and Bernard Yeung (2005), 'Corporate governance, economic entrenchment and growth', *Journal of Economic Literature*, **43** (3), September, pp. 655–720.

Nicoletti, Guiseppe and Stefano Scarpetta (2003), 'Regulation, productivity and growth: OECD evidence', *Economic Policy*, **36**, pp. 9–72.

Nickell, Stephen (1997), 'Unemployment and labour market rigidities: Europe versus North America', *Journal of Economic Perspectives*, **11** (3), pp. 55–74.

Nickell, Stephen (1999), 'Product markets and labour markets', *Labour Economics*, **6** (1), pp.1–20.

Nickel, Stephen, Luca Nunziata and Wolfgang Ochel (2005), 'Unemployment in the OECD since the 1960s. What do we know?', *Economic Journal*, **115**, pp. 1–27.

Pagano, Marco and Paolo F. Volpin (2005), 'The political economy of corporate governance', *American Economic Review*, **95** (4), pp. 1005–30.

Persson, Torsten, Gerard Roland and Guido Tabellini (2007), 'Electoral rules and government spending in parliamentary democracies', *Quarterly Journal of Political Science*, **2** (2), pp. 155–88.

Plümper, Thomas and Vera Tröger (2007), 'Efficient estimation of time invariant and rarely changing variables in panel data analysis with unit effects', *Political Analysis*, **15** (2), pp. 124–39.

Schumpeter, Joseph (1934), *The Theory of Economic Development*, Cambridge: Harvard University Press.

Scruggs, Lyle (2004), 'Welfare State Entitlements Data Set: A Comparative Institutional Analysis of Eighteen Welfare States', Version 1.0.

Shleifer, Andrei and Robert Vishny (1997), 'A survey of corporate governance', *Journal of Finance*, **52** (2), pp. 737–83.

Siebert, Horst (1997), 'Labor market rigidities: at the root of unemployment in Europe', *Journal of Economic Perspectives*, **11** (3), pp. 37–54.

Simeon Djankov, Rafael La Porta, Florencio López-de-Silanes and Andrei Shleifer (2006), 'The law and economics of self-dealing', *Journal of Financial Economics*, November.

Wasmer, Etienne and Philippe Weil (2004), 'The macroeconomics of labor and credit market imperfections', *American Economic Review*, **94** (4), pp. 944–63.

3. The impact of shareholding structure on large listed companies in France: time horizons and control

Jean-Louis Beffa and Xavier Ragot

INTRODUCTION

The shareholding structure of big companies in France has undergone profound changes since the nationalizations of the early 1980s. These changes are the result of action both by the state and by national and international financial markets, which have themselves evolved. Recent developments have confirmed research, showing that shareholding structure can equally contribute to improving the management of companies as it can also restrict their medium-term economic development (Streeck, 2003). In this domain, state action can help to facilitate the emergence of strategies in keeping with the long-term interests of the company and its stakeholders. The aim of this chapter is to distinguish between the different strategies of shareholders, so as to use this differentiation to put into perspective the recent evolution in shareholding in large companies in France. This analysis then leads to the presentation of possible measures to favour the medium-term development of companies.

A TYPOLOGY OF SHAREHOLDERS

The objectives and strategies of shareholders vary considerably, depending, for example, on whether they are family owners with a majority shareholding or institutional investors. This is particularly evident during debates and votes in annual general meetings (AGMs). This section presents a simplified typology of shareholders, which will then be applied to the recent history of French capitalism in the next section.

Corporate Control

Shareholders can either seek a return without directly influencing the choices made by companies, or seek to acquire power, with the aim of increasing the profitability of their investments. The first strategy is adopted by many collective savings funds, such as pension funds, which diversify their industrial investments to spread the risks, but consider them as portfolio investments. They sometimes vote in general meetings on resolutions concerning the general operating principles of companies, without commenting publicly on the companies' precise strategies (Downes et al., 1999). The second shareholder strategy is that of private equity funds and hedge funds. Their objectives may include the replacement of lacklustre management to increase economic efficiency, or, sometimes, the sale of assets to take advantage of temporary rises in their stock market value. Classically, the economic literature considers the nature of shareholder control in terms of the relations between three authorities. The first is the general meeting of shareholders, where resolutions are adopted by simple majority (ordinary general meetings) or by qualified majority (extraordinary general meetings), depending on the subject and on national law. The second is the board of directors, elected during general meetings and possessing a right of control over the management teams in direct contact with the day-to-day running of the company. The latter constitute the third authority. The relations between these three bodies are regulated by national laws, which determine the strategies available. For example, boards of directors enjoy greater independence in the United States than in the United Kingdom, as Margaret Blair (2003) has shown. In Germany, the independence of management teams is strengthened by the participation of employees in supervisory boards, within the context of the co-determination system. National legislation defines the general framework within which control strategies are developed. In particular, it may cover the constitution of groups of control, or the use of shares with multiple voting rights. Distinguishing between the strategies of different shareholders allows us to identify them along a first axis, according to their desire for control.

The Time Horizon of Investors

The time horizon provides the second axis along which the strategies of shareholders can be identified. Following the work of Adolf Berle and Gardiner Means (1932), it is common practice to differentiate between shareholders according to their desire for liquidity, that is, the possibility of selling an asset quickly at a satisfactory price. In the implementation of their strategy, the shareholders' desire for liquidity forces companies to turn away from risky investments, the economic results of which are revealed only over the long term. These sorts of investments may well be undervalued by the market. Thus, the desire for liquidity leads to behaviour that attaches more importance to the short term than to the long term. In this section, we differentiate investors directly according to the time horizon on which they focus. This is the most important factor influencing investment decisions. Studies on this subject generally refer to the 'short-termism' of economic agents that is said to lead to underinvestment in long-term projects. Other works (see, for example, Fama, 1998) take the opposite view, affirming that the efficiency of financial markets is the sole working hypothesis and concluding that there is an optimal investment horizon for financial markets and for companies. As the number of articles on this subject always rises after stock market crashes, we can expect a new series of works to appear shortly. Studies on the short-termism of investment decisions can be separated into those that focus on the short-termism of managers to the detriment of shareholders, and those that focus on the short-termism of shareholders to the detriment of companies.

Jeremy Stein (1989), for example, stresses the ability of management teams to manipulate their company results in order to boost share prices and their own earnings. Shareholders and analysts cannot prevent such practices, even if they are aware of the manipulation of results and of long-term underinvestment. A second series of works focuses on the myopia of shareholders imposing time horizons that are too short. These works analyse the evolution of stock market values and conclude that financial markets display excessive volatility (Shiller, 1989), irrational exuberance (Shiller, 2005) and short-termism in their evaluation of assets (Cuthbertson et al., 1997). Finally, a third series of works shows how the short-termist behaviour of corporate management is the result of financial imperfections, related to asymmetries of information (Froot et al., 1992), excessive volatility (Shleifer and Vishny, 1990) or the overoptimism of some investors, leading to financial bubbles. In particular, Patrick Bolton et al. (2005) show how the existence of excessive volatility caused by a small number of irrational investors can lead shareholders to impose modes of management compensation that encourage short-termist attitudes. The behaviour of managers is consequently the result of a pay structure that is biased towards short-termism in the interest of the shareholders. These works explain the existence of many forms of compensation, such as bonuses or stock options, which lead a number of actors to adopt a shorter time horizon than certain investment projects. They go on to show the possibility of different time horizons according to the type of shareholder. In particular, shareholders possessing sizeable control blocks, such as family

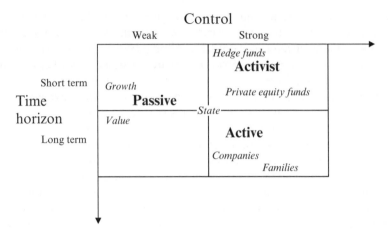

Figure 3.1   A typology of shareholders

shareholders, consider the return on their assets over the longer term (Anderson and Reeb, 2003).

Thus, the research enables us to understand the day-to-day functioning of companies that may be faced with very diverse types of shareholders. Some may value short-term financial profitability – sometimes 18 months for institutional investors, five to seven years for certain private equity funds – while others, such as family shareholders, have longer horizons. This time horizon for the valorization of assets provides a second dimension by which to differentiate shareholders.

Figure 3.1 gives a simple representation of the different types of shareholders. In the figure, the term 'growth' denotes the strategy of funds seeking fast-growing securities, while the term 'value' denotes the strategy of buying securities that the investor believes to be valued below their 'fundamental' value. In the latter case, the investor holds on to the securities until the other actors on the market have raised their estimations of the value. Investment funds can diversify their portfolios by acquiring both growth and value securities. Thus, the same investor can have a more or less short-term approach according to the strategy adopted for each company.

Figure 3.1 shows the average behaviour of each investor. The state has been placed in the middle because of the diversity of the strategies it follows in the companies it owns. Sometimes it is a passive investor, but it can be particularly active, for example, in defence-related companies or during major strategic movements. Lastly, the effectiveness of the state's role as an active shareholder in commercial companies is still open to debate. It would appear that it has no comparative advantages in this domain, contrary to the view that the state is the systematic guarantor of the long-term interests of companies. The question of whether there is room for improvement in the state's decisions as shareholder lies outside the scope of this chapter.

The figure does not take the degree of risk aversion into account as a means of differentiating between shareholders. Traditionally, risk aversion is presented as a key variable in financial economics. According to financial theory, if risk aversion is a key factor, then the most risky investments should have a higher return to compensate investors for the extra risk. Recent studies show that companies owned by family shareholders have higher long-term returns and lower risk than the average company (Anderson and Reeb, 2003; Sraer and Thesmar, 2007). Private equity funds, on the other hand, have higher volatility and lower returns than the average of returns on direct investment in company shares, largely because of the deduction of management fees (Phalippou and Gottschalg, 2009). Several hypotheses could account for these observations. Discussions with investors and analysts, however, always lead back to the time horizon of shareholders as the differentiating factor.

Now let us look at the different types of shareholders in more detail.

1. *Passive shareholders*   Passive shareholders take holdings in companies according to their level of risk and potential for growth. They make up portfolios in which they can arbitrate between risk and return. These investors, including, for example, most institutional investors, do not intervene directly in the choice of corporate strategies. Changes in their appreciation of the company are reflected in the buying and selling of securities. They thus have real but indirect influence, as their judgement on company performance may lead to a sale of shares that exposes the company to a takeover bid.

    In this way, these shareholders punish or reward *ex post* the quality of the management team's strategic orientations, without contributing *ex ante* to their definition. Management teams therefore have considerable freedom in defining long-term strategies. The risk, however, is that the most suitable strategies may not be appreciated by uninformed shareholders, resulting in share selling that brings down the price and heightens the risk of a takeover bid, or of an effective takeover that changes company strategy. The transparency and clarity of the strategy and of financial communication become essential. In this context, financial analysts have a very particular role to play, and their independence is crucial. According to Michael Goyer (2007), the majority of US institutional investors are passive, simply making portfolio choices. Only the hedge funds regularly seek to intervene, either to weigh on company strategies or to influence the stock market value over the short term.

2. *Activist shareholders*   Activist shareholders seek both a quick valorization of their investment and influence over company strategies. They can conduct leveraged buyouts (LBOs) and hostile acquisitions to speculate over the short term by breaking up companies. If a company is initially undervalued by the market, these operations can prove to be very lucrative. In such cases, it is easy to make short-term capital gains by sacrificing the long-term growth of the company, notably by paying out large exceptional dividends that drain the cash reserves, reducing research and development (R&D) expenditure, selling entities linked to long-term strategic positioning and calling into question the traditional progression of salaries. Stakeholders in the company suffer particularly from these strategies.

3. *Active shareholders*   Active shareholders seek to influence companies' strategies by possessing a large number of voting rights and/or seats on the board of directors. The archetype of such shareholders is the family shareholder. Family shareholders from CAC 40 include, for example, Bouygues, L'Oréal, LVMH, Pernod Ricard, Peugeot, PPR and Publicis. The controlling shareholder monitors company strategy closely, thus reducing the costs of information and coordination with managers – what economists call 'agency costs' (Stein, 2003). They are therefore prepared to accept a fall in share prices, provided it is of a temporary nature. These results confirm how important it is for shareholders to understand corporate strategies, both to detect management errors and to tolerate the fluctuations in share prices that are an inevitable part of business life.

4. *Private equity funds (leveraged buyout funds)*   Recent developments, marked by a long period of low interest rates and major financial innovations, have allowed for the fast growth of private equity funds, such as KKR, Blackstone or Carlyle, among many others. These investment funds acquire companies essentially by issuing debt, while at the same time possessing exclusive control. The degree of investment diversification of these funds, involving companies in very diverse sectors, leads to the formation of conglomerates, whose behaviour is different from that of industrial conglomerates. These investment funds optimize the financial structure of each company acquired – the equivalent of subsidiaries of industrial conglomerates. Furthermore, the mode of compensation of management teams is closely tied to the valorization of the companies acquired, especially at the time of resale, which is scheduled somewhere between three and 10 years after

the takeover. This mode of compensation helps to align the interests of the managers with those of the shareholders through paying out exceptional dividends to shareholders and providing generous profit sharing for the managers of the capital gains earned from reselling the companies (Jensen, 1997).

These organizations are very different from those of industrial conglomerates, which aggregate the cash flows from all their companies, so that the funds flow between the different entities. This allows them to pursue development strategies through takeovers or through internal growth in new activities. The efficiency of this internal capital market depends on the motivation and capabilities of the management teams (Stein, 2003). Industrial conglomerates, and large companies in general, also have the capacity to motivate their employees by offering career and promotion opportunities diversified throughout the company.

Finally, a question mark hangs over the capacity of LBO funds to allow companies to undertake risky development. We should start by setting apart the behaviour of the most activist funds, which seek to increase the profitability of their investment over the very short term by drastic restructuring or asset stripping. The large funds keep companies for several years in order to make capital gains from reselling them. We can, however, expect these funds to minimize the risks of valorization at the time of resale, which is probably less the case for shareholders who have no predefined horizon for reselling companies. Some LBO acquisitions have probably revitalized sluggish companies, but the average return appears to be low (Phalippou and Gottschalg, 2009), and the company is in danger of being re-evaluated even lower at the end of the complete economic cycle. The use of cash flow both for the payment of debts and for the remuneration of capital, both at high rates, diverts resources that would, in the case of industrial conglomerates, be devoted to R&D and international growth. We must also take into account the substantial drain on company cash constituted by start-up costs and management fees. Private equity funds will probably survive over the next few years, but uncertainties now hang over their development after the turbulence of the financial crisis. Interest rate and tax levels and the existence of target companies at relatively accessible prices are all necessary conditions for their continued existence (Armour and Cheffins, 2007).

5. *Dispersed ownership*   International comparisons of ownership structures have concluded that predominantly dispersed share ownership is rare on a national level. A first study (La Porta et al., 1999) reported

that only the United Kingdom, the United States and Austria had a majority of companies with dispersed ownership, that is, without blockholders representing more than 10 per cent of the share capital. A more recent study, however, covering a larger number of companies (Holderness, 2009), concluded that the concentration of ownership in the USA is in fact in line with the average for developed countries, and that the UK is the only exception, with a high proportion of companies with dispersed ownership. Likewise, Marco Becht and Colin Mayer (2001) studied the ownership and control of companies in different countries and found three forms of control. In continental Europe, companies are more likely to be controlled by private shareholders owning large blocks. The recent trends in France confirm the accuracy of this description. In the USA, control is more in the hands of the managers. Finally, in the UK, control appears to belong more to the market because of the lack of anti-takeover tools.

The recent dynamics in France and international comparisons both indicate that dispersed ownership structures with passive shareholders are more the exception than the rule. The presence of passive shareholders with large investment capacity, such as institutional investors, is not enough to halt the trend towards the concentration of company ownership. It is interesting to note that Becht and Mayer conclude that it is possible for managers to have considerable control over corporate strategy even in the presence of relatively concentrated ownership of their companies. Ultimately, however, this concentration will probably result in a strengthening of shareholder power. The repercussions on corporate strategy will depend on the time horizons of the shareholders whose power has been reinforced.

Now we shall use this typology briefly to outline the development of the shareholding structure of large French companies.

THE DEVELOPMENT OF THE SHAREHOLDING STRUCTURE OF LARGE FRENCH COMPANIES

After the period of nationalization, privatizations were accompanied by cross-shareholdings within the shareholdings of the large French companies. This structure made management teams relatively independent with regard to the shareholders, and at the same time interdependent on each other, thus adding importance to the role of mutual monitoring. The structure of cross-shareholdings has enabled companies to develop through their ties with other companies as shareholder of reference, rather than the state, which has been disappointing as a strategic partner.

This mode of shareholder intervention in corporate strategy – this shareholding regime, in other words – has proved to be unstable. The attitude of shareholders changed as a result of the international opening-up of financial markets and the taking of positions in the capital of French companies by investors from the UK or the USA, coupled with the take-over of control of the Union des Assurances de Paris, in which the AXA group had a central role. International shareholders, in particular, have regularly intervened to get companies to sell non-strategic holdings in order to strengthen their growth through this new source of finance. The 'uncrossing' of shareholdings has enabled French companies with the money to develop internationally, although with a dispersed ownership structure. The big companies have concentrated on their strong points at the level of international competition and developed their activities particularly in the emerging countries and North America. This can be illustrated by the examples of BNP, growing to become a universal bank of international size after its merger with Paribas, the transformation of Schneider, centred on industrial and domestic automation, or the development of Air Liquide, Lafarge and Saint-Gobain. Nevertheless, reference shareholders have continued to exist in the CAC 40: the state in the cases of Safran, EDF, GDF-Suez and Thales, and through the intermediary of the Caisse des Dépôts (CDC – a French public financial institution) in other sectors. Lastly, the presence of family shareholders has also proved to be crucial, as, for example, in the case of Peugeot, Michelin, Bouygues or L'Oréal.

Thus, the evolution of shareholder structure can be read in Figure 3.1 as a shift towards the left, in other words from active to more passive and dispersed shareholders. This evolution concerns only a proportion of companies due to the continued presence of companies with family capital.

Today, this passive and dispersed shareholding regime appears to be more unstable. A new class of investors is increasing its holdings in the capital of listed companies: Eurazeo, GBL, François Pinault, Bernard Arnault and Wendel have bought into the capital of Accor, Lafarge, Vinci, Carrefour and Saint-Gobain. They have acquired significant, but minority, interests in listed companies with the aim of influencing the strategy of those companies. The economic situation appears to be partly responsible for the instability of dispersed shareholdings. Favourable conditions of finance over the last few years have led to an increase in indebtedness, encouraging takeover strategies of undervalued companies by leveraged buyout, in other words, through high indebtedness. With this strategy coming to maturity because of the growing scarcity of target companies, or more simply due to the desire for more diversified strategies, share purchases have been directed towards large listed companies. Easy access to credit has therefore led, after several steps, to the emergence of actors with the wherewithal to buy large volumes of shares.

The choice of large listed companies with strategies judged to be suitable or improvable, and above all, the desire to be associated with strategic corporate decisions can align the behaviour of these investors with that of family shareholders. Although the former may defend long-term strategies by preventing hostile takeovers, they may also be tempted by the prospect of selling to make faster capital gains, unlike the family shareholders who are dedicated to making long-term investments in companies. The sudden turnaround in the credit market has imposed new constraints on LBO strategies. We shall not, therefore, be able to assess the stability of the new shareholding regime until the end of the current economic cycle.

This second evolution consists of a concentration of capital that can be read in Figure 3.1 as a return towards the right from passive shareholders to new, active shareholders. At present, it is difficult to predict how the latter will evolve, towards activism or towards contributing to the development of long-term strategy.

THE NEW ROLE OF THE STATE

The absence of a strategy with the long-term interest of the company as its objective is not necessarily the result of a problem of corporate governance, in the sense of the economic and legal relations between the shareholders and the executive management. It may also be the result of action by shareholders with short time horizons establishing incentive structures to achieve their own specific goals.

Faced with the differentiation in types of shareholders, the role of the state cannot be to impose a unique model on every company, but rather to contribute to the strengthening of long-term strategies in companies that need it. Indeed, innovation efforts and international development reveal their economic value only over long time periods. Economic fluctuations may lead to changes in shareholder structure to the detriment of long-term strategies. The public authorities have three levers at their disposal: the regulatory path to create and amend regulations concerning shareholder obligations, the role of the state as a direct or indirect investor, and lastly, its influence on the role of employees.

The regulatory path consists in making it more difficult for activist shareholders to take action based on short-term arbitrage when the other

BOX 3.1: THE EXAMPLE OF SAINT-GOBAIN

For Saint-Gobain, the sale of shares in companies such as Compagnie Générale des Eaux, Suez or BNP has facilitated the development of the group and its entry into the distribution sector, which now contributes to its growth and stability. This development has been accompanied by a shift towards regional activities, insulating the Group conglomerate from the main current factors of destabilization, namely the large differential in wage costs on an international level, the sharp rise in energy prices, and uncertainty relating to the accelerated rhythm and the form of technical change.

Nevertheless, the sale of Saint-Gobain shares by former corporate shareholders has left a fragmented capital structure in which the main shareholders are employees, institutional investors, the CDC and Areva, among others.

Figure 3.2 shows the evolution of shareholding from 1988 to 2007. First, we can observe a decrease in principal and small

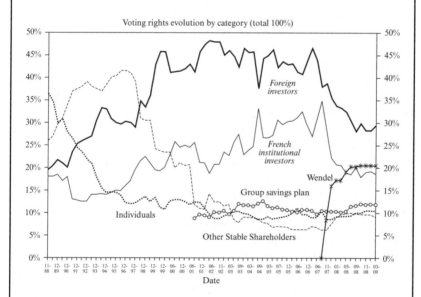

Figure 3.2   Evolution of the shareholding in Saint-Gobain, by voting rights

> shareholders to the advantage of institutional investors. This long
> evolution came to an end when Wendel obtained a stake in Saint-
> Gobain's capital. It is interesting to note that the entry of Wendel
> onto the Saint-Gobain board of directors has led to an agreement
> with the aim of reconciling the interests of different shareholders,
> particularly as regards the horizons of strategic investments. The
> agreement covers three essential principles. The first is support
> for the strategy approved by the board of directors and imple-
> mented by the executive management. The second is respect for
> the independence of the Group and equality in the treatment of all
> the shareholders. The third is shareholder stability and medium-
> term commitment.

shareholders are promoting long-term action. Several factors are linked to
the transparency of holdings to prevent creeping takeovers, or the question of voting rights in AGMs, recently debated. In this matter, there is no
question of limiting the takeover of companies for reasons of industrial
strategy, but rather of favouring shareholdings with a long-term strategic
horizon. It would be wise to reflect on the definition of creeping takeovers.
The current threshold defining a change in control (33 per cent of voting
rights) is too high, given the fragmentation of shareholdings. Lowering
this threshold could be a means of protecting minority shareholders.
Furthermore, the concept of change in control could be more directly
identified with actions taken in AGMs, such as the replacement of boards
of directors. The state could also intervene to modify incentive structures
in favour of long-term investments.

The state has substantial holdings in large companies, particularly
through the intermediary of the CDC. The *Fonds de Réserve des Retraites*
(Pensions Reserve Fund) has assets of over €30 billion and could become
an investor supporting long-term strategies. State shareholding is facing
its own difficulties, however. It must be active without being interventionist for reasons of political expediency. If it is more passive, it must not be
laxist; it must engage in understanding company strategies in order to fulfil
its supervisory role effectively.

Finally, long-term shareholding could be developed through an increase
in employee share ownership, which today represents only 5 per cent of
the capital of the CAC 40 companies. The slow development of employee
share ownership is probably due to uncertainty about stock market prices,
or even about the financial health of the company. Employees will only be
encouraged to invest their savings in the company that pays their wages if

that company is extremely solid. In the event of an economic downturn, the probability of being laid off may increase, and the value of their shares falls, creating difficult situations. In the large listed companies, however, there is still plenty of room for the expansion of employee shareholding. Another means of stabilizing the horizon of companies, while at the same time limiting the risk to employees' savings, consists in giving employees seats on the supervisory board, even if they are not shareholders, as is done in Germany (Boyer, 2005). A pillar of German capitalism can serve as reference: the presence of employee representatives corresponding to 20 per cent of the seats in listed companies improves motivation and strengthens the long-term strategy of companies. If the liaison between personnel is to be effective, the electoral body should include not only French employees, as in the current law, but all the employees in the European Union.

CONCLUSION

In conclusion, the evolution of financial markets and in the shareholdings of large companies over the last 25 years has enabled French companies to accelerate their modernization. In turn, this has allowed them to benefit from the internationalization of trade and new opportunities for development. Nonetheless, these companies are now vulnerable due to the fragility of their shareholdings. New shareholders may have industrial or financial aims that do not correspond to the companies' long-term development. To the list of shareholders whose interests are incompatible with those of the companies, we can add certain industrial shareholders from other geographical areas, who carry out strategic acquisitions to benefit from technology transfers without any real overall industrial gain. The vulnerability of French companies stems from the absence of a clear political choice as regards shareholder power. Two models appear to be possible: the UK model, in which shareholders enjoy far-reaching powers, and the US model (not to mention the German model), in which the boards of directors and supervisory boards are more independent and are intended to arbitrate between the divergent interests of the stakeholders (Aoki, 2007). This chapter argues in favour of the second model and shows that there exist means of action by which it can be achieved. Those means include foremost: redefining the concept of creeping takeover; clarifying the objectives of the state as shareholder; putting in place measures to prevent hostile takeovers, such as stock warrants; and, lastly, strengthening the role of employees when their interests coincide with the long-term interests of the company.

REFERENCES

Anderson, Ronald and David Reeb (2003), 'Founding-family ownership and firm performance: evidence from the S&P 500', *Journal of Finance*, **58** (3), pp. 1301–28.

Aoki, Masahiko (2007), *The Japanese Economy after the Flux Decade: Where Will Changes in Company Structure Lead? Prisme No. 10*, Paris: Cournot Centre for Economic Studies.

Armour, John and Brian R. Cheffins (2007), 'The eclipse of private equity', ECGI Working Paper, European Corporate Governance Institute, Bonn.

Becht, Marco and Colin Mayer (2001), 'Introduction', in Fabrizio Barca and Marco Becht (eds), *The Control of Corporate Europe*, Oxford: Oxford University Press, pp. 1–45.

Berle, Adolf and Gardiner Means (1932), *The Modern Corporation and Private Property*, New York: Macmillan.

Blair, Margaret (2003), 'Reforming corporate governance: what history can teach us', Working Paper 485663, Georgetown University Law Center, Washington, DC.

Bolton, Patrick, Jose Scheinkman and Wei Xiong (2005), 'Pay for short-term performance: executive compensation in speculative markets', *Journal of Corporation Law*, **30**, pp. 721–47.

Boyer, Robert (2005), 'What future for codetermination and corporate governance in Germany?', PSE Working Paper 39, Paris-Jourdan Sciences Économiques, Paris.

Cuthbertson, Keith, Simon Hayes and Dirk Nitsche (1997), 'The behaviour of UK stock prices and returns: is the market efficient?', *The Economic Journal*, **107** (443), pp. 986–1008.

Downes, Giles, Ehud Houminer and R. Glenn Hubbard (1999), *Institutional Investors and Corporate Behavior*, Washington, DC: AEI Press.

Fama, Eugene (1998), 'Market efficiency, long-term returns and behavioral finance', *Journal of Financial Economics*, **49**, pp. 283–306.

Froot, Kenneth, André Perold and Jeremy Stein (1992), 'Shareholder trading practices and corporate investment horizons', *Continental Bank Journal of Applied Corporate Finance*, **5** (2), Summer, pp. 42–58.

Goyer, Michel (2007), 'Institutional investors in French and German corporate governance: the transformation of corporate governance and the stability of coordination', CES Working Paper 07.2, Center for European Studies, Harvard University, Cambridge, MA.

Holderness, Clifford G. (2009), 'The myth of diffuse ownership in the United States', *Review of Financial Studies*, **22** (4), pp. 1377–408.

Jensen, Michael C. (1989, revised 1997), 'The eclipse of the public corporation', *Harvard Business Review*, **67** (5), pp. 61–75.

La Porta, Rafael, Florencio López-de-Silanes and Andrei Shleifer (1999), 'Corporate Ownership around the World', *Journal of Finance*, **54** (2), pp. 471–517.

Phalippou, Ludovic and Oliver F. Gottschalg (2009), 'The performance of private equity funds', *The Review of Financial Studies*, **22** (4), pp. 1747–76.

Shiller, Robert (1989), *Market Volatility*, Cambridge, MA: MIT Press.

Shiller, Robert (2005), *Irrational Exuberance*, Princeton, NJ: Princeton University Press.

Shleifer, Andrei and Robert Vishny (1990), 'Equilibrium short horizons of investors and firms', *American Economic Review Papers and Proceedings*, **80**, pp. 148–53.

Sraer, David and David Thesmar (2007), 'Performance and behavior of family firms: evidence from the French stock market', *Journal of the European Economic Association*, **5** (4), pp. 709–51.

Stein, Jeremy (1989), 'Efficient capital market, inefficient firm: a model of myopic corporate behavior', *Quarterly Journal of Economics*, **104** (4), pp. 655–69.

Stein, Jeremy C. (2003), 'Agency, information and corporate investment', in George M. Constantinides, Milton Harris and René M. Stulz (eds), *Handbook of the Economics of Finance*, 1A, Amsterdam: North-Holland, 2003, pp. 111–66.

Streeck, Wolfgang (2003), 'The transformation of corporate organization in Europe: an overview', in Jean-Philippe Touffut (ed.), pp. 4–44.

Touffut, Jean-Philippe (2003) (ed.), *Institutions, Innovation and Growth: Selected Economic Papers*, Cheltenham, UK and Northampton, MA, USA: Edward Elgar.

4. Questioning the legitimacy of shareholder power

Christophe Clerc

INTRODUCTION

It appears natural, a priori, that the ultimate power of decision in corporations should fall to the owners of the means of production. The shareholders are the owners; therefore it is they who should decide. This argument, which appears to be common sense, is the foundation of a school of thought in favour of increasing the power of shareholders in listed companies – the 'shareholder primacy' movement. This movement has enjoyed several notable successes: it has obtained the modification of representations,[1] of behaviours[2] and of the legal framework.[3] At an international level, this has resulted in a convergence of regulations towards the objectives it has defined.[4]

Many people oppose this movement, raising the fundamental question of the legitimacy of shareholder power: what justifies the pre-eminent position that shareholders have been given in the institutional architecture of corporations? I propose to examine this question in the context of commercial companies listed on the stock exchange, whose features make them an object of analysis in their own right.

The question of power in corporations has gained further importance from the fact that corporations have established themselves over the last two centuries as the principal institution[5] in the economic sphere and, more generally, as one of the most important institutions in the modern world,[6] alongside the state. By considering that profit should be the sole objective of corporations, one places them in a structurally conflict-provoking situation, where the law is a constraint that they must constantly seek to evade.[7] Who should have ultimate control, why and to what end are therefore questions of a significance that reaches far beyond the simple context of economics, finance and law: these are first and foremost anthropological and political questions.[8] This chapter does not set out to cover exhaustively the many debates provoked by the primacy movement,[9] but simply to ask a number of questions. As a point of departure, I shall present the triple paradox of shareholder primacy. I shall then explore the justifications put forward in support of this theory, and examine the implicit views underlying some of its key concepts. I shall then look at the legitimacy of state action in this domain from a historical perspective, before briefly proposing some alternative paths in the final section.

THE THREE PARADOXES OF SHAREHOLDER PRIMACY

Power to the Non-liable

Listed corporations are legal entities, in which the liability of shareholders is nearly always limited to the amount they have invested. If the company goes 'bankrupt',[10] the shareholders incur a loss, but only to the value of the price they paid to buy or subscribe to their shares.

That fact is well known. What is less well known is that investors have the choice to opt for forms of corporation that combine limited and unlimited liability. In French law, the *société en commandite par actions* distinguishes between limited partners, who are classic shareholders with limited liability, and managing partners, whose liability is unlimited. This is not specific to France; it is one of the oldest forms of company, which can be found in the Code of Hammurabi (ca. 1760 BC), among the Romans, in the Middle Ages and in modern times. It was still widespread in the nineteenth century and continues to exist today, in a minor form, notably in Italy, Germany, the United Kingdom and the United States (under the name of 'partnerships limited by shares'). In France, for example, the companies Michelin and Largardère have both adopted this legal status. Overall, however, this form has been abandoned in favour of companies where the liability of all the shareholders is limited.[11]

Several theoretical reasons help to explain the enthusiasm for limited liability, but the most important and most obvious is that: it enables shareholders to hope for unlimited profits while risking only limited losses. If this were betting, it would be called a 'winning formula'.

Let us now look at the theoretical implications and practical consequences of this system. From a theoretical point of view, jurists like to think that in legal systems that grant individuals an irreducible degree of freedom, each person should be liable for his actions. The limited liability of shareholders leads, however, to a radically opposite position: corporate law makes the shareholder non-liable. This position is all the more paradoxical in the theory of shareholder primacy, which seeks to give the shareholder both power and non-liability.

Let us take two examples. The first involves a company that is carrying out a restructuring demanded by the market. This could consist, for instance, in a reduction of capital or a debt-financed share buyback. The resulting lack of financial capacity, combined with changes in the economic environment, drive the company into bankruptcy. Although the shareholders profit from the reorganization, they are exempt from all liability.

In the second example, a company leases oil tankers. The shareholders, through the intermediary of the representatives they have elected to the board of directors (but who are directors in their own right, and not legal representatives of the shareholders), decide to adopt a minimalist safety policy. This choice results in an accident occurring, creating a huge oil slick. The shareholders can avoid the liability that they should, in principle, incur with regard to the clean-up costs. The same question arises for all activities liable to create large-scale damage, such as chemicals, nuclear power or genetically modified organisms (GMOs). Even with growing risks, the rule remains the same: the decision makers are not the payers.

It is true that company managers *are* liable. That fact, however, only heightens the paradox. The managers are either independent in their decision making, in both law and practice, in which case a transfer of liability is justifiable, or simply agents of the shareholders and must act in the latter's interest by following their instructions (whether these instructions are given individually, by a shareholder or group of shareholders, or transmitted by the market – the community of shareholders). The paradox of the *shareholder as non-liable decision maker* thus becomes striking.

From a practical point of view, the result of the principle of non-liability is clear: society as a whole plays the role of insurer for the risks taken by the shareholders. After all, why not? If one wants a dynamic society, it may be desirable to protect entrepreneurs from the risks they take. That raises two questions. First, in listed companies, the entrepreneur is not the shareholder who, whether an individual or a fund manager, simply manages a portfolio of assets. The executive manager is the real entrepreneur. The system is thus incoherent on this point. Second, there is a major problem of moral hazard: the insurance is free, the risk is largely determined by the behaviour of the insured party, and the insurer is granted no specific role in the internal control of the risk. What private insurer would accept such conditions?

The existence of this moral hazard raises two questions. The first is a question of principle: is there any justification for making a gift to share-holders of their 'insurance premium'? Or more precisely, to what extent does the existence of such a gift justify the demand for something to be given in return?

The second question is more technical, but equally important: how can society minimize its risk? In the absence of an internal solution (for instance, the presence of representatives of society on every board of directors), the path of regulation must be followed. This, however, has the 'defect' of being applied uniformly to every corporation, not only to those that throw caution to the wind in the hope of high profits, but also to those with prudent management. Using this type of argument, corpora-tions would use their considerable lobbying powers to keep regulations to a minimum.[12] The result is a difficult situation where regulation, although necessary, cannot be fixed at its optimal level.

Power without the Money

What is the use of a shareholder? From the company's point of view, it is legitimate to question the utility of each stakeholder. The shareholder can put forward three answers. First, shareholders provide the company with the capital it needs to develop. Second, they fulfil the functions of control and decision making. I shall not examine this second function, because although it does exist and is important, it is not specific to shareholders: one of the other stakeholders could perform it equally well. Third, by buying and selling shares on the stock market, the shareholder ensures the liquidity of the market. I shall not explore this third function either, because collectively, shareholders provide themselves with liquidity – the utility is therefore focused on the shareholders themselves rather than on the company.

The first and central role of the shareholder is therefore to provide capital. This idea needs to be defined more precisely, however: what counts is the money that flows into the company, that is, the capital subscribed on the primary market. The operations carried out by the shareholder on the secondary market are only of marginal interest to the company (they are of some interest in that through the share price, these operations inform the company about the way its decisions and its environment are perceived).

Over the last few years, both in France and abroad, in varying degrees and over different periods, shareholders have removed more money than they have invested in corporations, or have contributed almost nothing to their financing.[13] If shareholders do not fulfil the functions on which their legitimacy is founded, how can they lay claim to supreme power?

The Assumption of Power Justifying the Loss of Power

Several questions have been raised about the coherence of shareholder primacy theory. I shall mention one of these, which goes to the very heart of the primacy argument.

Central to primacy theory is the assertion that shareholders, whose claim on the company is not fixed, should be given sufficient power to ensure that they receive the payment they expect. As the legal system is unsatisfactory in this respect, shareholders have called for its reform in order to obtain the prerogatives they desire. Let us suppose that they are successful. They will then be able to ensure that they receive fixed payments. Consequently, the variables of adjustment will be the other stakeholders, as the shareholders will be able to juggle with wages, lay off employees, relocate activities, exert pressure on subcontractors, extend terms of payment, and so on. When the new system has become well established, the reversal of the situation will become obvious: de facto, the income of the shareholders will be fixed and that of the other stakeholders will be variable. The success of the primacy movement will undermine the very foundations of its reasoning.

Does this mean that we should oppose all the demands of shareholders? Not necessarily. But their justifications need to be more solid. And that is what I now propose to examine.

THE JUSTIFICATIONS OF SHAREHOLDER PRIMACY THEORY

Three main arguments are used to justify shareholder primacy. As we shall see, none of the three is indisputable.

Company Ownership

One of the most widely used arguments in favour of shareholder power stems from their supposed quality as 'owners' of the company. Although this idea has lost most of its theoretical credit among jurists, it is still frequently expounded in practice, finding expression, for example, in the following phrases: 'the shareholder is the owner of the firm', 'the shareholder is the real owner of the company' or 'the shareholder invests his money in the company; he is obviously the owner'.

There is no doubt that the shareholders are not the owners of the *firm*. They hold no rights over the tangible and intangible assets of the company. Otherwise, the personal creditors of the shareholders would be able to seize the company's assets in the event of the share-holders defaulting on the repayment of debts. Only the legal entity of the company can use the corporate assets and receive and dispose of the profits they produce in accordance with the decisions made by the managers. Whatever legal foundations it is based on, this regime is now applied universally for large listed companies. In English law, the situation is nicely summed up in the following sentence: 'Share is something of a misnomer, for shareholders no longer share any property in common' (Davies, 1997, p. 300).

Can one, therefore, assert that the shareholder is the 'owner of the company'? It is difficult to give precise meaning to this assertion. Envisaging the company as a legal entity (which it is, from a legal point of view), has its obvious difficulties: how can one be the owner of a person, or of the group of individuals that embody the legal entity? Can one say that the French are the owners of the French state? Or that members are the owners of their association?

It is no easier to make the shareholders owners from the perspective of a contractual theory of the company. If the company is simply a 'nexus of contracts', of what exactly could the shareholder be the owner? It is for this reason that the advocates of this theory have abandoned all reference to property rights in their argumentation (see Bainbridge, 1997, and Blair, 1995a).

The fact that the shareholders have invested money in the company does not change the above analysis. Investment is a transfer of funds made within a legal and contractual framework that confers certain rights and imposes certain obligations on the investor. Once invested, the money belongs to the company and no longer to the investor. The shareholding relation does have one specificity: it is an independent category of the law responding to the particular situation created by the emergence of the modern corporation. Linking it to property law is therefore inexact and pointless. At the very most, one can say that shareholders are the owners of their shares, in the sense that they have the use, benefit and disposal of them. This ownership, however, does not concern the company itself – it is attached to the security. This security is not a title deed. The ownership of such a security cannot, therefore, be a property right in itself. For this reason, an English author described the idea of considering the share as a property right as 'transcendental nonsense' (Ireland, 1999).

The legal situation of the shareholder is therefore that of the holder of a personal right on the company. The scope of the personal right may vary, but in its nature it is no different from other personal rights, such as that of the lender, for example.

The Risk Taken by Shareholders

Is the risk taken by shareholders a source of legitimacy for the power they demand? According to the theory, shareholders are residual creditors: they are paid only once the company's other creditors (suppliers, employees, banks and so on), who have a 'fixed' right to payment, have been paid. Should they have more rights because they take more risks?

Theoretical aspects

From a theoretical point of view, it is necessary to differentiate three different aspects of this question. First, can a particular and direct right of control over a specific risk be inferred directly from the existence of that risk? This principle is attractive, but it is not recognized as such in positive law. Risk is typically managed through regulation. On the one hand, regulation tends to limit the incidence of risk and repair the consequences. On the other, it organizes if need be, the potential victims so as to give them a collective right of representation. All this is done within a general framework of the balance of interests. It is not surprising, therefore, that supporters of shareholder primacy do not make direct use of this argument. They do put forward, however, a rather curious argument, according to which the shareholders should be given the power because, as they take the most risk, they are most able to pay the other stakeholders for this right (the 'price' taking the form of an addition to the fixed payment paid to the stakeholders in return for the power conferred on the shareholders). Corporate law and articles of association are, however, not the subject of real negotiations between the different stakeholders. Even when such negotiations do occur, there is not always a mechanism in place to ensure that the 'price' negotiated is actually paid. If it were real, the proposed operation would be a fool's bargain.

The second aspect is the division of labour resulting from risk-taking. According to Frank Knight (1933), the existence of an uncertain world leads to the appearance of two categories of individuals: those who are 'confident and venturesome' on the one hand, and those who are 'doubtful and timid' on the other. The former provide a guaranteed income to the latter in exchange for the results of their labour and the power of management. As for the latter, they only accept the assignment of the power of management, because they receive a guaranteed payment in return. The weakness of the reasoning is obvious. What characterizes investors in large listed companies is not so much their attraction to risk as the fact that they have capital to invest. Furthermore, the ability to diversify investments guarantees an amount of security that hardly requires the investor to be 'venturesome'.

The third theoretical aspect is richer. Power should be given to shareholders for reasons of economic efficiency.[14] As payments to shareholders are related to profit, it is in their interest to maximize that profit, and therefore to maximize the value of the firm, which is in line with the general interest. Moreover, the shareholders are the only party not structurally opposed to risk-taking at an appropriate level. Provided that the profitability is high enough to guarantee them their fixed income, the other stakeholders are supposed to oppose any strategy that might endanger their payment in the event of failure and bring them no additional compensation in the event of success.[15]

In its substance, the efficiency argument raises several issues. Apart from the fundamental questions concerning the validity of hypotheses about the rationality of economic agents and maximization under constraints, which reach far beyond the scope of this chapter, I shall examine three of these issues.

First, the shareholder primacy argument makes a very strong implicit hypothesis: that the shareholders protect their profit by creating wealth, and not by carrying out a simple transfer of wealth to their benefit and to the detriment of the other stakeholders. There is nothing to guarantee this result, and contradictory examples abound. Likewise, the shareholder primacy theory does not take into account negative externalities, which are assumed to be dealt with adequately elsewhere.

Second, if a risky decision by the shareholders is likely to endanger the payment of their fixed incomes to the other stakeholders, it is not illegitimate for them to have a say in the matter. When stakeholders have sufficient bargaining power, they never fail to protect themselves by negotiating the appropriate clauses – as is the case for banks.

Lastly, even if one accepts the foundations of the primacy argument, various examples illustrate how the shareholders' risk-taking can produce suboptimal results. Let us take, for example, the case of a company that pays 100 to the holders of fixed income rights. This company has the choice between project A, which is sure to bring in 100, and project B, which has a 50 per cent chance of bringing in 50 and a 50 per cent chance of bringing in 120. It is in the shareholders' interest to reject project A, which never gives them any return, in favour of project B, from which they can hope for a profit, even if the value of project A (100) is higher than the value of project B ($0.5 \times 50 + 0.5 \times 120 = 85$).

Empirical aspects

From a purely empirical point of view, the theory of risk suffers from serious limitations. One need only compare the situation of the shareholders to that of the employees with regard to risk.

Shareholders can select, diversify and control their risk. Even if they only invest in one company, shareholders have an important choice available to them: among the thousands of listed companies, they can choose the risk-return profile that best suits them. The possibility of diversification is an extension of this power of choice: each shareholder can invest in numerous companies, either directly or indirectly, at little cost, through the intermediary of investment funds. Controlling the risk is also easy. Upstream, the shareholder has large amounts of information about the company. This information is structured by the law and is extraordinarily detailed – especially if one thinks of the accounting rules and disclosure obligations imposed by stock market regulations. The information must be updated with defined frequency and new events likely to affect the stock market price must rapidly be brought to the attention of the market. In addition, the information is scrutinized by professionals – such as financial analysts and fund managers – and closely monitored by specialized, high-level public officials, whose numbers are surprisingly high compared to the number of companies they watch over. In the event of false information being disclosed, the shareholders have a right of action against the company. Downstream, when the risk is detected, shareholders can sell their holdings without delay at little cost. Finally, the market has increased the number of forms of risk coverage to such an extent that shareholders can now limit the risk with mathematical precision.

The situation of employees is diametrically opposite. The employee's power of choice is limited given the complexity of the combination of the jobseeker's profile (age, qualifications, experience, languages, nationality, mobility and so on). It also depends on the situation of the labour market and the time needed to recruit, which naturally leads to a limited choice for employees. In addition, the question of risk is not taken into account to any great degree, and diversification is almost impossible. In practice, an employee works for only one company. Risk management is also particularly difficult. Upstream, before being taken on, there is little or no organized information for the employee about the company he is going to join. Yet the employment contract, like all contracts, is incomplete, all the more so since there is little negotiation involved, and the employee is in a weak bargaining position. The control of this information – when there is any – is limited and its inaccuracy does not give the employee any right to compensation. Once the contract has been signed, the right to information remains limited, although there may be certain palliatives, for example, through the role played by works councils. Downstream, if the employee does detect a risk, his mobility is restricted – the advance notice required to leave the company and the time needed to look for another job are both counted in weeks and months, not in minutes and hours. Lastly, the value of an employee within a company is correlated to his specific investment. This investment is lost, however, by definition when he changes company. The management of risk by the employee therefore involves a loss of value that has no equivalent for the shareholder.

Thus, if one were to follow the theory of risk, the power of employees within the corporation would have to be increased. It appears that such a prospect would strike horror into the hearts of shareholder primacists. One need only read the work of Michael Jensen, one of the most often quoted pioneers of primacy theory to be convinced. According to Jensen, it is essential neither to deviate from the 'at-will' contract nor to attach too much importance to complying with the provisions of employment contracts (Jensen, 2000, p. 33).

The 'Single Master' Theory

There remains one last type of justification for shareholder primacy: shareholder power probably is not perfect, but it is still better than all the other solutions. The argument is based on the idea that one cannot serve several masters. In stakeholder theory, the managers must take into account not only the interests of shareholders, but also those of employees, customers, suppliers, local communities and so on. Because of the divergences between these different groups, the managers cannot make a rational decision, and so they favour their own specific interests.

Another argument, which is not relevant but nevertheless expressed, is based on rejection of the process of democratic decision making, dismissed in a few terse phrases for its 'inefficiency' (ibid., p. 52).

There are several problems with the theory of the single master. Within the very logic of primacy theory, where the managers take into account only the shareholders' interests, there are many divergences between majority and minority shareholders, preferential and ordinary shareholders, or even, within one and the same category, between shareholders with different investment horizons. Managers and shareholders make the best of it. In the UK, for example, the bylaws can provide for the power to designate a certain number of members of the board to be entrusted to a third party – a financial institution, for example. In that case, the board of directors is responsible for representing interests that may be contradictory (Fernandez, 2007, p. 16).[16] The solution found by English law is to consider that directors nominated by a third party only have a duty towards the company and not towards the person who nominated them.[17] More generally, the directors have a 'duty not to fetter discretion'.

Furthermore, in many legal systems that have not incorporated shareholder primacy, such as Germany, and where there is therefore no single master, the quality of industrial companies suggests that corporate executives are capable of taking the appropriate decisions for the good management of the company.

Lastly, this argument can never be sufficient in itself: if it is critical to have more than one 'master', one can choose who that might be. Shareholders are not the only possible choice.

THE PERSUASIVE POWER OF SHAREHOLDER PRIMACISM

Given the many doubts inherent in the shareholder primacy theory, one may wonder how it has succeeded in becoming dominant – although it has never ceased to be contested.

I shall not enter into the question of power relations here. The features that should be examined in such an analysis include notably the influence of collective investment vehicles (which can be considered, in functional terms, as a kind of unionization of shareholders with the aim of promoting their interests), the development of voting consulting firms, the role of activist shareholders, the influence of different member states in the legislative process of the European Union and the development of supervisory authorities focused on shareholders' interests.[18] There is such a wealth of content to be developed in this question that it needs a separate study.

In this chapter I shall examine only a few clearly identified concepts to show how a well-reasoned argument can be turned into a slogan. My intention is not to refuse theorists the right to sloganeer – everyone is free to propagandize their ideas – but, more modestly, to examine the semantic shifts involved and the representations that result from them. The concepts studied are those of the 'nexus of contracts', 'shareholder value' and 'shareholder democracy'. As a counterpoint, I shall also look at two primacy theories that have met with little interest: that of the 'potential shareholder' and that of the 'incompetent shareholder'.

The 'Nexus of Contracts'

The representation of the corporation as a 'nexus of contracts' lies at the heart of agency theory and shareholder primacism. It is normal to wish to look at what happens inside the 'black box' of the corporation and to extend that analysis by examining the relations between the corporation and external actors. The theory of the 'nexus of contracts' (which I shall refer to as 'nexism', for the sake of convenience), proceeds differently, however. On the grounds that legal entity is a fiction, nexism defines the company as 'a set of complex arrangements of many sorts that those who associate voluntarily in the corporation will work out among themselves' (Easterbrook and Fischel, 1991, p. 12). In this way, companies dissolve in the play of inter-individual relations, following a principle that somewhat recalls Margaret Thatcher's famous remark, 'There is no such thing as society . . .'. I shall briefly set out the (well-known) weaknesses in the reasoning before looking into the reasons for this presentation.

The first part of the argument appears to be commonsensical – companies are fictions. The parallel between physical entity and legal entity is taken a long way by the law: both live and die; they can own assets, incur debts, sue and be sued, be condemned in civil and penal law, and so on. For all that, nobody imagines that the process of attributing legal personality gives rise to a living being in flesh and blood. Having established that point, should one conclude that the legal personality of corporations should be completely disregarded? One would have to ignore the fact that all legal institutions – such as marriage, the state or property – are fictions. The same holds for rules of law, which exist only as mental representations. It would nonetheless be absurd to deny the reality of the legal system, which has a profound influence on the life of every person, and therefore of the rules that make it up. In this instance, the development of legal personality is one of the most far-reaching legal revolutions of the last 200 years in the business world. To dismiss this fact with a wave of the hand, in a few short phrases, is surprising to say the least.

The second part of the definition is a curious mixture, for the contracts concerned are not only those that connect the partners with each other, and the partners with the corporate executives, but all the company's contracts (Jensen, 2000, p. 1). Nexism is a theory of the firm before being a theory of governance. Such a theory, which places contracts at the heart of its analysis, is only worthwhile if it examines the real conditions of negotiation, execution and termination of those contracts. In particular, the following questions can be raised. What is the negotiating position of each party (for example, do employees have the choice of whether or not to work, do investors have the choice between investment and consumption)? What rights do the parties have in the context of negotiations? How are the negotiations organized (are they individual or collective)? What are the possible obstacles (the time that can be devoted to negotiations, the different parties' knowledge of the law, and so on)? Nexism does not examine these points. It starts from the principle that there is 'voluntary association', in other words free and informed association. The above questions provide a particularly strong working hypothesis, largely neglected by 'nexist' literature.

Nexism is not useful to agency theory.[19] One could easily come to the same conclusions without disregarding the legal personality of corporations. So why make it one of the foundations of shareholder primacy theory? Legal personality implicitly infers certain ideas, such as the permanence of the organization. Overnight, or almost, a corporation can see all its shareholders changed, its managers replaced, its customers and suppliers changed, all the contractual terms modified, and yet remain the same corporation. It is a mechanism that is astonishingly robust to change. The existence of a durable organization necessarily leads to a reflection on the creation and maintenance of the power relations that allow the entity to endure. Conversely, the existence of contractual relations between equals gives the picture of a moving world where everything is possible, provided it is contractualized. The shareholders are at the same level as the other stakeholders, but they are the weakest of them all: as they have only the right to a residual payment, to the 'crumbs', they have the right to be protected so that these crumbs are not taken away by those who have the right to the comfort of a fixed payment. Agency theory further shows that shareholders should be particularly wary of corporate managers, suspected *ad libiditum* of being lazy and thieving. The shareholders thus become the victims. Protecting them can then become a politically correct objective for legislators.

'Shareholder Value'

The only truly ingenious aspect of the concept of shareholder value lies in the semantic innovation it contains. In itself, the idea is not original: it affirms that shareholders in a company producing lower returns on capital than the average among its peers have an interest in moving their investment to a competing firm with higher-than-average returns.

It is the vocabulary used that is innovative. The term 'profit', which has controversial connotations and narrow perimeters, is abandoned. The technical term that covers the notion of value is 'return on capital', dividends, share buybacks and reductions of capital. The more elegant term of 'value' is retained, however: 'creating value' sounds better than 'improving the profitability of capital'. This term also avoids mention of the creation of wealth, as shareholder value can be created through the simple transfer of wealth to the shareholders, to the detriment of the other stakeholders.

A company whose profitability is lower than average is said to 'destroy shareholder value'. The abuse of language is patent, as such a company may still be creating wealth and distributing it to its shareholders. For the latter, however, the company represents an opportunity cost, because it is not doing as well as its peers. If one applied this reasoning to the school system, one would have to consider a pupil with good but below-average marks as 'destroying knowledge value'. Would telling him this be the best way to encourage him? This vocabulary is in fact a way to designate as illegitimate managers whose results (annual, half-yearly or quarterly) fall below the average. This stigmatization is advantageous to the shareholder: it is a tool for exerting permanent pressure on a sizeable proportion of companies, as, by definition, there will always be companies with below-average results. Another advantage is that even when profitability is steadily increasing, the stigmatization remains. If one were to apply this reasoning to employees, then one would have to affirm that paying below-average wages 'destroys wage value', even when wage levels are rising. This brings out the inflationary character of the process. Finally, the construction of a comparison group made up of 'comparable' companies is very subjective, giving shareholders an additional lever for demanding higher returns.

'Shareholder Democracy'

There are certain principles, the simple pronouncement of which is enough to win support. They are the most dangerous. The power of seduction they exert leads people to accept them as a premise before even examining them. 'Shareholder democracy' is one such principle. Through being invoked by shareholders of large listed companies, taken up by journalists, consecrated by the public authorities and incorporated into reflections on corporate governance, the concept assumes the value of a paradigm. Can one be against democracy? A recent study commissioned by the European Commission[20] leads us to raise the question: is 'shareholder democracy' a founding principle or a useful slogan?

The notion of shareholder democracy is based on a parallel drawn between the corporation and political society, with the shareholder in the role of the people, the general meeting as the parliament and the board of directors as the government. If democracy is *the power of the people, by the people, for the people*, then the corporation should be *the power of the shareholders, by the shareholders, for the shareholders*. But where society applies the principle of 'one man, one vote',[21] corporations give more votes to those who, being richer, possess more shares. In political science, the system that associates power with wealth has a name: 'plutocracy'.[22] What is improperly called 'shareholder democracy' should strictly, therefore, be called 'shareholder plutocracy'. In reality, however, these comparisons have little pertinence: there is nothing in common between a political system that guarantees our status as citizens and a set of rights and duties attached to the quality of partner. Misusing the term 'democracy' does nothing to inform the debate.

Thus, the appellation 'shareholder democracy' is first and foremost a slogan, exploiting the concept of democracy to justify an increase in shareholders' powers. One should nonetheless examine the possibility that this slogan, however inappropriate, may nevertheless be the synthetic expression of underlying principles.

The idea that all shares of the same nominal value should have the same voting rights attached to them is central to the concept of 'shareholder democracy': equal rights for equal investments. This concept, known by jurists under the name of the 'proportionality principle', has been popularized in the slogan 'one share, one vote', based on the model of 'one man, one vote'.

Is the 'proportionality principle' truly a 'principle'? The European Commission, when it commissioned the study mentioned above, requested an analysis of *deviations* from the 'proportionality principle': a way of explicitly affirming the existence of a principle and of implicitly stigmatizing such 'deviations'. The study set out to analyse the mechanisms that fail to respect the proportionality principle, called control enhancing mechanisms, or CEMs. The study demonstrated that proportionality is not a 'principle': out of the 19 countries studied, not one applies it. On the contrary, the EU report clearly showed that in every country studied, the applicable law authorizes a number of CEMs – between five and 11 per country. At least seven CEMs are available in every country but one. Furthermore, these CEMs are widely used, particularly in EU countries. On average, 44 per cent of the companies in the sample use CEMs (the sample being composed of large capitalizations and companies recently floated on the stock market). Regarding large capitalization only, 52 per cent of companies make use of CEM.

Finally, it has been clearly established that the so-called 'proportionality principle' has no historical foundation. On the contrary, the beginnings of modern corporate law were characterized by an attraction towards the 'one man, one vote' regime. That principle comes closer to the principle of shareholder democracy, but not in the sense that the shareholder primacy movement would like to give it.

The Theory of the 'Potential Shareholder'

According to this theory, if one must choose one sole master for the corporation (as per the single master theory), then that should be the shareholder for the following reason: any stakeholder can become a shareholder, whereas the reverse is not true. For example, an employee can buy shares in order to defend his interests (by asking for wage rises or dividend cuts at the AGM), whereas a shareholder cannot become an employee (and ask for wage cuts).

This argument has been advanced in all seriousness. It is easy to understand its lack of success.

The Theory of the 'Incompetent Shareholder'

The theory of the incompetent shareholder is more interesting (Easterbrook and Fischel, 1991, p. 11). According to this theory, the interest of shareholder primacy is that it enables rich but incompetent shareholders to entrust their money safely to (relatively) poor but competent corporate managers. This achieves the desirable objective of directing financial flows towards investment.

There are nevertheless serious doubts about the suitability of a model that maintains wealth in the hands of incompetent people. One might prefer a system that ensures the transfer of wealth to competent managers, so that the economy ultimately benefits from the enlightened choices of rich and competent shareholders.

Finally, this theory reflects an image of the idle, rentier shareholder, uninterested in the 'body corporate'. It is therefore unsurprising that it should be largely omitted from primacist literature.

All in all, however, the watchwords of shareholder primacy have been sufficiently convincing to bring about a good number of reforms that tend to strengthen the power of shareholders. They have led to a weakening in the will of the public authorities to find balanced solutions, raising questions about the legitimacy of state action in this matter.

THE LEGITIMACY OF STATE ACTION

Implicitly or explicitly, shareholder primacy puts to the test the legitimacy of state action in the domains that concern it. Yet, as I now hope to show, one would have to take an extremely short view to forget everything that corporate law owes to state action. Only legislation could ensure the transition from partnership to joint-stock company, which is the model of modern corporations. The question that could be asked, however, is why the transition between the two models has been so slow.

The Parallel Evolution of Partnerships and Joint-stock Companies[23]

The triumph and decline of partnerships

For the Romans, the common-law company was the *societas*, based on consent, contribution and shared interest (the partners were united by the *jus fraternitatis*, which established reciprocal relations of brotherhood between them). It resembled the current form of the undeclared partnership and was characterized by three main features. First, there was no separation between the assets of the partner and the company. Consequently, each partner had the right to withdraw his contributions, and creditors of the partners had a right over the company's assets. Second, the *societas* had no permanence: any partner could request its immediate dissolution at any time, and any clause to the contrary was invalid. Third, there was no provision for any corporate body: all the partners had the power (and even the duty) to manage the company, and there was no mutual power of representation among partners.

In the Middle Ages, two forms of company can be clearly distinguished. The first was the *commenda*, used in maritime and associating an entrepreneur, possibly a navigator or merchant (the *tractator*), and a provider of funds (the *commendator*). The life of the company was limited to the duration of the trade expedition. The profits were typically shared out according to custom, depending on whether the entrepreneur contributed nothing (in which case he received one quarter of the profits) or one-third of the capital (which gave him the right to half of the profits). The contracts show that certain obligations were sometimes imposed on the *tractator*, such as not to marry without the consent of the *commendator*, or not to play dice (or other gambling games). Legally, the *commenda* lay on the boundary between company contract and loan contract. The first of these qualifications, generally chosen, had the advantage of avoiding the prohibition of usury.[24] It was founded on the *risk* taken by the partner.[25]

The other common legal form of partnership in the Middle Ages was the *compagnia*, which initially brought together above all members of the same family. In companies that adopted the technique of *affrèrement* ('brotherhood'), all the assets were pooled together and the partners lived together ('one bread, one wine, one purse'). Liability, originally extended to the partners' collateral kin, was later restricted to the partners themselves – it was, of course, unlimited.[26] The duration of the contract varied: it could commit the partners for life (for family-based firms) or on the contrary for the duration of the shared project. Gradually, the rule became established that the signature of one partner committed all the partners when the corporate name was used.

In the seventeenth and eighteenth centuries, the legal forms of the firm became more complex: the French Royal Decree of 1673 distinguished between the *société générale* (similar to the modern general partnership), the *société en commandite* (limited partnership – a continuation of the *commenda*) and the *société anonyme* (heir of the Roman *societas*, similar to the modern undeclared partnership). Although they moved away from the medieval family community, the essential characteristics of these

partnerships remained the same. The firms were of limited size. Their existence was often secret. Their form was consensual, and the bylaws were
often reproduced in writing a verbal agreement of which it conserved the
original form (in dialogue).

Broadly speaking, there was no clear separation of company assets
or of limited liability during this period. Contracts frequently contained
clauses giving the partners explicit property rights over the assets of the
firm.[27] While the status of *société en commandite* should, in principle, have
protected the company's assets against creditors, the principle was not
firmly established, and judgments to the contrary were still being made in
the eighteenth century.

In 1804, the French civil code stayed with a traditional conception of
the firm, stipulating that, 'A firm is established by two or several persons
which agree by a contract to appropriate property or their industry for a
common venture with a view to sharing the benefit or profiting from the
saving which may result therefrom'. In fact, this chapter draws largely
on earlier definitions written by expert jurists such as Jean Domat and
Robert-Joseph Pothier, who were jurisconsults in the seventeenth and the
eighteenth century, respectively. One again finds the notions of contractual
consent, contribution and *affectio societatis*.

In the nineteenth century, partnerships started to enter into competition
with joint-stock companies, although the latter had been in existence for a
long time. This heralded the beginning of the decline of partnerships.

The law at the origin of joint-stock companies
Joint-stock companies have existed since Antiquity. In Rome, for instance,
the concession of tax collecting to publicans or the salt mines was operated
in this form.

In Italy, in the Middle Ages, legal measures were introduced to organize
the limited liability of partners in *commandites*, with the aim of attracting
capital. This was the case in Florence, for example (statutes of 1408 and
1495), and then in Bologna, Lucca and Rome. In France, in a prolonga-
tion of these statutes, the Royal Decree of 1673 made provision for the
limited liability of fund providers investing in *sociétés en commandite*.

Joint-stock companies burgeoned with the development of large companies, funded directly through the intervention of the public authorities.
The model for these was the Dutch East India Company, founded in 1600,
or, in France, the *Compagnie des Indes Orientales*, founded in 1664. These
companies were characterized by having a large number of shareholders
(the term 'shareholder' came into use in 1606), a real internal organization
and the attribution of a more or less complete form of legal personality.
In addition, the Royal Charter by which they were constituted usually

granted them privileges or trading monopolies that guaranteed their success. In France, the end of the eighteenth century saw the development of forms of company that exploited the technique of *commandite* to limit the liability of partners. These 'false *commandites*', with vague bylaws, only had limited success, however.

Joint-stock companies only really emerged in the nineteenth century. In France, the Civil Code of 1804 did not directly mention the legal personality of companies, but it did set out the rules leading to its recognition, as the Court of Cassation observed in a landmark decision in 1834. The Code of Commerce of 1807 confirmed the limited liability of silent partners (while forbidding them from interfering in the management of the *société en commandite*) and created the typical form of joint-stock companies: the *société anonyme* ('*anonyme*' – anonymous in English – because the names of the partners remain unknown, not appearing in the corporate name). Both in France and abroad, however, the real emancipation of joint-stock companies occurred later. In France, it was only from 1867 on that joint-stock companies could be created without prior authorization from the public authorities.

The United Kingdom followed a similar path to France.[28] In the seventeenth century, the traditional firms of the Middle Ages (*commenda* and *societas*) gave way to the development of chartered companies, which were endowed with legal personality but did not confer limited liability on their partners, and joint-stock companies. The development of a stock market for shares, regardless of whether the companies had legal personality, led to the formation of a speculative bubble, the bursting of which led to the passing of the Bubble Act in 1720. This Act subjected the obtaining of legal personality to the approval of King or Parliament. As a consequence, the corporate form that developed was the 'unincorporated association', which had no legal personality. Such firms frequently used the legal technique of establishing a trust to guarantee the proper use by managers of the assets dedicated to the firm's operations ('deed of settlement companies'). This system was not modified until the nineteenth century. The Bubble Act was repealed in 1825. Then a law passed in 1844 allowed the incorporation of joint-stock companies endowed with legal personality upon simple registration of the constituent acts.[29] In 1852, a court ruling recognized the possibility of limiting the liability of partners towards creditors of the company, provided that the creditors were expressly informed.[30] As this judicial recognition did not, however, give the mechanism sufficient simplicity and transparency, the Limited Liability Act of 1855 (modified in 1856) was passed to give companies the benefit of limited liability, subject to their meeting fairly simple conditions, such as having at least seven partners and affixing the word 'limited' to their corporate name. From a symbolic point of view, the separation between partners and company was completed by a law of 1862 making provision for partners to 'form companies' and not to 'form themselves into a company'.[31]

In the United States, the movement happened later; the dates vary from state to state, but it was not until the second half of the nineteenth century that it gradually became possible to create joint-stock companies without the authorization of state legislatures and to benefit from limited liability.

The Slow Transition from Partnership to Joint-stock Company

Legal personality makes the company a subject of law in its own right. The company owns an estate that is distinct in legal and accounting terms from the assets of its partners, the pledge of its creditors, as well as organs to represent it in dealings with third parties. This represents a tremendous simplification for the company in its contractual relations and a source of legal security for third parties. The partners can also benefit from limited liability. Given these advantages, it is surprising that the technique of legal personality has spread so slowly, especially since, as noted above, it has existed since Antiquity.

It should be remembered that the creation of legal personality and the granting of limited liability have always been closely linked to a process of state authorization. It could not be otherwise: the acquisition of legal personality and the limitation of liability to the value of the capital invested cannot result solely from the desire of the parties concerned. The relative (*inter partes*) effect of contracts constitutes an obstacle: how can a contract signed between partners be binding *vis-à-vis* parties who have contracted with the company? A clause would have to be included in all the company's conditions of sale and purchase stipulating that such parties recognize the existence of the legal personality of the firm, which would be a particularly cumbersome and unsure mechanism (any party could refuse to accept these conditions). In addition, it would be of no use against third parties whose claims are not of contractual origin, such as victims of accidents or beneficiaries of tax and social security contributions. Lastly, states with a civil-law tradition impose succession laws (for example, the existence of protection rights for heirs), and nearly every state taxes successions: it is obviously not possible to create a legal entity that makes it possible to evade these legal rules without legislative permission.[32] Indeed, the pre-eminent role of the law in the incorporation of modern companies has been recognized by the European Court of Justice in its Daily Mail ruling.[33]

Moreover, the opposability to third parties of limited liability and legal personality presupposes that the appropriate public notices have been posted. To be useful, these notices must be governed by conditions that are known to everyone. Only the law can impose such a uniform and therefore effective regime of public notification. The failure of *commandites* in France, under the *ancien régime*, was largely due to the fact that the Royal Decree of 1673 subjected the granting of limited liability to the realization of formalities of public notice. As the business world forcefully rejected this proposal (threatening to relocate companies abroad if this law were really applied to them), the rule fell into disuse, and the existence of limited liability was thrown into a state of ambiguity. Thus, the emergence and development of legal personality and limited liability have always depended on action by the public authorities (such as, laws, statutes, decrees, orders or charters), defining and enforcing the necessary rules of substance and notification.

Over a long period, the state has not always had the strength or ambition to enact and enforce such rules, and this has put a brake on the development of legal personality. In addition, the slowness of the development of legal personality can probably also be attributed to a certain distrust on the part of states. Legal entities are potentially immortal. They can accumulate unlimited quantities of assets, meaning that their power could therefore end up rivalling that of the state. The same question had already arisen during the Middle Ages in the case of religious orders, and the problem worsened with the irruption of legal personality into the economic sphere. In this respect, the English case of the Company of Merchants of Great Britain Trading to the South Seas is illuminating: this company became so powerful that in 1719 it could offer to take up the whole national debt. By corrupting certain ministers, it also obtained the right to pay off that debt in company shares. The fervour with which the public greeted this scheme was equalled only by the profundity of the bankruptcy that followed. This was the context in which the above-mentioned Bubble Act was passed.

The state, without whom companies would not exist in their modern form, therefore has the legitimacy to regulate their essential features. This legitimacy is all the greater since, as already noted, companies are institutions that occupy a pre-eminent position in society.

THE PATHS OF REFORM

Demonstrating that the theoretical foundations of shareholder primacy are fragile and that the state has the legitimacy to intervene is not enough. I have shown that shareholders do not have the legitimacy to monopolize power, but it still remains to indicate the directions that reform could take, or the existing mechanisms that should be retained.

The Paths of Reflection

First and foremost, reform means establishing principles, identifying a method and modifying representations. As far as the principles are concerned, I can put forward three: efficiency, which remains a key concern under any hypothesis; justice, both for its own sake and as a factor of efficiency (an unjust system being ultimately inefficient); and pluralism, adopting the principle that there is almost certainly no one optimal model and that each corporate form must be set in its specific legal, economic and cultural context.

The method is based on a necessary widening of the field of research. The governance movement is too focused on the UK and US models. It would be useful for more detailed and more numerous studies to be devoted to other countries, such as Germany, Japan, the Netherlands, Denmark, France, Italy or Spain, and so on. Above all, these studies should not simply carry out an appraisal using the criteria of shareholder primacy; they must identify the intrinsic strengths and weaknesses of these models and examine them within their specific legal and institutional contexts.

The modification of representations of the company is a useful or even essential preliminary to any significant reform. This does not mean looking for models in which shareholders have no power, but strengthening the foundations of systems in which they do not have *all* the power. Several directions can be envisaged for this research.

The position of the employee

The question of the respective positions of the shareholder and the employee provides a good point of departure. Legally, the former makes a contribution while the latter hires out his services. This dichotomy is not necessarily well founded, however. One can perfectly well consider that both make a contribution: the former of money (or other assets), the latter of time. As it happens, this analysis is corroborated by the existence in law of the concept of 'contribution in the form of services'. A comparative analysis grid could be drawn up, focusing on contribution, payment and risk. For example, if the capital contributed is lost in an unsuccessful venture, it may be recovered through another investment; the contribution of time, however, if it is considered to be lost, cannot be recovered elsewhere. The payment expected by the shareholder is composed of hoped-for distributions of profit and added value. What employees expect in return for their labour is more complex, consisting of not only their wages, but also diverse hopes for the future such as wage rises, promotions or career. In addition to the loss of their contribution, risk also concerns the hoped-for payment; this risk affects both the shareholders and the employees. As seen above, whereas the former can cover their risk, or at least limit it by diversifying their asset portfolio, the latter have no control whatsoever over the risk. A large part of the employee's risk stems from decisions made by the shareholder, to the extent that the shareholder can impose restructuring or relocation, increase the indebtedness of the company, change strategy or even sell the company. Relations between employees and shareholders should therefore be appreciated in the light of this analysis grid.

Team production

As far as the role of managers is concerned, some of the most fruitful research comes from team production theory, developed in particular by Margaret Blair.

As its point of departure, this theory focuses on the production process. Drawing on the works of Armen Alchian and Harold Demsetz (1972), it defines team production as a process in which several types of resources are used (including labour, finance, ideas and so on), the finished product is more than the sum of the intermediate products of each resource used, and the resources come from several different people.[34]

In addition, the production process is supported by firm-specific investments, which are made by members of the team to the benefit of the team. These may include, for example, the funding of particular equipment, training to use this equipment, particular unpaid efforts with a view to developing the enterprise, investments in customer relations, or the building of roads or facilities by the local community to service this centre of production. The characteristic shared by these investments is that they are wholly or partly lost if the joint enterprise fails, if the author of the specific investment leaves the team or if one of the team members appropriates for him- or herself all the profit resulting from the team's work (what team production theorists call a 'hold-up' (Klein et al., 1978). When a company implements team production methods, it is in the team members' interest to maintain durable relations in order to make the most of their specific investments. It is difficult to measure the exact value of specific investments, but first estimates show that they are far from negligible: a US study valued these investments at about 15 per cent of total wages, higher, that is to say, than total company profits (Topel, 1990; Blair, 1995b).

Who should have the power in the team? Who should be the *team leader*? This raises two questions. Should the function be exercised inside or outside the team? Should the controller be a residual creditor?

It has been shown that the very logic of team production, as proposed by Alchian and Demsetz, gives precedence to internal control (Rebérioux, 2007). It is advisable to choose someone who is sufficiently close to the production process, because when the team leader has control power over the whole team, he must be able to determine the contributions of each member accurately in order to pay them according to their true worth. This proximity between the manager and the company also results in a more perceptive understanding of the risks taken and opportunities available, in contrast to 'external' managers who may be less competent and suffer from considerable cognitive bias.

Team production theory also shows that one should avoid choosing a team leader who might appropriate for himself the whole profit of the team, failing which the team members may be discouraged from making specific investments. Moreover, if the law institutionalizes a system that authorizes 'hold-ups', then the potential victims have every interest in seeking to minimize the damage that this may inflict on them, either by demanding pay rises or by reducing their effort. Therefore, the team leader should not be the residual creditor. Thus, the twin requirements of proximity and neutrality rule out shareholders from this role, in favour of company managers, defined as 'mediating hierarchs'.

By making the manager a 'mediating hierarch', not answerable solely to the shareholders, but taking into account the constraints of the other stakeholders, team production theory opens the way to a more dynamic and entrepreneurial view of the company. This approach can usefully be combined with the study of trust as a mechanism to reduce agency costs.

The concept of profit
The literature on team production leads to a rethinking of the concept of profit, which is no longer considered as a payment used to remunerate shareholders, but as the sum of surpluses produced out of the relations with all the stakeholders. In big corporations, this approach enhances the value of one of the essential sources of profit: the capacity to organize the flows of input and coordinate the skills of everyone (Charreaux and Desbrières, 1998).

Paths for Action

There are three main sources of inspiration for establishing or maintaining non-primacist systems if one remains within the broad framework of the most widespread forms of company (excluding cooperatives, for example, from the analysis).

Power to the board of directors
The first system gives predominance to the board of directors. The model here is that of corporate law in Delaware, characterized by protection of the board's decision-making powers.

The board of directors enjoys considerable prerogatives not only in the management of the company, but also in domains directly affecting the shareholders' interests, such as the distribution of dividends. The founding principle of the allocation of powers makes the board of directors the centre of decision-making power. Pursuant to the fiduciary duties of directors, these powers must be exercised, and the shareholders cannot encroach upon these prerogatives. Moreover, the directors are protected in their actions by the 'business judgment rule'.

This system is interesting in that it favours greater responsiveness in running the business by providing managers not only with sufficient room for action but also with real independence that gives them the *legitimacy* to act.

Power-sharing between the stakeholders

The second system ensures the representation of the interests of the different stakeholders within the company. Germany provides a good case in point.

In the traditional version of this model, companies have a shareholder of reference.[35] Banks play an important role in the control of companies and can have seats in the different corporate bodies. For the biggest companies, the codetermination system gives half the seats on the supervisory board to worker representatives. Lastly, cross-shareholdings between companies have created a web of inter-company relations, and therefore a form of corporate control over the actions of companies.

The German system has evolved. Following the privatization of Deutsche Telekom in 1996, which boosted popular shareholding in Germany, and the creation of the Neuer Markt in 1997, the legal framework was reformed to strengthen shareholders' rights. Thus, for example, the KonTraG law of 1998 regulated the voting right of banks over shares held on deposit and prohibited the creation of shares with multiple voting rights and voting ceilings. A law passed in 2000 (but applicable in 2002) also changed the tax system for added values to facilitate the sale of cross-shareholdings. Nevertheless, codetermination was maintained and the 2001 law on takeover bids has given the supervisory board (where the workers' representatives sit) the power to authorize defence strategies to repel takeover bids.[36]

This system is of interest for two reasons. First, it provides a large space for negotiating and seeking consensus, with the result that corporate decisions enjoy greater adhesion from all stakeholders. Second, by giving employees a voice in the event of takeover bids, it gains more trust *vis-à-vis* individual long-term strategies involving specific investments. All in all, the system appears to be more equitable, and by winning greater trust, it can increase corporate profitability by raising everyone's personal motivation and reducing control costs.

The corporate interest

In the last model, the managers are the guardians of the interest of the company as a whole. The corporate interest, distinct from the interests of each stakeholder, is placed at the heart of the managers' duties.

Reference to the corporate interest serves two purposes. First, it limits the powers of the managers, who can no longer act solely in their own interest. This is a negative function, purely protective and preventive, with retroactive application. In a more dynamic, positive and forward-facing way, corporate interest also serves to give a direction, an objective, to the managers' actions. Corporate interest thus fits perfectly into the legal theory of power. That power is purpose based and directed towards an objective. It is used to defend an interest that remains partly distinct from the holder of that power who has certain powers over others (see Gaillard, 1985, and Le Nabasque, 1986). The managers' purpose is to further the corporate interest, which is distinct from the managers' interest. The company provides a natural setting in which powers are balanced and diverging interests are synthesized. Conceived in this way, corporate interest is the instrument by which conflicts can be transcended. Making managers, on the other hand, the subservient principals of shareholders robs them of their legitimacy. By pursuing exclusively the latter's interest, managers become the puppets of the shareholders and their powers are weakened, symbolically and effectively, to the advantage of the investors. The company then risks losing its capacity to integrate opposing forces and to create something that serves the interests of all the stakeholders. As one author so rightly said, 'We cannot construct corporate law by denying the conflicts of which companies are the theatre' (Le Cannu, 2003, our translation).

The concept of corporate interest has the favour of courts, which attribute to it precisely that integrative function – source of balance between the different parties, and therefore of social peace. To illustrate this approach, I shall take the examples of France, the UK and the United States.

In France, the concept of corporate interest is not defined anywhere in law,[37] and the texts that refer to it are dispersed throughout the code of commerce,[38] so that no unified regime is established a priori. One important text – article 1833 of the civil code, which refers to 'the common interest of the partners' – could, however, be used to reject the concept of corporate interest (as some law professors advocate) (see Schmidt, 1994 and 1995). Case law has nonetheless taken up the concept and makes wide use of it: it is employed, for example, to limit the abuse of law in the relations between shareholders, to define when managers may be held liable for mismanagement, to determine whether it is appropriate for a court to designate a provisional director within a company, or to establish whether there were reasonable grounds for the dismissal of a manager (conditioning the possible award of damages to such a manager).

By giving full effect to the theory of corporate interest, case law confirms that the company is much more than a 'nexus of contracts': it is an institution. Thus, several rulings by the Appeal Court have refused to consecrate the contractual theory of the firm, indicating, for example, that 'although in its old conception, which remains that of the civil code, that the corporation is a contract, it cannot be denied that it constitutes much more than a contract'[39] or that, 'the corporation [is] rather an institution, that is to say, a corporate body surpassing individual will.[40] The Court of Cassation has evoked the 'contractual value' of bylaws, which is a way of giving them effect without recognizing the contractual theory of the company.[41]

As the concept of corporate interest is not defined by law in France, this question has been the subject of diverse reflections. One of the most oft-quoted definitions comes from the MEDEF (national confederation of French employers) and the AFEP (French association of private businesses), for whom the corporate interest should be understood as the interest of the company, that is, 'the superior interest of the legal entity itself, that is to say the company, which is considered as an autonomous economic agent, pursuing its own objectives, distinct notably from those of its shareholders, employees, creditors (including the tax authorities), suppliers and customers, but which corresponds to their common interest, which is to ensure the prosperity and continuity of the company'.[42] This definition contains the two classic features of the theory, namely the independence of the concept of corporate interest, which cannot be reduced to that of the stakeholders, and the teleological perspective of this concept, as the firm is assigned objectives of 'prosperity' and 'continuity'. Without giving a general, abstract definition of corporate interest, case law has specified some of its features, including conservation of the 'durability of the company'.[43] In the event of a takeover bid, it has also been established that the corporate interest 'should not be confused with that of a few shareholders or a group of shareholders', and that it depends on 'the conditions, notably financial, under which the sale takes place'.[44] The price offered should be taken into consideration, but it cannot be the sole criterion of the corporate interest.

In the UK, the concept of corporate interest is traditionally given a particular place in the system of obligations imposed on managers. For historical reasons, these duties are divided into those deriving from common law, namely the duty of care, and those deriving from equity, namely fiduciary duties. The latter include the duty of loyalty, which is traditionally defined as the duty to act 'bona fide in what they consider – not what a court may consider – is in the interests of the company'.[45] It is clear that this interest can be distinct from that of the shareholders or the company creditors: in a 1990 decision, for example, the House of Lords recognized the right of managers of a company in financial trouble to sell an asset at a price below the maximum they could obtain, provided that they justified the choice of buyer in terms of the latter's guarantees offered to the employees.[46]

In the United States,[47] the concept of corporate interest arises notably on the occasion of takeover bids. In this context, the issue is that of the managers' power, or duty, to fight hostile takeover bids by establishing defence mechanisms, such as poison pills, for example. The *Unocal v. Mesa Petroleum* (1985) ruling[48] was the landmark decision on the question of defences, setting out the principle of a new criterion by which the managers' decisions should be examined: 'enhanced scrutiny'. For a defence to be valid, the managers of the targeted company must prove, in particular, that they have reasonable grounds to believe that there is a 'danger' for the company,[49] showing their good faith and due diligence. In examining this danger, the board of directors can take into account, among other things, 'the impact on the "stakeholders" other than the shareholders (that is, the creditors, customers, employees and perhaps even the wider community)'. This jurisprudence was enshrined by the *Revlon v. MacAndrews* (1986) decision,[50] which dealt specifically with the question of the interests to be protected as a priority by the managers of the target company in the event of a takeover bid. At the end of a complex and subtle line of reasoning, the Court decided, essentially, that a distinction should be made between two cases: if the directors do not participate in the sale of the company, they can defend the 'corporate bastion' (and the different interests attached to it) against the bid; in the opposite case, the directors become auctioneers who must 'maximize the value of the company in a sale to the benefit of the shareholders'.[51] This decision was confirmed by the Time-Warner ruling,[52] made in 1990, which was the occasion for the Court to start by recalling two principles: first, that 'the board of directors . . . is not under any per se duty to maximize shareholder value in the short term, even in the context of a takeover', and second, that the directors can determine that 'the present stock market price is not representative of true value or there may indeed be several market values for any corporation's stock'. The Court then specified two cases[53] in which, by application of the Revlon jurisprudence, the board of directors has the duty of maximizing shareholder value: (i) when the company has embarked on an organized process of auction with the aim of selling itself or carrying out a reorganization leading to a break-up, and (ii) when a company, in reply to a takeover bid, abandons its long-term strategy and seeks an alternative deal entailing a break-up of the company. The targeted company can therefore choose to pursue its strategy by defending its independence, which is a clear manifestation of the consideration given to a form of corporate interest.

Thus, a real place has been given to corporate interest in France, the United Kingdom and the United States. The concept is also particularly vigorous in the rest of continental Europe. It therefore constitutes a path that is both rich in lessons and promising for all kinds of reflection on the distribution of power in companies.

CONCLUSION

Although the shareholder primacy movement has enjoyed undeniable success, its theoretical foundations are shaky and empirical evidence of its advantages are lacking. In this context, the political question of the legitimacy of shareholder power deserves to be examined. This should be done not with the intent of going from one extreme to the other, but with the aim of determining the appropriate degree of shareholder power and finding suitable means by which to safeguard the interests of the other stakeholders. All this should be done while protecting the company from the moral hazard resulting from the non-liability of shareholders.

The historical analysis of companies brings to light the considerable debt that the modern company owes to intervention by the public authorities. It is therefore perfectly normal that joint-stock companies, which are legal creatures of the state, should be governed by rules ensuring that their use remains in keeping with the interests of society.

NOTES

1. In this regard, we should note the increasing number of reports (of which the Cadbury Report, in the United Kingdom, was the precursor), of institutions (such as the ICGN – Institute of Corporate Governance Network) and principles of 'soft law' (notably through codes of good conduct or the OECD Principles of Corporate Governance). The rule of 'comply or explain' is also used in the same way.
2. One of the most important changes has been the development of variable pay for managers as a means of aligning their interests with those of the shareholders. The powerful rise of shareholder activism is part of the same movement.
3. Note, in this regard, the adoption by the European Union of directives relating to takeover bids, transparency and shareholder rights, as well as the adoption of International Financial Reporting Standards (IFRS). Paradoxically, the United States has been less

active in adapting its legal and regulatory framework to the demands of shareholder primacy.

4. For a critical analysis of this movement of convergence, see Armour et al. (2007).

5. Here, the term 'institution' is used in the legal sense, referring to the idea of a legally organized collective structure. Dean Maurice Hauriou (1906) defined it as 'a group of people, organized in an enduring way for the realization of an idea'.

6. In particular, corporations exert great influence over the location of production and research activities. They also direct the contents of these activities. Furthermore, they intervene actively in the political domain through negotiations with social partners, lobbying and the funding of election campaigns.

7. In France, the Court of Cassation – the French supreme court for civil, business and criminal matters – recognized, for a time, the corporate interest of bribes paid to leading French politicians (Cass. crim. 6 Feb. 1997, 'Mouillot' case, D. 1997, 334) before returning to its traditional jurisprudence in the Carignon case (Cass. crim. 27 Oct. 1997, D. aff. 1997, 1438). The Court of Cassation was uncomfortable with the grounds it gave for this judgment: it had to affirm, *in abstracto*, that any misdemeanour committed by the corporation is contrary to its corporate interest in that it 'exposes the legal entity to an abnormal risk of penal or fiscal penalties against itself or its managers and damages its credit or reputation'. This involves an irrefragable presumption of conflict between infringements of the law and corporate interest, a presumption which, however desirable it may be, remains a fiction. In another vein, the film 'The Corporation' is a study (exclusively inculpatory) of the 'psychology' of corporations for which profit is the sole motive. It illustrates the dangerous drifts that can result from this.

8. The role of the experts is important, but it is not everything. It should not be forgotten that finance is simply a branch of economics, which is itself part of anthropology. This means that one must advance with caution, examine hypotheses carefully and always mistrust general conclusions and too-perfect systems. As for jurists, their vocation for intervening in this debate is limited to three points: as technicians, they possess the tools to construct the practical compromises that can be found; they may also be cognizant of the different compromises that have been established in the past or in other countries; finally, by their training, they are sensitive to the overall coherence of systems and their justification.

One cannot afford to abandon a critical attitude towards the 'Law and Economics' movement: not to deny the often stimulating contributions it has made, but to demarcate its limits. The experts – especially in this domain – are not free from ideological a prioris. Their conclusions can be paradoxical, and, over time, the systems they have designed rigidify. The intervention of experts always raises the classic problem of 'hidden information'; this is also true in the relations between experts in governance and political decision makers. In this respect, the explanation and discussion of starting hypotheses is particularly sensitive. As Ronald Coase so rightly said, 'Economic theory has suffered in the past from a failure to state clearly its assumptions. Economists in building up a theory have often omitted to examine the foundations on which it was erected. This examination is, however, essential not only to prevent the misunderstanding . . . but also because of the extreme importance for economics of good judgment in choosing between rival sets of assumptions' (Coase, 1937, p. 386).

9. In particular, and although it is fundamental, I shall not examine the question of the rationality of markets. On the cognitive biases of traders who deal on (and make up) markets see Fenton-O'Creevy et al. (2005).

10. Here the term is used in a broad sense, covering any organized procedure at the end of which the corporation's creditors may not be paid because the corporation is insolvent.

11. The expansion of the limited liability model can also be observed in the consultant professions (such as lawyers) where there is a trend towards the adoption of structures with limited liability (in the United States), such as limited liability partnerships, or LLPs).

12. The standard argument, not entirely without good sense, is that one must not penalize everyone a priori simply to guard against a few black sheep.
13. In the United States, for example, over the 1981–96 period, the net share issues (issues minus buybacks) of non-financial companies were negative, to the tune of US$700 billion (Ireland, 1999). According to the AMF (French Financial Market Authority) annual report for 2007, there was a negative total of €500 billion in 2006 and more than €600 billion in 2007; in France, net share issues totalled €21 billion in 2007, similar to the figure for 2006, after being close to zero for the years 2003, 2004 and 2005.
14. The relation between the quality of residual owner and the attribution of power was first expressed by Armen Alchian and Harold Demsetz in 'Production, information costs, and economic organization' (1972, p. 782). It was taken up notably by Erik Furubotn and Svetozar Pejovich, in their analysis of property rights (1972, p. 1137).
15. This is an interesting aspect of the theory. It would be worth conducting empirical studies into the respective attitudes of shareholders and other stakeholders (particularly employees) towards risk-taking. Generally speaking, it is regrettable that studies into this type of question focus so intently on synthetic variables such as the stock market price, which rarely leads to useful conclusions, and so little on the validity of their central hypotheses, which could give rise to vast psychological and sociological surveys.
16. English law, however, provides for a double limit to this mechanism: if the third party has the power to designate more than half of the directors, he or she cannot obtain the forced execution of that right. In addition, shareholders keep the ability of dismissing the directors thus designated.
17. *Kuwait Asia Bank EC v. National Mutual Life Nominees Ltd* [1991] I AC 187 (Privy Council), in Fernandez (2007, p. 17).
18. On the development of takeover law in the United States and the United Kingdom, see the study of John Armour and David Skeel (2006), which clearly illustrates the dynamics at work.
19. It should be noted that nexism is even in contradiction with the theory of the firm as expounded by Ronald Coase in his 1937 article on the nature of the firm (Coase, 1937). For Coase, the power to give instructions to employees (characteristic of the employment relation) was the dividing line between the inside and the outside of the 'firm'. The combination of nexism and agency theory causes that distinction to disappear.
20. This study gave rise to a report, published on 17 May 2007, entitled, 'Report on the Proportionality Principle in the European Union', commissioned by the European Commission to serve as the foundation for possible reform of the 'proportionality principle'. This study is available on the EC website at: http://ec.europa.eu/internal_market/company/shareholders/indexb_fr.htm.
21. Companies have used this system in the past, notably during the first half of the nineteenth century, but it has been largely abandoned since then.
22. 'Monarchy and tyranny he [Socrates] considered to be both forms of government, but conceived that they differed [greatly] from one another; for a government over men with their own consent, and in conformity with the laws of free states, he regarded as a monarchy; but a government over men against their will, and not according to the law of free states, but just as the ruler pleased, a tyranny; and wherever magistrates were appointed from among those who complied with the injunctions of the laws, he considered the government to be an aristocracy; wherever they were appointed according to their wealth, a plutocracy; and wherever they were appointed from among the whole people, a democracy' (Xenophon, 1859).
23. For the historical aspects of corporate law, see notably Lévy-Bruhl (1938), Sicard (1953), Lefebvre-Teillard (1985) and Hilaire (1986). For English law, see notably Farrar (1988) and Fernandez (2007).
24. The prohibition of usury was justified by texts from the Old Testament ('Thou shalt not lend upon usury to thy brother', Deuteronomy 23-20; 'He does not lend at usury or take excessive interest', Ezekiel, 18-17) and the New Testament ('do good, and lend, expecting nothing in return', Luke, 6-35). From these texts scholars deduced the principle of

the 'sterility of gold': gold is a vile metal that cannot reproduce itself; interest plays on time, whereas time belongs only to God and not to men. Dante put usurers in the seventh circle of hell, further in than violent people. The Reform, under the impetus of Calvin, led to the absolute prohibition of usury being abandoned in Protestant countries: in England, for example, only excessive rates of interest were banned from the sixteenth century on (the legal limit being fixed at 10 per cent and then, in 1713, at 5 per cent).

25. There were – already – financing packages put together to obtain the legal qualification of company (to get around the prohibition of usury) while avoiding the taking of risks. In England, for example, the practice of the 'triple contract' (*contractus trinius*) combined a partnership contract, insurance on the capital invested and insurance on the profit. See Fernandez (2007, p. 8).

26. Unlimited liability, by extending the legal personal right of creditors, facilitated companies' access to credit.

27. Technically, this meant that shares in companies possessing real estate were themselves considered to be real estate.

28. On the evolution of corporate law in England, see in particular Ireland (1999).

29. In the meantime, in 1837, a ruling had confirmed the principle that the shareholders are not the owners of the company's assets (*Blight v. Brent*, 1837, 2 Y&C Ex 268).

30. *Hallett v Dowdall* (1852) 21 LJ QB 98.

31. The limited liability of partners was also strengthened with the decline, over the course of the nineteenth century, of the practice of issuing shares of which the nominal value was not entirely liberated on issuance.

32. It is true, however, that some rulings in France have granted legal personality to groups that do not benefit from it by law: for example, works councils, group committees, unofficial trade unions, 'companies' of joint ownership of ships. These decisions, however, are essentially marginal rectifications of legislative oversights with hardly any effect on the economic sphere.

33. '[C]ompanies are created by national law and exist only by virtue of that national legislation and the latter therefore determines its incorporation and functioning' (*ECJ*, 27 September 1988, ECR 1988, 5483).

34. '1) several types of resources are used . . . 2) the product is not a sum of separable outputs of each cooperating resource . . . and 3) not all resources used in team production belong to one person' (Alchian and Demsetz, 1972, p. 779).

35. In 1990, about 90 per cent of listed companies had a reference shareholder possessing more than 25 per cent of their capital (Jenkinson and Ljungvist, 2001, p. 397).

36. On the evolution of the German system, see in particular Gordon (2003).

37. The question of the insertion of a definition was debated during the examination of the 1966 bill on companies, but was rejected (see JOAN CR, 12 June 1965, pp. 2031–5).

38. In the French code of commerce, texts mentioning the company's interest deal with (i) the accomplishment of acts of management, in SARL and SNC (limited companies and general partnerships), 'in the interest of the company' (articles L. 221–4 and L. 223–18), (ii) the misappropriation of company assets (articles L. 241–3 and L. 242–6), and (iii) the criteria of validity of voting agreements (article L. 233–3). In the civil code, article 1848 refers to acts of management in civil society organizations.

39. Paris, 26 March 1966, Gaz. Pal. 1966.I.400.

40. Reims, 24 April 1989, Gaz. Pal. 1989, 2, somm. 431.

41. Cass. Civ. 1ère, 15 July 1999, Bull. Joly, Nov. 1999, §261.

42. AFEP – MEDEF Report, 2003 (our translation).

43. Cass. Com. 18 June 2002, Bull. Joly 2002, p. 1221, note by Stéphane Sylvestre.

44. CA Paris 15 March 2000, JCP E 2000, p. 1046, note A. Viandier (affaire Groupe André/ Atticus). The Appeal Court of Paris had already refused to give partners' interests precedence over the interests of the company in a ruling of 5 April 2002 (RJDA 3/03 no. 270).

45. *Re Smith and Fawcett Ltd* [1942] Ch 304, p. 306.

46. *Re Welfab Engineers Ltd* [1990] BCLC 833.

47. The jurisprudence quoted comes from the State of Delaware, the most representative in this matter.
48. *Unocal Corp. v. Mesa Petroleum Co.*, Delaware Supreme Court, 1985, 493 A. 2d 946. The decisions quoted in this paragraph concern the State of Delaware, which has the highest concentration of large listed companies in the United States.
49. This danger is described as 'a threat to the corporate policy' or 'a danger to corporate policy or effectiveness'.
50. *Revlon, Inc. v. MacAndrews & Forbes Holdings, Inc.*, Delaware Supreme Court, 1986, 506 A. 2d 173.
51. 'The directors' role changed from defenders of the corporate bastion to auctioneers charged with getting the best price for the stockholders at a sale of the company' (*Revlon, Inc. v. MacAndrews & Forbes Holdings, Inc.*, 1986).
52. *Paramount Communications, Inc. v. Time, Inc.*, Delaware Supreme Court, 1990, 571 A. 2d 1140.
53. While stipulating that other cases of application could be envisaged.

REFERENCES

Alchian, A. and H. Demsetz (1972), 'Production, information costs, and economic organization', *American Economic Review*, **62**, pp. 777–95.

Armour, J. and D.A. Skeel (2006), 'Who writes the rules for hostile takeovers, and why? The peculiar divergence of US and UK Takeover Regulation', CBR Working Paper 331, Centre for Business Research, University of Cambridge.

Armour, J., S. Deakin, P. Sarkar and M. Siems (2007), 'Shareholder protection and stock market development: an empirical test of the legal origins hypothesis', CBR Working Paper 358, Centre for Business Research, University of Cambridge.

Bainbridge, S.M. (1997), 'Community and statism: a conservative contractarian critique of progressive corporate law scholarship', *Cornell Law Review*, **82**, pp. 858–73.

Blair, M. (1995a), 'Corporate ownership: a misleading word muddies the corporate governance debate', *Brookings Review*, **13** (1), pp. 16–19.

Blair, M. (1995b), 'Rethinking assumptions behind corporate governance', *Challenge*, November/December, pp. 12–18.

Charreaux, G. and P. Desbrières (1998), 'Gouvernance des entreprises: valeur partenariale contre valeur actionnariale', *Finance Contrôle Stratégie*, **1** (2), pp. 57–88.

Coase, R. (1937), 'The nature of the firm', *Economica*, **4** (16), pp. 386–405.

Davies, P. (1997), *Gower's Principles of Modern Company Law*, London: Sweet & Maxwell, 6th edition.

Easterbrook, F.H. and D.R. Fischel (1991), *The Economic Structure of Corporate Law*, Cambridge, MA: Harvard University Press.

European Commission (2007), 'Report on the Proportionality Principle in the European Union', available at: http://ec.europa.eu/internal_market/company/shareholders/indexb_fr.htm (accessed 10 August 2007).

Farrar, J. (1988), *Farrar's Company Law*, London: Butterworths.

Fenton-O'Creevy, M., N. Nicholson, E. Soane and P. Willman (2005), *Traders, Risks, Decisions, and Management in Financial Markets*, Oxford: Oxford University Press.

Fernandez, M. (2007), 'Le Contrôle de l'entreprise par ses fournisseurs de crédit dans les droits français et anglais', Thesis, University of Paris II.

Furubotn, E.G. and S. Pejovich (1972), 'Property rights and economic theory: a survey of recent literature', *Journal of Economic Literature*, **10** (4), pp. 1137–62.

Gaillard, E. (1985), *Le Pouvoir en droit privé*, Thesis, University of Paris I, Paris: Economica.

Gordon, J. (2003), 'An international relations perspective on the convergence of corporate governance: German shareholder capitalism and the European Union, 1990–2000', ECGI Law Working Paper 06/2003, European Corporate Governance Institute, Brussels.

Hauriou, M. (1906), 'L'Institution et le droit statutaire', Rec. Acad. Législ, Toulouse.

Hilaire, J. (1986), *Introduction historique au droit commercial*, Paris: PUF.

Ireland, P. (1999), 'Company law and the myth of shareholder ownership', *Modern Law Review*, **62** (1), pp. 32–57.

Jenkinson, T. and A. Ljungvist (2001), 'The role of hostile stakes in German corporate governance', *Journal of Corporate Finance*, **4** (7), pp. 397–446.

Jensen, M.C. (2000), *A Theory of the Firm*, Cambridge, MA: Harvard University Press.

Klein, B., R. Crawford and A. Alchian (1978), 'Vertical integration, appropriable rents and the competitive contracting process', *Journal of Law and Economics*, **21** (2), pp. 297–326.

Knight, F.H. (1933), *Risk, Uncertainty and Profit*, London: London School of Economics and Political Science.

Le Cannu, P. (2003), *Droit des sociétés*, 2nd edn, No. 138, Paris: Domat-Montchrestien.

Lefebvre-Teillard, A. (1985), *La Société anonyme au XIXème siècle*, Paris: PUF.

Le Nabasque, H. (1986), 'Le Pouvoir dans l'entreprise: essai sur le droit de l'entreprise', Thesis, University of Rennes I.

Lévy-Bruhl, H. (1938), *Histoire juridique des sociétés de commerce en France aux XVIIème et XVIIIème siècles*, Paris: Domat-Monchrestien.

Rebérioux, A. (2007), 'Shareholder primacy and managerial accountability', CLPE Research Paper 1/2007, Comparative Research in Law and Political Economy, York University, Toronto.

Schmidt, D. (1994), 'De l'intérêt commun des associés', JCP 1994, I, 3793 and 3800 bis.

Schmidt, D. (1995), 'De l'intérêt social', JCP E, 1995, I, 488.

Sicard, G. (1953), *Les Moulins de Toulouse au Moyen Age*, Paris: A. Colin.

Topel, R.C. (1990), 'Specific capital and unemployment: measuring the costs and consequences of job loss', in A.H. Meltzer and C.I. Plosser (eds), *Studies in Labor Economics in Honor of Walter Y. Oi*, Amsterdam: North-Holland, pp. 181–214.

Xenophon (1859), *The Memorable Thoughts of Socrates*, Book IV, Ch. 6, translated by Eugène Talbot, *Oeuvres Completes de Xénophon*, Volume I, Paris: Hachette.

5. Corporate governance, labour relations and human resource management in the UK and France: convergence or divergence?

Simon Deakin and Antoine Rebérioux

INTRODUCTION

Numerous studies have examined the role that labour plays, or might play, in corporate governance (see, for example, Blair, 1995; Aoki, 2001, chapter 11). In addition, the potential of ownership structure and of corporate governance practices (alongside product market conditions) to shape employment conditions has received a lot of attention. The relationship between the stock market and the labour market have been analysed at the macroeconomic and macro-legal levels, notably through the concept of 'institutional complementarities' (Hall and Soskice, 2001; Ahlering and Deakin, 2007; Barker and Rueda, 2007; Black et al., 2007). The key idea is that a financial system that favours liquidity, as in the United States or the United Kingdom, may limit the possibilities for employee commitment and cooperation within enterprises, but facilitate the reorganization of corporate activities. These studies stress, at a first level of interaction, the relationship between the spheres of finance and employment. More recently, some works have explored the influence of stock markets on human resource management (HRM) practices and working conditions at the micro level (see, for example, Gospel and Pendleton, 2005; Jackson, 2005).

Parallel to these developments, the comparative literature on corporate governance systems has made important progress over the last decade. The conventional distinction between an 'outsider' (US–UK style) model and an 'insider' (German, Japanese or French) model is now increasingly questioned by studies taking into account the national and international trajectories of rules regulating stock markets, listed companies and labour. For example, in continental Europe and Japan, changes in securities law and in corporate law, together with the growing liquidity of financial markets, have increased the sensitivity of managers to the interests of external shareholders (Fanto, 1998; Cioffi and Cohen, 2000; Aoki, 2007). This has led some authors to identify a convergence between the continental European or Japanese systems of corporate governance and the US or British model (Hansmann and Kraakman, 2001). At the same time, the 'managerialist' features of the US system are increasingly highlighted (see, for example, Stout, 2007). In this regard, it has been suggested that the evolution of corporate and labour laws in the UK, for example, is by no means reducible to a pure shareholder-oriented model of governance (Armour et al., 2003).

In this chapter, we study the effects of corporate governance, and more precisely of a stock market listing, on HRM practices, through a UK–French comparison. The rationale for this comparison is twofold. First, corporate governance systems in France and the UK appear to be increasingly similar, albeit with some continuing legal and institutional differences, some of which are clear-cut. These differences make it possible to interpret the contrasting empirical observations that we report here, and to draw some conclusions on the relationships between the spheres of finance and labour. Second, two very similar datasets (the WERS survey in the UK and the REPONSE survey in France) have been used by a number of authors specifically to assess the link between stock market pressure and HRM practices. Thus, a body of knowledge now exists against which theories can be tested. We rely on these studies to develop our argument.

We report evidence that corporate governance does matter for HRM: establishments of listed companies are more involved in the use of 'high commitment' (or 'high road') HRM practices than others.[1] We also report evidence that this involvement is slightly stronger for French listed companies than for UK ones, a divergence that is mainly related to differences in the way labour laws operate in the two countries.

The chapter is ordered as follows. The next section sets out the relevant dynamic features of the UK and French corporate governance systems (including, where relevant, employment regulation), with the aim of identifying their main similarities and differences, and the implications these might have for the link between the stock market and employment relations. The third section provides an overview of the (likely) effects of the stock market on employment relations, on the basis of the theoretical and empirical literature. The fourth section discusses and synthesizes the empirical evidence that comes out from the exploitation of the French and UK workplace-level datasets (REPONSE and WERS). The final section concludes, by stressing the role of labour regulation in the management of the business firm.

CORPORATE GOVERNANCE IN THE UK AND FRANCE: DIVERGENCES AND CONVERGENCES

At first sight, the UK and France represent two clear cases of the division of national systems of production into 'liberal market' and 'coordinated market' regimes (Hall and Soskice, 2001). UK corporate governance is centred on the idea of 'shareholder value management', with companies run principally for the benefit of shareholders, who are regarded as the owners of the business. There is a high degree of stock market liquidity, and share ownership is dispersed. There is no institutionalized voice for labour at the level of the firm, and employment law provides few constraints on restructurings. As a result, management has considerable flexibility in developing HRM strategies aimed at maximizing shareholder returns, including the use of financial and other performance-based incentives for workers, while minimizing commitments to job security. At the same time, the short-term time horizon under which management is operating limits the possibility of enduring labour–management partnerships, with negative implications not only for job stability and employee well-being, but also, potentially, for training and, ultimately, for labour productivity.

France, on the other hand, is a system in which the concept of shareholder primacy enjoys no obvious legitimacy. On the contrary: the prevailing legal conception of the firm is based on the idea that managers serve the 'company interest' over and above those of the shareholders or of any other corporate constituency. Share ownership is relatively concentrated by international standards, as a result of continuing cross-shareholdings among listed companies and the legacy of state ownership of and influence over large industrial and financial enterprises.[2] Employment protection is backed by labour law and worker voice is institutionalized mainly through legally mandated enterprise committees. This ensemble of rules and institutions qualifies the influence of capital markets while encouraging high levels of investment in human resources: with no choice but to comply with stringent labour laws and to seek consensus with employee representatives, management has to follow a high-productivity route if the firm is to remain competitive.

The description we have just given is nonetheless too simplistic, and it gives an overly static presentation of the two systems. Both have been subject to considerable institutional change in the past decade, together with shifts in ownership structure and in the relationship between industry and finance. The result has been to see the two countries moving closer together, at least in the sense of functional convergence, as opposed to the formal approximation of laws and practices. This convergence makes it difficult to identify the precise areas of similarity and difference, and complicates the task of identifying appropriate hypotheses for empirical testing concerning the impact of corporate governance on employment relations.

Let us first consider the issue of the institutional framework. In the two systems, certain deeply embedded concepts, or principles of company law, can be identified, which give expression to basic values in the sphere of corporate governance. In the words of the Viénot report (1995) on corporate governance in France:

> In Anglo-American countries the emphasis is for the most part placed on the objective of maximizing share values, whilst on the European continent and in France in particular the emphasis is placed more on the company's interest . . . Company's interest can be defined as the overriding interest of the corporate body itself, in other words the company considered as an autonomous economic agent, pursuing its own aims as distinct from those of its shareholders, its employees, its creditors including the tax authorities, and of its suppliers and customers; rather, it corresponds to their general, common interest, which is that of ensuring the survival and prosperity of the company. (p. 8; our translation)

The Viénot report was commissioned by the French employers' federations, MEDEF and AFEP, and was responsible for a significant repositioning of French corporate governance towards a shareholder value approach. It is significant that, even in this context, its authors felt it necessary to reassert the concept of a distinctive 'company interest', identified with the enterprise in and of itself, and extending beyond the separate interests of each of the different stakeholder groups. Indeed, a long tradition in French legal thinking insists that the managers of the enterprise must not be identified as the agents of the shareholders, on the grounds that this would undermine the organizational integrity of the firm. This 'institutionalist' or 'managerialist' approach to the legal theorization of the business enterprise informs the strict regulation of collective redundancies in France, emphasizing the unity, in this respect, of labour law and corporate law in that system (Paillusseau, 1999; Aglietta and Rebérioux, 2005, p. 43).

Thus, the French system of company law essentially sees the business enterprise as having an *organizational* dimension that rests on the contributions made by a number of stakeholder groups, and not simply a *financial* dimension which describes the contribution of the shareholders. This divergence of approach operates at a fundamental conceptual level, so that even the legal terms used to define the business enterprise are not precisely analogous. The UK law concept of the 'company', for example, refers to a financial relationship between managers and investors; there is no equivalent to those concepts that recognize the enterprise's organizational dimension, such as the French *entreprise*. This longstanding legal tradition is carried over into the modern corporate governance codes: beginning with the Cadbury Code of 1991, these formally exclude labour and other 'stakeholder' interests from participation in company-level governance, in favour of the principle of managerial accountability to shareholders.

Nevertheless, it would be a mistake to ignore altogether the 'managerialist' dimension of UK company law. This comes close to the notion of the 'company interest' in the concept of 'enlightened shareholder value', which the government-sponsored Company Law Review suggested, in the early 2000s, as a central, defining objective for the UK corporate enterprise. This notion 'requires directors to act in the collective best interests of shareholders, but recognizes that this can only be achieved by taking due account of wider interests', including those of employees (Company Law Review Steering Group, 2000, pp. 14–15). It could be argued that this did nothing more than restate a basic principle of UK company law. Whether or not that is an accurate description of the historical context to the Steering Group's proposal, the inclusion of a new formula for directors' duties in the Companies Act 2006 signals a subtle shift towards a pluralist or multi-stakeholder conception of the firm. This imposes a duty on directors to act in such a way as to 'promote the best interests of the company', and provides that in fulfilling that duty a director must

> (so far as reasonably practicable) have regard to – (a) the likely consequences of any decision in the long term, (b) the interests of the company's employees, (c) the need to foster the company's business relationships with suppliers, customers and others, (d) the impact of the company's operations on the community and the environment, (e) the desirability of the company maintaining a reputation for high standards of business conduct, and (f) the need to act fairly as between the members of the company. (Companies Act 2006, section 172)

This provision is an indication of the degree to which UK company law is currently moving away, if only very slightly, from the standard 'shareholder value' position with which it is conventionally associated.

In this regard, the redefinition of directors' duties is not an isolated example. UK law, in contrast to that operating in the United States, for example, provides significant voice rights to employee representatives in the event of a major event affecting the organization of the enterprise, such as a restructuring or business transfer. Thanks in large part to the influence of EU law, a large-scale redundancy or transfer of a significant part of the business triggers an obligation to inform and consult employee representatives over the implications of the event in question for workers' interests. Although there is no veto right and no 'status quo clause' requiring the unravelling of corporate restructurings if these obligations are not met, legal sanctions for breach of the relevant rules have been tightened in recent years and, in finely balanced cases, can alter the outcome of commercial negotiations, with implications for job security (Armour and Deakin, 2003). The UK regime on takeover bids will also, in the future, be affected by requirements to take into account employee interests. As part of the steps taken to implement the Thirteenth Company Law Directive in the UK – a measure which, for continental systems, represents a significant step towards a shareholder-oriented takeover regime like that of the UK's City Code – bidder and target companies subject to UK law will, for the first time, have to disclose in detail their plans for future restructurings or redundancies, a step that is likely to open up new opportunities for employee representatives to influence the takeover process, as they do on the continent (Deakin, 2007). A further step towards strengthening employee voice is the recent implementation in the UK of the EU Information and Consultation Directive, although as yet its influence is limited (Hall, 2006).

Conversely, there are aspects of the French legal framework that contradict the standard picture of France as a 'coordinated market system'. There is a case for saying that France has always occupied a middle position between the Anglo-American systems and the more strongly corporatist, German-influenced ones. Codetermination, in the sense of board-level representation for workers, does not formally exist in French law: two members of the *comité d'entreprise* (works council) may take part in meetings of the board of directors (or supervisory board), but without voting rights. If a two-tier board structure similar to the German model is an option for listed companies, very few adopt it. Moreover, the French *comité d'entreprise* is a very different institution from the German works council: it has representatives of both workers and managers and is chaired by a representative of the employer. Although French workers, through the works council and other representative bodies, have significant rights of co-participation in decisions affecting the organization of the firm,[3] employee voice is not as deeply institutionalized at the workplace level as it is in Germany. Union influence within the workplace is limited and is, moreover, a comparatively recent development, having been encouraged in legal reforms of the 1980s. The enforcement of employers' legal obligations depends on active state intervention through the labour inspectorate and judicial intervention to a much greater degree in France than in either Germany or the UK.

French company law has seen far-reaching changes in the direction of strengthening shareholder rights in the past five years. The 'New Economic Regulation' of 2001 and the Financial Security Act of 2003 were designed

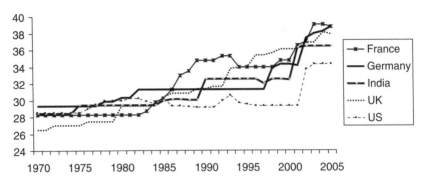

Sources: Conway et al. (2008), with kind permission of John Wiley & Sons; Lele and Siems (2007).

Figure 5.1 Shareholder protection in five countries, 1970–2005 (60 variables)

to protect the position of minority investors and to enhance information flows to the general body of shareholders. Capital market laws have been progressively transformed, largely along the lines of the financial disclosure requirements of the US Securities and Exchange Commission (SEC) model, since the mid-1990s. Some elements of the predominantly Anglo-American model of the corporate governance codes have also been adopted.

Figure 5.1, which is based on Lele and Siems (2007), illustrates the extent of convergence between the company law rules of the two countries and puts it into a broader international context. It provides a measurement of change in the rules of core company law, including some which have taken the form of 'default rules' for listed companies under the terms of corporate governance codes. A higher score on the index indicates a higher degree of legal protection for shareholder interests (the methodology used to construct the index is set out in Lele and Siems). It can be seen that for much of the period covered by the index, but in particular since the mid-1990s, French law has provided stronger shareholder protection than US law, and has been roughly comparable to UK law. The laws of all the countries covered in this index – France, Germany, India, the USA and the UK – have been moving in broadly the same direction of greater rights for shareholders, largely as a result of the international diffusion of the corporate governance code model, and of the harmonization of company laws within the EU.

Figure 5.2 describes the same process of change for labour law (Deakin et al., 2007). Here, it can be seen that there is greater evidence of divergence, with French labour law, as a whole, providing for a considerably higher level of protection than UK labour law. UK labour law, however, has

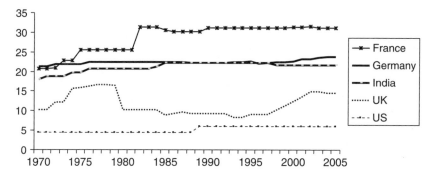

Sources: Conway et al. (2008), with kind permission of John Wiley & Sons; Deakin et al. (2007).

Figure 5.2   Labour regulation in five countries, 1970–2005 (40 variables)

been strengthening again since the mid-1990s, in part thanks to changes in the law of employee representation associated with the implementation of EU directives concerning information and consultation rights.

This is not to suggest that some important differences do not remain. A core feature of the British system remains the City Code on Mergers and Takeovers, which, it has been argued, focuses managerial attention in listed companies on the short-term financial interests of shareholders (Deakin et al., 2003). Takeover defences are very rarely put in place prior to a bid, in large part thanks to the Code; the Code and related aspects of the Listing rules underpin the principle of one-share, one-vote, which is regarded as imperative by many institutional investors. In France, by contrast, legislation implementing the Thirteenth Directive in March 2006 allowed the board of directors to issue warrants providing the right to new stock to existing shareholders in the face of a hostile takeover bid, subject only to majority shareholder approval at an ordinary meeting. This provides a powerful poison-pill-like defence against takeovers (Shearman & Sterling LLP, 2006). In a significant point of difference from the UK, the principle of one-share, one-vote is still not recognized by most large listed companies in France, diluting minority shareholder influence and providing managers with a level of protection from the market for corporate control.

In terms of share ownership structure, France is traditionally much closer to Germany than to the USA and the UK, but there have been important changes in the last decade (see also Carlin, Chapter 1 in this volume). The concentration of ownership is still high: blockholdings are fairly common. Cross-shareholding between major non-financial companies, even if it is decreasing in importance, is still far more prevalent than

Table 5.1   Ownership of common stock (as a % of outstanding shares) for listed companies in three countries, 2002

Ownership	UK	France	Germany
Households	14.3	6.5	22.9
Non-financial companies	0.8	20.2	11.7
Government	0.1	3.6	1.9
Banks	12.6	12.6	33.5
Institutional investors*	40.0	26.0	12.0
Foreign	32.1	31.2	18.1
Total (rounded)	100	100	100

Note: * Pension funds, mutual funds and insurance companies.

Source: Tirole (2006, p. 37).

in the Anglo-American systems (Thomsen, 2004, pp. 306–8). Nevertheless, there has been a considerable increase in institutional investors, national (mainly mutual funds) and foreign (mainly US and UK pension and mutual funds). By the end of 2003, non-resident investors owned 43.9 per cent of the outstanding share of CAC 40 companies and almost 35 per cent of the shares of all listed companies. In the UK, the proportion of shares held by institutional investors is very high and has been rising steadily for the past four decades; even here, there has been a significant recent change, with the proportion of foreign ownership increasing rapidly since the mid-1990s. Table 5.1 presents the distribution of ownership for UK, French and German listed companies in 2002. It appears that, to some extent, the French distribution is now more similar to the UK than to the German one. In particular, the activity of institutional investors is much higher in France and the UK than in Germany.

The evolution and comparison of levels of stock market capitalization in each of these jurisdictions reflect this pattern of change (see Figure 5.3). Since the end of the 1990s, the French level of stock market capitalization has been greater than the German one, representing more than 100 per cent of the GDP in 2006 (against 53 per cent in Germany).

As shown in Table 5.2, this growth in French stock market capitalization is not due to a rise in the number of listed companies, but rather to an increase in the volume of security transactions, directly related to the growing importance of institutional investors.

Figure 5.3 and Table 5.2 also make it clear that the UK significantly outperforms France and Germany in terms of the level of stock market activity.

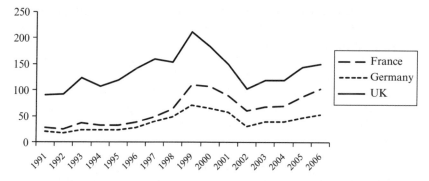

Note: Non-domestic equities are excluded. For example, the UK line refers to UK listed companies listed on the London Stock Exchange.

Sources: Conway et al. (2008), with kind permission of John Wiley & Sons; Eurostat.

Figure 5.3 *Stock market capitalization (as a % of GDP) in three countries, 1991–2006*

Table 5.2 *Number of listed companies in three countries, 1995–2006*

Year	London Stock Exchange	Euronext Paris	Deutsche Börse
1995	2502	904	–
1996	2623	891	–
1997	2513	900	–
1998	2423	962	662
1999	2274	969	851
2000	2374	966	983
2001	2332	936	983
2002	2824	873	934
2003	2692	817	866
2004	2837	787	819
2005	3091	749	764
2006	3256	730	760

Source: Fédération Internationale des Bourses de Valeur (FIBV), Autorité des Marchés Financiers (AMF).

To sum up this section: notwithstanding their different histories and trajectories, there are signs of functional convergence between the UK and France in the corporate governance area. In particular, the rules and practices protecting minority shareholder rights have strengthened at a time when institutional shareholder ownership, already predominant in the UK, has been growing in France. Both countries have experienced an increase in foreign institutional ownership. Thus, external shareholders are in a relatively strong position to impose transparency and financial return requirements on corporate insiders. Nevertheless, pressure from external shareholders may be expected to be somewhat higher in the UK, where the stock market is more liquid and ownership more dispersed than in France; conversely, labour rights are more deeply entrenched in France.

THE EFFECTS OF STOCK MARKET LISTING ON HUMAN RESOURCE MANAGEMENT: THEORY AND EVIDENCE

In a capitalist system, it is clear that every company has to achieve a level of profitability that allows it to cover the cost of capital. Over and above this level, the requirements of profitability will be more or less intense according to the macro-institutional context that underlies the different national varieties of capitalism (Hall and Soskice, 2001; Amable, 2003). In essence, the increasing role played by the stock market and by minority shareholders in corporate governance strengthens the requirement for financial returns on the part of listed companies. Competing to attract household savings, investment funds seek to offer the highest possible profitability (at a given level of risk) to their beneficiaries, through the valuation of the securities composing their portfolio. As a result, institutional investors come to advocate new forms of corporate management, based on the maximization of 'shareholder value'. A conspicuous example of a strategic turn by listed companies in reaction to the increasing pressure of the stock market is reported by Sigurt Vitols (2002), with the 'Big Three' German integrated chemical/pharmaceutical companies: Hoechst, Bayer and BASF. While these companies tended in the immediate postwar period to prioritize growth (in particular through diversification) and investment over profitability, the transformation in corporate governance in the mid-1990s led them to focus on stock price and financial profitability. In the case of Hoechst, this involved a radical change of business model, with the abandonment of the integrated strategy.

Shareholder value-based management models are all founded on the same principle: there is 'creation of shareholder value' when the (financial) profitability achieved by the company (the return on equity – ROE) is higher than the profitability expected by the market (the cost of equity capital for the firm). The most widely used metric of shareholder value creation, the concept of 'economic value added' (EVA), expresses this principle most clearly. Corporate executives are requested to maximize shareholder value in each financial period; in turn, this should guarantee a positive movement in the firm's share price. By contrast, any 'destruction' of shareholder value (positive financial profitability, but returns below the cost of capital) runs the risk of provoking a fall in the price of the company's shares. From an operational point of view, as managers have no direct influence over the cost of capital, the requirement of shareholder value creation ultimately comes down to a requirement for the maximization of financial profitability.[4]

In the context of the management of labour, several authors claim that shareholder value-based management induces a 'low-road' approach to HRM (Hutton, 1996; Porter, 1997). On the one hand, a need to prioritize shareholder and financier interests implies that firms have a lower capacity to commit to their employees. This argument is supported by Margaret Blair (1995), who argues that the implementation of shareholder primacy might deter workers from investing in firm-specific human capital. On the other hand, labour costs are the main component of operating costs. As such, they provide the most direct leverage to increase net profits for a given level of total turnover. Put differently, (short-term) financial requirements result in a cost-cutting-oriented type of HRM.

At a macro, national level, the 'varieties of capitalism' (VOC) approach sets out a similar hypothesis, by stressing the institutional complementarities that are likely to form between the stock market and the labour market (Hall and Soskice, 2001; Amable et al., 2005; Goergen et al., 2006; Black et al., 2007). The key idea is that a financial system that favours liquidity may limit the possibilities for employee commitment and cooperation within enterprises, but facilitate the reorganization of activities.

On these bases, it is possible to state some predictions regarding the impact of capital market pressures, deriving from stock market listings, on labour management.

- A shareholder-value-oriented approach to managing a business results in low job tenure for at least two reasons. First, it favours periodic restructuring (collective redundancies) to meet financial targets, or following a hostile takeover (or to fend one off). Second, companies might be prone to using short-term (fixed-term) labour contracts. The overall result is a low level for average job tenure in companies subject to the pressure of minority shareholders.
- In the same vein, it implies a low level of investment in human capital. Once again, different mechanisms are at stake. The limitation of training expenditure is a basic strategy for reducing (indirect) labour costs. Also, the lack of commitment by employees might

dissuade business firms from investing in apprenticeship-type training. On the other hand, the lack of commitment by firms will also
discourage employees from bearing the opportunity cost of firm-
specific training.

- A third common prediction relates to remuneration policy, and more
  precisely to the intensive use of performance related pay (PRP) by
  firms engaged in (shareholder) value creation. The rationale for PRP
  in a shareholder-value-oriented business model is twofold. First,
  PRP provides high-powered incentives for workers and top executives that might help to meet financial requirements. In particular,
  share option schemes and employee share ownership plans (ESOPs)
  directly align corporate insiders' interests with those of minority
  stockholders. Second, PRP is a powerful tool for achieving labour
  cost (wage bill) flexibility. This flexibility is particularly important
  when financial profitability is the crux of corporate strategy: the possibility for employers to pay, on a selective and reversible basis, individual or collective (profit-sharing schemes) bonuses allows them to
  diminish labour costs in the case of a market downturn. In turn, it
  makes it possible to avoid any short-term decrease in profitability
  and the (subsequent) sanction of the stock market. In sum, a liquid
  capital market should support the use of stock options, ESOPs and
  individual and collective bonuses.

Some articles have tested some of those propositions, on a comparative,
cross-sectional, basis. Boyd Black et al. (2007) provide a first systematic
approach in this vein, for OECD countries. As a proxy for (minority)
shareholder pressure, they use two variables: a measure of trading activity
and new stock issues over a three-year period, corrected for the number of
listed firms and the ratio of the number of merger and acquisition (M&A)
deals to population in millions (averaged over the first half of the 1990s).
The unemployment rate and trade union density are introduced as control
variables in the regressions. They find a negative effect of market liquidity on job tenure, measured by different proxies. They do not, however,
observe any impact of stock market or M&A activity on training. Last but
not least, they find a positive influence of market liquidity on the use of
employee stock ownership plans. As a conclusion, the idea of a low road
for labour management stemming from financial market pressure is only
partially corroborated: job tenure is lowered, but not training.

As interesting as they are, these predictions are restricted to the comparative analysis of national systems. As such, they cannot take into account
infra-national, micro diversity – an important point when considering firm
strategies.[5]

At a micro level, three empirical studies can be highlighted for the way that they link together the study of corporate governance transformations and changes in the management of labour: Rubinstein and Kochan (2001), Jackson et al. (2005) and Deakin et al. (2006).[6]

Saul Rubinstein and Thomas Kochan (2001) provide a detailed account of Saturn, a US vehicle manufacturer set up as an experimental partnership between General Motors and the United Auto Workers union. This seminal study revealed the difficulty management faced in articulating the priority granted to shareholders' interests and the building up of a framework involving long-term commitment between employers and employees.

Simon Deakin et al. (2006) report case-study evidence based in particular on a series of interviews conducted in UK companies since the mid-1990s. Their objective was to assess the degree of compatibility between stock market liquidity and cooperation in labour relations. At a first level, their study shows that partnership arrangements with employees are vulnerable to shareholder pressure. Yet, they also found that different mediating strategies may be available to help deal with financial-return requirements without adopting a low-road/low-equilibrium approach to labour management. In particular, they found that labour law rules favouring worker voice (information and consultation), as well as product market regulation fostering competition based on quality rather than price, might favour cooperative strategies between employers and employees. In sum, those devices make it possible to base profit strategy on a set of high commitment HRM practices.

This result echoes the conclusion reached by Gregory Jackson et al. (2005).[7] Their analysis synthesizes a series of studies looking at the changes in HRM in German listed companies subject to increasing stock market pressure. They observe a tendency towards reducing the number of salaried staff, falling back on a stable core of employees. In most cases this occurred without mass redundancies due to the use of voluntary departures, early retirement and so on. Within companies, average wage level tended to rise, while the use of individual and collective bonuses was becoming more widespread. They suggest that the strong institutionalization of worker involvement in German companies, through collective bargaining and codetermination rights (for works councils and at the board level), has not been damaged to any great extent by the transformation of corporate governance towards a more market-based system. To some extent, codetermination has even facilitated corporate restructuring in a way that has proved to be beneficial for the remaining workforce: the evolution of codetermination towards an insider-oriented, efficiency-driven model (rather than a political instrument aiming at reforming or even overthrowing the capitalist system) is somewhat consistent with the need for high financial returns, which is implicit in an active and liquid stock market system. Sigurt Vitols (2004), looking at the influence of the rise to power of investment funds on German corporations, similarly observes the emergence of a hybrid model, termed 'negotiated shareholder value'. In this model, minority shareholder requirements for financial return have to be negotiated with corporate insiders, and these negotiations generally alter the nature of those requirements.

The case studies carried out by Jackson et al. (2005) and Deakin et al. (2006) reveal a subtler picture than the 'low-road hypothesis' conventionally stated in the literature: partnership arrangements with workers as well as an increase of the average wage level are possible, despite pressures for financial return coming from shareholders. This might even suggest a 'high-road' scenario, in which financial return requirements are delivered on the basis of a long-term horizon through heightened investments in human capital. Yet two observations qualify this possibility. First, additional investments in human resources appear to be restricted to a limited number of permanent or 'core' employees: in the German case, listed companies that adopted shareholder value practices reduced total employment. Second, the choice of a high-road strategy for the management of labour appears to be closely connected to the existence of devices (legal or organizational) supporting worker voice.

The use of micro (firm or workplace-level) data to assess the impact of the stock market on labour management might deepen our understanding, for it combines the possibility of obtaining statistical representative results with the ability to differentiate among organizations at the infranational level (Pendleton and Deakin, 2007). For example, it should be possible to test whether workplaces belonging to listed companies whose equity capital is mostly held by financial investors have distinctive HRM practices and whether those practices are more of a 'low-road' or 'high-road' nature. The next section presents some research along those lines by examining the UK and French cases.

SOME FINDINGS BASED ON ESTABLISHMENT-LEVEL SURVEY DATA

One of the advantages of a French/UK comparison is that relatively similar datasets are available, which provide a uniquely detailed map of workplace relations in the two countries: the Workplace Employee Relations Survey (WERS 2004) for the UK[8] and the 2004 *Relations Professionnelles et Négociations d'Entreprise* survey (REPONSE 2004) for France.[9] The questionnaires on which the datasets are based are not identical, but there are many similarities; REPONSE has been, to a large degree, modelled on WERS. Those surveys consist of three sets of questionnaires (one addressed to a management representative, one to an employee representative and one to a small number of employees) for a representative sample of establishments. Whereas the WERS 2004 survey includes the public sector, REPONSE 2004 does not.

In both surveys, the information supplied on HRM practices, work organization and industrial relations is very rich. If the data pertain mainly to the establishment level, there is also information available on stock market quotation and the distribution of the company's equity capital.

Corinne Perraudin et al. (2008) merged the REPONSE database – consisting of 3,000 French establishments with 20 or more employees, representative of the private sector (excluding farming) – with an administrative source that provides information about the individual characteristics of workers and the amount of wages paid at each establishment.[10] They end up with a linked employer–employee database (LEED), providing a large quantity of information on the competitive environment of these establishments, the distribution of equity ownership and their HRM practices for the year 2004. In relation to the structure of equity ownership, they constructed a variable that divides the sample into three categories: establishments belonging to non-listed companies, establishments belonging to listed companies in which institutional investors are not the main category of shareholders and, finally, establishments belonging to listed companies in which (minority) institutional investors are (collectively) the main category of shareholders. This variable can be considered a proxy for the degree of 'financialization' of the companies concerned, that is, the degree of financial pressure exercised by the capital market on management. By definition, non-listed companies are not directly subject to the requirements of profitability imposed by the stock market. Conversely, listed companies in which institutional investors are the largest category of shareholders are the most directly concerned by the stock market rationale of maximizing profitability. Listed companies in which financial investors are not the main category of shareholders lie somewhere between the two.

A series of econometric regressions[11] were then performed to estimate the influence of this corporate governance variable on different HRM practices, controlling for a large set of dimensions. These dimensions related to the structural characteristics of the establishment (sector of activity, number of employees, age, turnover level of the company), the commercial context in which the establishment operates (market share, the predictability of demand for its products, the activity's development, the existence of an unusual variation in activity during the last year, and the competitive strategy adopted) and the socio-demographic characteristics of the workforce (proportion of managers and supervisors, technicians and professionals, clerical and frontline workers, proportion aged under 40 and proportion of women).

The main results were the following.

- There was a particularly strong tendency to use agency workers or subcontractors among establishments belonging to listed companies, whether or not institutional investors were the primary category of shareholders. On the other hand, those establishments made significantly less use of fixed-term labour contracts. Establishments subject to stock market pressure therefore tended to mobilize commercial contracts (use of temporary employment agencies and subcontractors) rather than employment contracts (fixed-term contracts) to meet their temporary personnel needs.

- Being listed on the stock market – whatever the composition of the body of shareholders – distinctly increased the probability of using individual bonuses for managerial employees and collective bonuses for all employees; Jackson et al. (2005) obtained a similar result for Germany. Thus, agency workers, subcontractors and bonuses enable the company to vary its labour costs by modulating both the volume of labour employed (via temporary workers and subcontractors) and the remunerations (via bonuses).

- Net (hourly) wage levels, both average and median, were higher in establishments belonging to listed companies, and more so when the main category of shareholders consisted of institutional investors.[12] It suggests that there is a rent-sharing within establishments belonging to listed companies; wages did not follow a rationale of cost minimization. Again, this result echoes that of Jackson et al. for German firms: although they observed that the pressure exerted by financial markets led companies to reduce the workforce, they also found that the wages paid to the remaining employees tended to rise.

- Being listed was positively linked to higher levels of training expenditure: it had a significantly positive influence on the likelihood of the firm spending more than 3 per cent of the wage bill on training.

- Being listed on the stock market had a negative influence on increases in the size of the workforce. It had no significant effect on workforce reductions, however. Again, whether or not the equity capital of the firm was owned primarily by institutional investors, growth in staff numbers was less frequent in establishments belonging to listed companies. Such a strategy allows the firm to build the workforce around a relatively limited core group of employees. From a cost perspective, it makes it possible not only to reduce the number of employees to whom rent is shared and a high level of training expenditure is offered, but also to limit the costs of labour turnover by stabilizing the core workforce.

To sum up, these estimations establish a particular HRM profile, which is associated with a stock market listing in France. The presence or otherwise of institutional investors in the firm studied does not qualitatively change the results, although it generally strengthens the coefficients. This HRM profile is characterized by two main features. First, stock market pressure favours strong variability in labour costs, achieved through wage flexibility and the substantial use of temporary contracts. Among the latter, the use of commercial contracts (agency workers or subcontractors) is favoured rather than the use of fixed-term employment contracts. Second, listed companies tend to adopt a high-road rather than a defensive or low-road strategy towards dealing with labour costs. Wage levels and training expenditure are relatively high. Nevertheless, analysis of their practices in terms of variations in workforce size (marked by a reluctance to recruit) and their considerable use of external forms of temporary work arrangements underline the fact that these investments in human resources are concentrated on a relatively limited number of core employees.

In the UK case, a number of studies have been devoted to the analysis of the links between corporate governance (legal form and ownership) and HRM practices on the basis of the WERS survey. Suzanne Konzelmann et al. (2006), examining WERS 1998, found that a corporate governance regime that privileges remote stakeholders (as is the case in public listed companies) tends to operate as a constraint on the delivery of commitment-based HRM. This analysis used public company status as a proxy for being listed, since WERS 1998 did not distinguish between listed and non-listed companies. Andrew Pendleton and Simon Deakin (2007), carrying out a preliminary analysis of WERS 2004 that did contain this distinction, found no statistical difference between listed establishments and non-listed ones in terms of either long-term commitment with employees or consultative practices. Controlling for size and sector, they also did not observe any significant impact of being listed on training effort by firms.

A different approach was taken by Konzelmann et al. (2007). They grouped the corporate governance variables in WERS 2004 into a series of composite categories that included public sector organizations, listed companies, non-listed public companies, private companies, owner–member/public interest firms (a group including mutuals and cooperatives), partnerships and self-proprietorships. They found that public sector organizations (where taxpayer/government pressure is strong) and listed companies were more likely to report that they had joint consultation procedures with employees. In the employee survey, however, only partnerships and self-proprietorships were positively associated with consultation. Employees in the public sector and in listed companies were less likely than in other categories to report that they had a degree of control over their work, and employment in listed companies was negatively associated with a perception of job security. Stress was positively associated with employment in the public sector and in listed companies. Job satisfaction levels were lowest in listed companies, followed by the public sector, and highest in owner–member firms, partnerships and self-proprietorships. Employees in listed companies were also significantly more likely to report a lack of trust than those in other groups.

A direct comparison between the UK and France, using WERS 2004 and REPONSE 2004, was carried out by Neil Conway et al. (2008). By excluding the public sector component of the WERS survey, a high degree of homogeneity between the WERS and REPONSE samples was achieved. The choice of variables in this study was influenced by the need to have a common frame of reference across the two questionnaires. More precisely, six (dependent) variables were selected in the management questionnaire: the level of training provided for by the employer, the autonomy granted to workers (degree of control over their work), the importance of team working (percentage of employees involved in formally designated teams), the use of individual PRP, the use of collective PRP and the degree of worker involvement in the negotiation of targets (concerning profitability, growth, budget constraint, wage bill, quality or security). The same set of control variables were introduced into the (logistic) regressions: establishment and organization sizes, establishment age, sector, market share, the activity's development (growth, decline, stability) and the composition of the workforce in the establishment (by reference to the proportion of white-collar workers).

In the UK, listing is positively and significantly associated with team working and PRP (individual and collective). In France there is evidence of a significant positive relationship between listing and team working and PRP (individual and collective), as in the UK. In addition, in France listing is significantly and positively related with all human resource intensity variables except engagement over targets. The link with listing is particularly strong for two practices: collective PRP and team working. Altogether, these results indicate that establishments of listed companies are relatively more involved in the use of high commitment HRM practices than others, and this is especially the case in France.

Summing up, there is some evidence in the empirical research that we have surveyed to suggest that French listed companies are adopting high-road HRM practices as a way of responding to the particular mix of stock market pressures and additional institutional constraints to which they are subject. Evidence that external shareholder pressure is influencing HRM is to be found in the studies that demonstrate the statistical link between being listed (whether or not the equity capital in question predominantly is held in the form of mutual and other investment funds) and the adoption of a particular bundle of HRM techniques. These techniques include a reluctance to increase workforce numbers, greater use of agency labour and subcontractors, higher levels of training, the use of PRP and other incentive devices, and increased remuneration for those workers keeping their jobs. This may indicate a move to a model of 'negotiated shareholder value' (see Vitols, 2004) in which rents are shared by shareholders and a core of well-protected, and highly incentivized and remunerated workers. This route is the most feasible one available as a means of maintaining overall competitiveness, given the high intensity of worker involvement in French companies. In the UK case, even if the hypothesis of a 'high road' in HRM is not fully corroborated, there is at least no support for the existence of a constraint linked to stock market pressure.

CONCLUSION

In this chapter we have reviewed evidence on the relationship between corporate governance and human resource management in the UK and France, looking specifically at the way in which stock market pressures influence the way that listed companies treat their employees. The two systems are, to a degree, converging, at least at the level of formal law and regulations: France has adopted a more shareholder-friendly legal regime over the past decade. The pattern of share ownership in France is also changing, with a greater role for overseas investors and a higher level of stock market activity, although cross-shareholdings are still much more widespread than is the case in the UK. In the UK, dispersed share ownership remains the norm, together with a high level of liquidity in the stock market. UK-based institutional investors remain a powerful influence, but as in France, overseas ownership is growing.

How does this shifting pattern of corporate ownership and governance affect labour relations and HRM? An important factor is the strength of labour law in the two countries. In France, labour law is strong and appears to operate as a 'beneficial constraint' on management (Streeck, 1997): negotiated shareholder value, based on rent-sharing between shareholder and the core workforce, is the predominant pattern. Nevertheless, non-core groups, in the contingent workforce represented by the growing part of the workforce employed via agencies and through subcontractors, are becoming excluded from this rent-sharing process. In the UK, labour laws remain weak, despite some adjustment to the mainland European model of employee information and consultation rights. Given weak labour laws and intense financial pressures, there is some evidence that listed companies are somewhat less inclined than French companies to adopt high commitment HRM practices.

NOTES

1. Paul Edwards and Martin Wright (2001), in an assessment of the literature, broadly define high commitment HRM practices as: 'some combination of: schemes to promote employee discretion and autonomy, such as formally designed teamworking, quality circles or problem-solving groups; systems of communication that allow for upward communication of employee suggestions as well as downward communication from management; and serious attention to developing employee skills. They may . . . also deploy merit or performance based pay and other features of HRM' (p. 570).
2. Ownership concentration is also favoured by legal devices, such as double voting rights or voting caps to protect against hostile takeovers (see Cozian et al., 2005, p. 290), as well as shareholder pacts (p. 305).
3. For example, similar to a shareholder or a group of shareholders holding more than 5 per cent of equity capital, the *comité d'entreprise* has the right to submit proposals to be included with a company's proxy statement. Another important right is the possibility for the *comité d'entreprise* to call in an expert accountant, in order to obtain an expert evaluation of the information communicated by the employer.
4. For a more detailed discussion on value-based management, see Cooper et al. (2000); Froud et al. (2000a and 2000b); Lordon (2000); Hossfeld and Klee (2003); and Rebérioux (2007).
5. For a discussion on this point, see Goergen et al. (2006).
6. Vitols (2002) is more concerned with global business strategy than with labour management per se.
7. See also Jackson (2005).
8. Jointly sponsored by the Department of Trade and Industry, the Advisory, Conciliation and Arbitration Service (ACAS), the Economic and Social Research Council, and the Policy Studies Institute.
9. Carried out by the Research and Statistics Department of the French Ministry of Labour (DARES).
10. The DADS (*Déclarations administratives de données sociales*, collected by the National Institute for Statistics and Economic Studies, INSEE) represent an exhaustive administrative source of information on wages.
11. Using the ordinary least squares method, dichotomous logit or multinomial logit estimations, according to the nature of the explained variables.
12. For a similar approach that attempts to explain mean wage in the establishment

through employer (including ownership) and employee characteristics, see Earle and Telegdy (2007).

REFERENCES

Aglietta, M. and A. Rebérioux (2005), *Corporate Governance Adrift. A Critique of Shareholder Value*, Cheltenham, UK and Northampton, MA, USA: Edward Elgar.

Ahlering, B. and S. Deakin (2007), 'Labour regulation, corporate governance and legal origin: a case of institutional complementarity?', *Law and Society Review*, **41** (4), pp. 865–908.

Amable, B. (2003), *The Diversity of Modern Capitalism*, Oxford: Oxford University Press.

Amable, B., E. Ernst and S. Palombarini (2005), 'How do financial markets affect industrial relations? An institutional complementarity approach', *Socio-Economic Review*, **3**, pp. 311–30.

Aoki, M. (2001), *Toward a Comparative Institutional Analysis*, Cambridge, MA: MIT Press.

Aoki, M. (2007), 'Whither Japan's corporate governance?', in M. Aoki, G. Jackson and H. Miyajima (eds), *Corporate Governance in Japan: Institutional Change and Organizational Diversity*, Oxford: Oxford University Press, pp. 427–48.

Armour, J. and S. Deakin (2003), 'Insolvency and employment protection: the mixed effects of the Acquired Rights Directive', *International Review of Law and Economics*, **22**, pp. 443–63.

Armour, J., S. Deakin and S. Konzelmann (2003), 'Shareholder primacy and the trajectory of corporate governance', *British Journal of Industrial Relations*, **41** (3), pp. 531–55.

Barker, R. and D. Rueda (2007), 'The labor market determinants of corporate governance reform', CLPE Research Paper 5, Comparative Research in Law and Political Economy, York University, Toronto.

Black, B., H. Gospel and A. Pendleton (2007), 'Finance, corporate governance, and the employment relationship', *Industrial Relations*, **46** (3), pp. 643–50.

Blair, M. (1995), *Ownership and Control. Rethinking Corporate Governance for the Twenty-first Century*, Washington, DC: Brookings Institution.

Cioffi, J. and S. Cohen (2000), 'The state, law and corporate governance: the advantage of forwardness', in S. Cohen and B. Gavin (eds), *Corporate Governance and Globalization. Long Range Planning Issues*, Cheltenham, UK and Northampton, MA, USA: Edward Elgar, pp. 307–49.

Company Law Review Steering Group (2000), *Modern Company Law for a Competitive Economy: Developing the Framework*, London: DTI.

Conway, N., S. Deakin, S. Konzelmann, H. Petit, A. Rebérioux and F. Wilkinson (2008), 'The influence of stock market listing on human resource management: evidence for France and Britain', *British Journal of Industrial Relations*, **46** (4), pp. 631–73.

Cooper, S., D. Crowther, M. Davies and E. Davis (2000), 'The adoption of value-based management in large UK companies: a case for diffusion theory', paper presented at the 23rd annual Congress of the European Accounting Association, Munich, 29–31 March.

Cozian, M., A. Viandier and F. Deboissy (2005), *Droit des sociétés*, 18th edn, Paris: Litec.

Deakin, S. (2007), 'Is the "modernisation" of company law a threat to employee voice within the enterprise? A British Perspective', in U. Jürgens, D. Sadowski, G.F. Schuppert and M. Weiss (eds), *Perspektiven der Corporate Governance*, Baden-Baden: Nomos, pp. 235–57.

Deakin, S., P. Lele and M. Siems (2007), 'The evolution of labour law: calibrating and comparing regulatory regimes', *International Labour Review*, **146**, pp. 133–62.

Deakin, S., R. Hobbs, D. Nash and D. Slinger (2003), 'Implicit contracts, takeovers and corporate governance: in the shadow of the city code', in D. Campbell, H. Collins and J. Wightman (eds), *Implicit Dimensions of Contract*, Oxford: Hart, pp. 289–331.

Deakin, S., R. Hobbs, S. Konzelmann and F. Wilkinson (2006), 'Anglo-American corporate governance and the employment relationship: a case to answer?', *Socio-Economic Review*, **4** (1), pp. 155–74.

Earle, J. and A. Telegdy (2007), 'Ownership and wages: estimating public–private and foreign–domestic differentials using LEED from Hungary, 1986–2003', NBER Working Paper 12997, Cambridge, MA.

Edwards, P. and M. Wright (2001), 'High-involvement work systems and performance outcomes: the strength of variable, contingent and context bound relationships', *International Journal of Human Resource Management*, **12**, pp. 568–85.

Fanto, J. (1998), 'The role of corporate law in French corporate governance', *Cornell International Law Journal*, **31**, pp. 31–91.

Franks, J. and C. Mayer (1996), 'Hostile takeovers and the correction of managerial failure', *Journal of Financial Economics*, **40**, pp. 163–81.

Froud, J., C. Haslam, S. Johal and K. Williams (2000a), 'Restructuring for shareholder value and its implications for labour', *Cambridge Journal of Economics*, **24** (6), pp. 771–98.

Froud, J., C. Haslam, S. Johal and K. Williams (2000b), 'Shareholder value and financialization: consultancy promises, management moves', *Economy and Society*, **29** (1), pp. 80–110.

Goergen, M., C. Brewster and G. Wood (2006), 'The boundaries of governance: the effects of the national setting and ownership changes on employment practice', ECGI, Finance Working Paper 136/2006, European Corporate Governance Institute, Brussels.

Gospel, H. and A. Pendleton (2005), *Corporate Governance and Labour Management: An International Comparison*, Oxford: Oxford University Press.

Hall, M. (2006), 'A cool response to the ICE regulations? Employer and trade union approaches to the new legal framework for information and consultation', *Industrial Relations Journal*, **37** (5), pp. 456–72.

Hall, P. and D. Soskice (2001), 'An introduction to varieties of capitalism', in Hall and Soskice (eds), *Varieties of Capitalism: The Institutional Foundations of Comparative Advantage*, Oxford: Oxford University Press, pp. 1–70.

Hansmann, H. and R. Kraakman (2001), 'The end of history for corporate law', *Georgetown Law Journal*, **89**, pp. 439–68.

Hossfeld, C. and L. Klee (2003), 'Performance reporting on EVA by French and German companies', 2nd workshop on Performance and Management Control, Nice, September.

Hutton, W. (1996), *The State We're In*, London: Vintage.

Jackson, G. (2005), 'Stakeholders under pressure: corporate governance and labour management in Germany and Japan', *Corporate Governance*, **13** (3), pp. 419–28.

Jackson, G., M. Höpner and A. Kurdelbusch (2005), 'Corporate governance and employees in Germany: changing linkages, complementarities, and tensions', in H. Gospel and A. Pendleton (eds), *Corporate Governance and Labour Management: An International Comparison*, Oxford: Oxford University Press, pp. 84–121.

Konzelmann, S., F. Wilkinson and N. Conway (2007), 'Corporate Governance and employment relations' CBR Working Paper 355, Centre for Business Research, University of Cambridge.

Konzelmann, S., N. Conway, L. Trenberth and F. Wilkinson (2006), 'Corporate governance and human resource management', *British Journal of Industrial Relations*, **43**, pp. 541–67.

Lele, P. and M. Siems (2007), 'Shareholder protection: a leximetric approach', *Journal of Corporate Law Studies*, **17**, pp. 17–50.

Lordon, F. (2000), 'La Création de valeur comme rhétorique et comme pratique. Généalogie et sociologie de la valeur actionnariale', *L'Année de la régulation*, **4**, Paris: La Découverte, pp. 117–67.

Paillusseau, J. (1999), 'Entreprise, société, actionnaires, salariés, quels rapports?', *Chronique*, Recueil Dalloz, pp. 157–66.

Pendleton, A. and S. Deakin (2007), 'Corporate governance and workplace employment relations: the potential of WERS 2004', *Industrial Relations Journal*, **38** (4), pp. 338–55.

Perraudin, C., H. Petit and A. Rebérioux (2008), 'The stock market and human resource management: evidence from a survey of French establishments', *Louvain Economic Review*, **74** (4–5), pp. 541–86.

Porter, M. (1997), 'Capital choices: changing the way America invests in industry', in D. Chew (ed.), *Studies in International Corporate Finance and Governance Systems: A Comparison of the US, Japan and Europe*, Oxford: Oxford University Press, pp. 5–17.

Rebérioux, A. (2007), 'Does shareholder primacy lead to a decline in managerial accountability?', *Cambridge Journal of Economics*, **31** (4), pp. 507–24.

Rubinstein, S. and T. Kochan (2001), *Learning from Saturn*, Ithaca, NY: Cornell University Press.

Shearman & Sterling LLP (2006), 'Implementation in France of the Takeover Directive and the New French Poison Pill: How Does it Affect Defensive Measures Available to French Companies?', 6 April, Client publication.

Stout, L. (2007), 'The mythical benefits of shareholder control', *Virginia Law Review*, **93**, pp. 789–809.

Streeck, W. (1997), 'Beneficial constraints: on the economic limits of rational voluntarism', in J. Hollingsworth, J. Rogers and R. Boyer (eds), *Contemporary Capitalism: The Embeddedness of Institutions*, Cambridge: Cambridge University Press, pp. 197–219.

Thomsen, S. (2004), 'Convergence of corporate governance during the stock market bubble: towards Anglo-American or European standards?', in A. Grandori (ed.), *Corporate Governance and Firm Organization: Microfoundations and Structural Forms*, Oxford: Oxford University Press, pp. 297–317.

Tirole, J. (2006), *The Theory of Corporate Finance*, Princeton, NJ: Princeton University Press.

Viénot, M. (1995), *Le Conseil d'administration des sociétés cotées*, Report of the joint CNPF-AFEP committee, Paris.

Vitols, S. (2002), 'Shareholder value, management culture and production regimes in the transformation of the German chemical–pharmaceutical industry', *Competition and Change*, **6**, pp. 309–25.

Vitols, S. (2004), 'Negotiated shareholder value: the German variant of an Anglo-American practice', *Competition and Change*, **8** (4), pp. 357–74.

6. Corporate social responsibility as a contractarian model of multi-stakeholder corporate governance: normative principles and equilibrium properties

Lorenzo Sacconi[1]

INTRODUCTION

The aim of this chapter is to develop a fully-fledged theory of corporate social responsibility (CSR) that is both normatively convincing and which provides an implementable model of multi-stakeholder corporate governance. My use of 'normative' here lies in the same vein as welfare economics and economic ethics: it is concerned with proposals of desirable reforms of economic institutions that improve social well-being and consistency with social justice and fairness according to an ethical assessment based on the idea of impartial, *ex ante* unanimous agreement, in other words, the 'social contract'.[2] Questions about the implementation of a given normative model, such as what kind of rules should provide for it, what incentives and individual motivations should support it, whether or not legal enforcement should be required, and whether it may rely on self-enforceability are important as well. I shall define the normative model in the first part of the chapter and develop a theory of implementation in the second. In the last three sections, I shall outline a multiple strategy for solving the problem of endogeneity and self-sustainability of a CSR norm or social standard understood according to the normative model.

From the normative perspective, a CSR theory should answer the following questions. Is the proposed normative model uniquely defined? Does it provide a clear-cut normative meaning? How can it solve possible clashes among legitimate claims and interests that risk making its implications ambiguous? Is it impartially justified? Does it have the capability to induce efficient levels of economic investments? What kind of impact might it have on values such as economic welfare, distributive justice and social stability?

In order to answer these questions, in this chapter, I develop an argument in favour of CSR as a normative model of corporate governance in the multi-stakeholder and multi-fiduciary perspectives. There are, however, some well-known challenges that must first be squarely faced. I refer to these as 'Jensen's challenges to the stakeholder model' (Jensen, 2001). The first challenge is the commonly accepted prejudice that due to the multidimensionality of the objectives pursued by a company adhering to the stakeholder approach, its objective function must be ill-defined and incapable of endowing managers and directors with a clear normative goal to guide them in their conduct, or provide a bottom line whereby their performance becomes assessable. Moreover, the lack of a unique goal improperly enlarges managerial discretion and makes the board's fiduciary duties and accountability owed to shareholders devoid of any precise content, whereby it may be concluded that the indefiniteness of a multiple objective function opens the way to managerial malfeasance.

In its defence, I shall show that the CSR model of corporate governance is built on a well-defined company objective function, which is at least as precise as the 'profit-maximization' goal that microeconomic theory traditionally attributes to the firm. I make this statement without giving up the tenet that the corporate goal must not be defined as an attribute of the corporation – seen as a holistic and collectivist entity on its own – but should be reduced to the goals and interests of its constituencies – in my view, the corporate stakeholders. In so far as the CSR model derives the corporate objective function from a social contract theory of the firm, managers and directors cannot behave with arbitrary discretion. On the contrary, they are constrained by the principles of contractarian ethics, which makes it possible to derive the fiduciary duties owed to each company stakeholder. The social contract model thus helps to curb managerial remiss and abuse of authority carried out against the legitimate interests of all the non-controlling corporate stakeholders, who are in many respects under-protected by incomplete contracts. Most importantly, the social contract model counteracts the presumption that CSR, while expressing laudable concerns for social issues, would be unable to account for the proper nature of the firm as an economic institution. As I shall show, the CSR model answers questions concerning the very nature of the firm, and offers explanations and arguments for how the corporation might emerge as an economic institution run to the mutual advantage of all its stakeholders.

Once the normative model has been developed, the reader will wonder whether the model corresponds to real-world incentives and interests that drive the economic interactions between real-life economic agents. Subsequently, I shall thus concentrate on the implementation of this normative model.

To implement a model, one must seek endogenous mechanisms that are based on a realistic account of economic agents' preferences and beliefs, and which are capable of rendering the model's implementation self-sustainable. First, it requires verifying if the model's own basic system of interaction (the corporate realm of the interaction among firms and their stakeholders) could stand up by itself without strong sanctions and inducement from the outside. This does not exclude the support that could be provided by a change in regulation – as long as some legal frameworks have been developed to support a different normative model of the corporation – or by the social and legal institutions based in different social subsystems (in other words, the legal system or civil society).[3] Nevertheless, the essential point for an implementation theory is to see whether the model can be sustained through the equilibrium rational choices made by the agents participating within its socially interactive context (involving interactions among companies and stakeholders, which is a domain wide enough to allow for a large array of situations).

The idea of self-sustainability immediately leads one to think that the implementation of the CSR normative model should be a matter of self-regulation and voluntariness. This is also a basic tenet of the second part of this chapter. One must grasp, however, that there is a large gulf between the two ways in which voluntariness and self-regulation may be understood, and they must not be confused. On the one hand, there is the view (see Jensen, 2001) that voluntariness and self-regulation coincide with shareholder value maximization in the long run. According to this view, CSR is only a matter of wise strategic management with the aim of achieving long-term shareholder value maximization through the appropriate means (including stakeholders understood as means). On the other hand, there is the idea, which I actively support, that voluntariness must coincide with the development of and voluntary adhesion to social norms and social standards explicitly formulated through a process of social dialogue between companies and their stakeholders. This simulates the social contract model, such that these explicit norms are able to generate by themselves the incentives and motivations that allow them to be largely endogenously self-enforced.

In this chapter the implementation problem is studied from a non-cooperative game theoretical perspective, as the problem of whether – due to the roles played by explicitly formulated CSR social norms – a mutually advantageous equilibrium profile of behaviours may emerge endogenously from the interaction between the firm and its stakeholders, wherein the normative model is put into practice. The emphasis is on the role that an explicit utterance of CSR norms may play in the emergence of behaviours that implement, by means of endogenous incentives, exactly that norm as an equilibrium point in the firm and stakeholders' interaction. The game of reference is the trust game, a game where the possibility that a firm is abusing its stakeholders' trust – that is, not complying with a model of fair cooperation with them – is consubstantial. In this context, an explicit CSR norm or social standard that incorporates the idea of multi-stakeholder governance is shown to be helpful in an essential way. By using it as a cognitive device, it becomes possible to describe the game so that several types of reputations based on different levels of conformity to the CSR model may be developed even if unforeseen contingencies are involved (see also Sacconi, 2000, 2007b). This answers the question about the existence of equilibria and – if they exist – how to recognize them when implementing the CSR normative model of governance.

A DEFINITION OF CORPORATE SOCIAL RESPONSIBILITY

According to many views, 'corporate social responsibility' is a form of corporate strategic management that sets corporate standards of conduct at a level higher than mandatory legal constraints, and envisages itself as a system for the *governance* of transactions between a firm and its stakeholders.[4] It is clear that here 'governance' is no longer the set of rules simply allocating property rights and defining the owners' control over the company's management. Instead it resembles the neo-institutional view whereby the firm, like the contract and other institutional forms, is a 'governance system' that establishes diverse rights and obligations in order to reduce 'transaction costs' and the negative externalities due to economic transactions.

I therefore propose the following definition of CSR: a model of extended corporate governance whereby those who run a firm (entrepreneurs, directors, managers) have responsibilities that range from fulfilment of their fiduciary duties towards the owners, to fulfilment of analogous fiduciary duties towards all the firm's stakeholders.

Two terms must be defined in order for the foregoing proposition to be clearly understood.

1. *Fiduciary duties*   It is assumed that a subject has a legitimate interest but is unable to make the relevant decisions, in the sense that s/he does not know what goals to pursue, what alternative to choose, or how to deploy his/her resources in order to satisfy his/her interest. S/he, the *trustor*, therefore delegates decisions to a *trustee* empowered to choose actions and goals. The trustee may then use the trustor's resources and select the appropriate course of action. For a fiduciary relationship

– this being the basis of the trustee's authority *vis-à-vis* the trustor – to arise, the latter must possess a claim (right) towards the former. In other words, the trustee directs actions and uses the resources made over to him/her so that results are obtained that satisfy (to the best extent possible) the trustor's interests. These claims (that is, the trustor's *rights*) impose fiduciary duties on the agent who is entitled to authority (the trustee), which s/he is obliged to fulfil. The fiduciary relationship applies in a wide variety of instances: tutor/minor and teacher/pupil relationships; in the corporate domain, the relationship between the board of a trust and its beneficiaries, or according to the predominant opinion, between the board of directors of a joint-stock company and its shareholders, and more generally between management and owners (if the latter do not run the enterprise themselves). The term 'fiduciary duty' therefore means the duty (or responsibility) of exercising authority for the good of those who have granted that authority and are therefore subject to it.[5]

2. *Stakeholders*   This term denotes individuals or groups with a major stake in the running of the firm and who are able to influence it significantly (Freeman and McVea, 2002). A distinction should be drawn, however, between the following two categories.

- *Stakeholders in the strict sense*   Those who have an interest at stake, because they have made specific investments in the firm (in the form of human capital, financial capital, social capital or trust, physical or environmental capital, or for the development of dedicated technologies, and so on). They are investments that may significantly increase the total value generated by the firm (net of the costs sustained for that purpose), and which are made specifically in relation to *that* firm (and not in any other) so that their value is idiosyncratically related to the completion of the transactions carried out by or in relation to that firm. These stakeholders are reciprocally dependent on the firm, because they influence its value but at the same time – given the specificity of their investment – depend largely on it to satisfy their own well-being (lock-in effect).
- *Stakeholders in the broad sense*   Those individuals or groups whose interest is involved, because they *undergo* the 'external effects', positive or negative, of the firm's transactions, even if they do not directly participate in the transaction. Thus, they neither contribute to, nor directly receive value from the firm.

It is evident that these two categories cannot be completely separated. For example, a manufacturer in a developing country who supplies a component for an industrial good assembled in a Western European country is essentially dependent on his/her contract. Moreover, with his/her low labour costs (due to the customer's market power), the manufacturer makes a crucial contribution to the European firm's profits. If, at the same time, a mature technology is used, however, s/he can easily be replaced by the European firm, whose dependence on the supplier is therefore limited (in short, the reciprocal dependence relation is not symmetrical).

We can now appreciate the scope of CSR defined as an extended form of governance. It extends the concept of fiduciary duty from a mono-stakeholder setting (where the sole stakeholder to whom fiduciary duties are owed is the owner of the firm) to a multi-stakeholder one in which the firm owes fiduciary duties to *all* its stakeholders (the owners included). Classifying stakeholders on the basis of the nature of their relationship with the firm must thus be regarded as an important gauge in assigning these further fiduciary duties.[6]

'ABUSE OF AUTHORITY': THE ECONOMIC BASIS OF EXTENDED FIDUCIARY DUTIES OWED TO CORPORATE STAKEHOLDERS

Let us now inquire into whether economic theory provides support for the thesis that the firm has 'further' responsibilities towards its stakeholders. According to neo-institutional theory (Williamson, 1975, 1986; Grossman and Hart, 1986; Hart and Moore, 1990; Hart, 1995; Hansmann, 1996), the firm emerges as an institutional form of 'unified transactions govern-ance' intended to remedy imperfections in the contracts that regulate exchange relations among subjects endowed with diverse assets (capital, labour, instrumental goods, consumption decisions and so on). These assets, if used jointly, are able to generate a surplus over the cost of their use, which is higher than in the case of their separate use by each asset holder. Contracts by which these asset holders regulate their exchanges are nonetheless incomplete: they do not include provisos covering unforeseen events, either due to the costs of drafting them, or because the cognitive limits of the human mind make it impossible to predict all possible states of the world. Yet for these assets to be used in the best manner possible, specific investments must be made: investments undertaken with a view to the value that they may produce within an idiosyncratic contractual rela-tion. That means that the surplus generated with respect to the costs sus-tained by each party to the exchange is determined by the undertaking of *specific* activities with *specific* counterparts (suppliers, customers, employees, financiers and so on). Let us assume that parties behave opportunistically (that is, they are egoists who act with astuteness). Thus, once the investments have been made, contractual incompleteness means that the terms of the contract can be renegotiated, so that the party in a stronger *ex post* position is able to appropriate the entire surplus, thereby expropriating the other stakeholders. If, however, agents expect to be expropriated, they will have no incentive to undertake their investments at the optimal level. This expectation of unfair treatment gives rise to a loss of efficiency at the social level.

The firm responds to this problem by bringing the various transactions under the control of a hierarchical authority – the authority, that is, of the party that owns the firm, and through ownership is entitled to make decisions over the contingencies that were not *ex ante* contractible. Unified governance supplements incomplete contracts with authority relations through the vertical and horizontal integration of the units that previously made separate contributions. The firm is therefore a special contractual form: when contracts lack provisos contingent on unforeseen events, they can be 'completed' with the 'residual right of control', which entitles its holder to decide what should be done about decisions not *ex ante* contractible – that is, decisions 'left over' from the original contract and that become available only when unforeseen situations arise.

The residual right of control underpins authority: those parties entitled to residual right of control may threaten the other parties of the contract with exclusion from the physical assets of the firm, thereby ensuring that *ex ante* non-contracted decisions are taken *ex post* to their own advantage. They are thus safeguarded against the opportunism of the other stakeholders, and they are able to protect the expected value of their investments in situations where contract incompleteness provides margins of discretion when residual decisions have to be made. There is therefore an efficiency rationale for the idea of the firm as a 'unified governance' of transactions: if one party (a class of stakeholders) has made a specific investment of greater importance than that made by the others at risk, then that party should be granted the property right, and with it, the right to make 'residual' decisions. This is also the basis for regulating the delegation of authority from the owners to directors or managers by corporate governance rules when the owners themselves are not able to directly exercise the entire residual right of control. Fiduciary duties owed to the owners must guarantee that delegated exercise of residual rights of control by the board of directors or managers will maintain or improve the efficiency of their original allocation to the selected class of stakeholders.

One should not underestimate, however, the risks of the firm *qua* unified governance. Due to contract incompleteness, there is not just one single stakeholder at risk. Multiple stakeholders often undertake specific investments (investments in human capital, investments of trust by consumers, investments of financial capital, investments by suppliers in raw materials, technologies and instrumental goods). Contracts with these stakeholders are also incomplete.

If, however, a firm brings its contracts with certain stakeholders (labour contracts, obligations towards and relations with minority shareholders) under the authority of a party who is allocated control over residual decisions (for example, the controlling shareholder group) – and more generally if a party is enabled by its de facto power to exercise discretion over *ex ante* non-contractible decisions concerning implicit or explicit contractual relations with the other stakeholders (consumers, customers, suppliers, creditors and so on) – what is there to ensure protection of the investments and interests that are different from those of the controlling stakeholder? If fiduciary duties are linked only to ownership, the stakeholders without residual right of control will not be protected by the fiduciary duties of those running the firm.

The inherent risk is thus an abuse of authority (Sacconi, 2000). Those wielding authority may use it to expropriate the specific investments of others by exploiting 'gaps' in contracts. The gaps persist even under a system of unified governance, which means simply allocating to only one stakeholder the right to 'fill' those gaps with its discretionary decisions. Those in a position of authority are able to threaten the other stakeholders with exclusion from access to physical assets of the firm or from the benefits of the contract, to the point that those stakeholders become indifferent to accepting the expropriation or forgoing the value of their investments by withdrawing from the relationship. Thus the entire surplus – including its part produced through efforts and investments carried out by the non-controlling stakeholders – will be appropriated by the controlling party. Again forward-looking stakeholders will be deterred from entering the hierarchical transaction with the controlling party. In general, this will produce an internal 'crisis of legitimacy' between firm and stakeholders (a crisis in the relationships between the organizational authorities and participants in the organization) and an external 'crisis of trust' (in relationships with stakeholders who have entered into contractual or external relations with the organization). Various stakeholders will *ex ante* have a reduced incentive to invest (if they foresee the risk of abuse), while *ex post* they will resort to conflicting or disloyal behaviour (typically possible when the asymmetry of information is inherent in the execution of some subordinate activity) in the belief that they are being subjected to abuse of authority. In the economist's jargon, this is a 'second best' state of affairs (less than optimum): all governance solutions based on the allocation of property rights to a single party may approximate social efficiency, but they can *never* fully achieve it. This much is acknowledged by the theoreticians of contractual incompleteness when they point out that the allocation of the residual right of control induces the party protected by that right to overinvest, while those less protected are induced to under-invest. The consequence is a shortfall with regard to the social optimum (Grossman and Hart, 1986; Hart, 1995).

On the other hand, if the stakeholder category entitled to exercise owner-ship (the double right of controlling residual decisions and claiming residual revenue; see Hansmann, 1996) is selected on the basis of its ability to mini-mize total costs deriving from the summation of contractual costs borne by various stakeholders and costs of exercising authority, it is by no means certain that a solution will be found that reduces each of those costs to a minimum (that is, reduces the opportunism suffered by each stakeholder to a minimum). It may be sufficient for the solution to emerge if, for example, the governance costs of one class (the capital holders, for example) are low enough to counterbalance a relative increase in the contractual costs borne by another class (the workers, for example). The fact is that the relative (in) efficiency depends on manifest or simply expected unfairness: the separa-tion between efficiency and fairness (a myth of neoclassical economics) is no longer feasible when one faces the real-life problem of working out acceptable solutions for the governance of transactions.

When CSR is viewed as 'extended governance', it completes the firm as an institution of transactions governance (Sacconi, 2000). The firm's legitimacy deficit (whatever category of stakeholders is placed in control of it) is remedied if the residual control right is accompanied by further fiduciary duties towards the subjects at risk of abuse of authority and deprived of the residual control right. At the same time, this is a move towards greater social efficiency, because it reduces the disincentives and social costs generated by the abuse of authority. From this perspective, 'extended governance' should comprise:

- *the residual control right* (ownership) allocated to the stakeholder with the largest investments at risk and with relatively low govern-ance costs, as well as the right to delegate authority to professional directors and management;
- *the fiduciary duties* of those who effectively run the firm (administra-tors and managers) towards the owners, given that the latter have delegated control to them; and
- *the fiduciary duties of those in a position of authority in the firm (the owner or the managers) towards the non-controlling stakeholders*: the

obligation of running the firm in a manner in which these stakeholders are not deprived of their fair shares of the surplus produced from
their specific investments, and that they are not subject to negative
externalities. [7]

A number of recent economic and legal models of governance support
this view of CSR. For example, the firm can be seen as a 'nexus' of specific
investments regulated by incomplete contracts, rather than as a nexus of
simple contracts, and therefore as a team of actors cooperating to produce
a surplus from those specific investments (Rajan and Zingales, 2000).
Based on a similar view that combines different theories of the firm – the
theory of incomplete contracts with that of team production – is the model
of multi-stakeholder governance developed by Margaret Blair and Lynn
Stout (1999, 2006). This view regards corporate governance structures
as a form of prevention against opportunistic behaviour among the N
members of the team making specific investments. When applied to a
public company, this model translates into a board of directors acting as a
mediating hierarchy: an authority system charged with the task of finding
the appropriate balance in the protection of diverse interests. The (controversial) legal basis for this form of 'impartial governance' exercised by
the board of directors and by management in the US joint-stock company
is the 'business judgement doctrine': the manager's use of a standard of
professional conduct that insulates his or her choices against claims by
shareholders (Blair and Stout, 1999; see also Meese, 2002).
   Many unanswered questions nevertheless remain. Does a criterion exist
with which to give more precise specification to these extended duties,
and from which it is possible to derive a strategic management standard
of sufficient clarity such that the 'extended governance' model cannot be
accused of entailing higher governance costs than the traditional 'narrow'
corporate governance view? What norms are effective for the implementation of CSR? What is the role of company law with respect to other parts
of the law that impose constraints on corporate behaviour? And what
role can be played by self-regulation? I shall address these questions in the
sections that follow.

THE SOCIAL CONTRACT AS A CRITERION
FOR THE FAIR BALANCE OF STAKEHOLDERS'
INTERESTS

If a firm is a team of participants with specific investments, then the meta-
phor of a 'bargaining game' among multiple stakeholders can be applied.

These stakeholders must agree on a shared action plan (a joint strategy), which allocates tasks among the members of the team so that the contribution of each of them is efficient (because it produces the maximum surplus net of each stakeholder's costs). At the same time, each stakeholder wants to get as much utility as possible from the agreement. Bargaining is thus typically a mixed interests game. Although it is in stakeholders' common interest to cooperate – as this enables them to produce a surplus that would otherwise be impossible – conflict nevertheless persists among them over the distribution of the value created. Choosing the joint strategy implies answering the question of what is due to each stakeholder and what each of them can expect from the firm in exchange for its contribution, so that each stakeholder may agree on that joint strategy. The question thus arises as to how the stakeholders' interests can be balanced against each other, and what claims on the firm should be considered the appropriate basis for the management's fiduciary duties. 'Stakeholder', in fact, is a descriptive term. It reminds us that a variety of classes of individuals have interests at stake in the running of the firm, and that they may sometimes advance conflicting claims. The use of the term 'stakeholder', however, does not provide a *criterion* with which to balance claims when they are mutually conflicting.

To answer the question, it is necessary to have a criterion that makes it possible to identify the balance that *any* stakeholder would accept as the basis for its voluntary cooperation with the firm. We thus need an *impartial* criterion. It is here that ethics – understood as a set of impartial criteria for collective choice-making – comes into play as part of the firm's governance and strategic management.

I suggest the 'social contract' among the stakeholders of the firm (Sacconi, 1991, 2000) as the ethical criterion. By 'social contract' I do not mean any real-life bargain, but a 'touchstone' from which one can assess the diverse outcomes of the day-to-day running of the firm. In other words, the social contract is the agreement that would be reached by the representatives of all the firm's stakeholders in a hypothetical situation of impartial choice.[8] Corresponding to the notion of 'social contract' is the following multi-stage deliberative procedure, which generates impartially acceptable agreements.

1. Force, fraud and manipulation must be set aside.
2. Each party comes to the bargaining table with only its capacity to contribute and its assessment of the utility of each agreement or non-agreement proposed (dispensing with any form of threat other than its possible refusal to agree).
3. The bargaining status quo must be set at a level such that each stakeholder breaks even regarding the cost of its specific investments. Each

stakeholder must thus obtain from the social contract at the least reimbursement of the cost of the specific investment it has contributed to the surplus (otherwise the bargaining process would permit opportunistic exploitation of the counterparty's lock-in situation). The distribution of the surplus is regulated by the social contract, as well as by the corresponding deliberative procedure on the basis of 'initial endowments' thus defined.

4. Each party in turn puts him-/herself in the position of each of the other parties. For each position, s/he can accept or reject the contractual alternatives proposed.[9]
5. If solutions are found that are acceptable to some stakeholders but not to others, these solutions must be discarded and the procedure repeated (which reflects the assumption that cooperation by all stakeholders is recognized as necessary).
6. The terms of the agreement reached are therefore those that each stakeholder is willing to accept from its particular standpoint, meaning that the non-empty intersection of the joint strategies and relative distributions is acceptable to each of them.

Note that this intersection is necessarily *non-empty*, for otherwise the game would not allow a cooperative surplus. In other words, it would not be the case that joint action by the parties may produce something more than their separate actions and that at least one surplus distribution proves to be reciprocally advantageous (if it must be so, then there exists at least one agreement acceptable to all).

THE SOCIAL CONTRACT AND A UNIQUELY DEFINED OBJECTIVE FUNCTION OF THE FIRM

The main objection brought against CSR is that the multi-stakeholder approach to a firm's governance leaves the management without a clearly stated and uniquely defined 'bottom line' to be used as a benchmark against which to evaluate its success or failure (Jensen, 2001). The consequence, the argument goes, is that the management exploits this situation to pursue its personal interests. It comes up with every possible device to conceal its essentially self-dealing behaviour behind the interests of other stakeholders. The critics of CSR maintain that whereas it is easy to check managerial strategy (among the alternatives available at any particular time) against the criterion of increasing as much as possible the firm's profits and to make management comply, it is much more difficult in the case of 'stakeholder value', since this consists of numerous dimensions to be maximized simultaneously (the interests of the various stakeholders). Consequently, stakeholder value contains an intrinsic contradiction: the strategy that simultaneously pursues the conflicting, or at best divergent, goals of the various stakeholders is ultimately left to managerial discretion.[10]

This objection does not apply to the model of the social contract of the firm proposed here, which by no means ignores the existence of a distributive conflict, but instead resolves it by identifying a bargaining equilibrium that permits mutual cooperation among the members of the team.

A counterpart of the contractarian ethical decision procedure given in the previous section is a mathematical model of bargaining whose solution is as exactly computable as the profit function in microeconomic theory. Hence, one can simply substitute profit maximization by maximization of the solution function to the bargaining game, taking this function as the proper (perfectly computable) objective function.[11] This solution is simultaneously an answer to both the problem of cooperation and that of distributive conflict among the stakeholders. Moreover, if the bargaining set is well defined (and if one accepts the Nash, Harsanyi and Zeuthen postulates of bargaining theory), the solution is defined uniquely, so that the set of admissible solutions is reduced to one single alternative. Hence, the best pursuit of the interest of the stakeholder controlling the firm is equivalent to the solution of the bargaining problem among all the stakeholders. (In any event, various theories of bargaining yield solutions that closely resemble each other; David Gauthier (1986) and Ehud Kalai and Meir Smorodinsky (1975) for example, provide slight changes to the basic Nash solution. For the purposes of this study, identifying a set of 'close' solutions compatible with the idea of rational bargaining appears sufficient.)

What does this solution say? On the assumption that the external effects on third parties with no influence on the transactions are minimized by selection of the forms of cooperation that damage them least, one may proceed as follows. Net of the initial (pre-bargaining) position or status quo, in which coverage of the costs of specific investments by each stakeholder must be included, the calculation is made of the value for each stakeholder of each cooperative outcome from joint action plans. The set of these values (or better, the set of these vectors of values) is the outcome space, associating with each joint action plan (joint strategy) an allocation of the cooperative surplus (positive or nil) to the players. Rational bargaining takes place within this space among players seeking to obtain the highest possible share of the cooperative surplus, to the detriment of the others' shares. This happens only once the players have accepted the need for reciprocal agreement, for in its absence they would be unable to

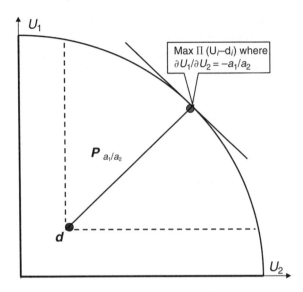

*Figure 6.1   A cooperative bargaining game with two players and the Nash
solution in a symmetrical case*

obtain anything more than the initial position (status quo). Calculable
within this space is the Nash bargaining function – the product of the
utilities of the various stakeholders with specific investments, that is, an
aggregative function of their utilities. Where the product (the aggrega-
tion) is maximum, there is a bargaining equilibrium – a rational agreement
among the participants in the social contract – corresponding to the Nash
bargaining solution (Nash, 1950; Harsanyi, 1977) (see Figure 6.1 for an
example with two players).

Specifically, let us consider a case with two players, 1 and 2, and let
us assume that the solution is a point in space R^2 enclosed between the
positive Cartesian axes U_1 and U_2, each of which measures the utility for
a player of the outcomes of the cooperative game (see Figure 6.1). The
space therefore represents the outcomes subject to bargaining in terms of
the players' utility value (that is, their payoffs). The standard analytical
assumption is that the payoff space is convex and compact. The payoff
space P therefore has an efficient frontier (in the upper-right positive
ortant), which represents the set of outcomes for which the players' utilities cannot be increased by an alternative agreement without reducing the
utility of at least one other player. Below this frontier are agreements
for which gains are still possible for both players; above it, are outcomes
infeasible by any agreement or joint plan of action. All points in the space

represent different possible values of the coalition among the two players. In fact, only when both players agree on the solution of the game can they leave the status quo *d*, which is represented by a point interior to the space, so that they may benefit from cooperation. The characteristic function of the coalition between the two players is therefore super-additive (it is better to agree than not to agree). Obviously, of interest are only those agreements for which there is an efficient allocation. But on what point among those on the frontier should the agreement fall? The Nash solution states that the players will agree on the joint strategy corresponding to the point of the frontier where the following holds:

$$\text{Max}\,\Pi_i(U_i - d_i) \text{ (where } i = 1, 2 \text{ denotes the various participants in the bargaining),}$$

where U_i is the utility of the generic stakeholder *i* for the cooperative transaction that it undertakes with the firm, and d_i the cost of the specific investments made by *i* in order to participate in the joint action plan (that is, *i* always at least recoups the cost of its specific investment). The solution hence assumes that bargaining should provide each player with at least a net advantage, which is the difference between the share of the surplus received and the status quo value. As a consequence of additional rationality postulates, these net individual advantages can be identified such that the *product* of all of them is the maximum among those in the set of the possible outcomes of the cooperation. One may say that this is the collective choice function adopted by the members of the coalition in the light of their bargaining in order to resolve the problem of their joint action. It is coherent with the proportionality of the remunerations with the relative utilities, because the ratio in which the shares of the surplus a_1/a_2 are distributed is proportional to the ratio between the marginal variations in the players' utilities $\partial U_1/\partial U_2 = -a_1/a_2$ (Brock, 1979; Sacconi, 1991, 1997). Based on Nash's postulates (1950) and those of Zeuthen–Harsanyi (see Harsanyi, 1977), this solution expresses a bargaining equilibrium built on the individual rationality of the players.

This equilibrium does not need operational interpersonal comparisons of utility (which operationally are problematic) in order to be calculated (interpersonal comparisons can be confined to the interpretative level).[12] It obeys, in fact, simple axioms of individual rationality in bargaining, such as: the decision to grant a concession according to the expected personal utility given the probability that the counterparty will accept or refuse it; the decision not to make a concession that one would not expect the counterparty to make in a similar situation; conditions of mutually expected rationality, such as expecting that the willingness of acceptance by the counterparty depends on a symmetric probabilistic assessment of the first party's behaviour; not expecting the counterparty to accept something that oneself would not accept; and so on (see ibid.).

If these postulates are taken literally, they can, of course, be criticized for being unrealistic. What matters for my purposes here, however, is that these postulates are a good approximation of rational behaviour in a hypothetical (that is, ideal) bargaining situation among stakeholders (for it is a *normative* model being developed here, one that is no less normative than that of profit maximization).

Moreover, the outcome of the bargaining game can be interpreted as the solution that is coherent with a notion of distributive justice. On the assumption that it is possible to unify the unit's measuring utility, we find that the bargaining solution computed always distributes the advantages proportionally to 'relative needs' or to the relative marginal variations in the intensity of personal utilities (Brock, 1979; Sacconi, 1991, 1997, 2000). Because it is located in the upper-right frontier of the space of the bargaining outcomes, it fulfils the requirement of social efficiency (no advantage from cooperation is lost) and at the same time corresponds to an intuitive notion of fairness.

THE EMERGENCE OF EXTENDED FIDUCIARY DUTIES FROM THE SOCIAL CONTRACT OF THE FIRM

Thus far, the social contract has been presented as a normative deliberative procedure making it possible to identify the terms of an agreement that would be acceptable from an impartial standpoint – that is, from the viewpoint of any of the stakeholders – so that it can be adopted as a standard of behaviour by, for example, the mediating hierarchy proposed by Blair and Stout. The social contract can also furnish a reconstruction – understood as a 'potential explanation' – of how bargaining has given rise to a firm with fiduciary duties *both* towards the owners *and* towards all the stakeholders (that is, socially responsible).

Consider a 'state of nature' prior to the creation of the firm. Bilateral transactions among stakeholders regulated by incomplete contracts are subject to reciprocal opportunistic behaviour, with the consequence that prohibitive bargaining costs render them inefficient. At the same time, the parties to those transactions are entirely unconcerned about the negative external effects of their transactions on other agents, who although they do not participate, are nevertheless affected. This is a Hobbesian scenario in which the life of economic transactions among agents is 'solitary, poor, nasty, brutish, and short'.[13] The stakeholders thus address the problem of creating an association whereby all their transactions can be undertaken in accordance with agreed-to rules and are therefore not subject to contract costs, while at the same time the negative effects on those who do not participate in the benefits from the transactions are reduced to a minimum. The 'first social contract' of the firm (*pactum unionis*) is nothing other than the agreement that the stakeholders reach *among themselves* to set up the association (the '*just* firm'). They negotiate the association's constitution, which consists of a common plan of action (joint strategy) to which each of them contributes either by carrying out a positive effort or by simply refraining from applying his/her veto. This *first social contract* of the firm stipulates as follows:

1. rejection of shared plans of action that generate negative externalities for those not participating in the cooperative venture or, if these negative externalities are essential for the production of the cooperative surplus, a compensation of third parties so that they are rendered neutral;
2. production of the maximum surplus possible (difference between the value of the product for its consumers, who belong to the association, and the costs sustained by each stakeholder to produce it); and
3. a distribution of the surplus that is 'fair', or rationally acceptable to each stakeholder in a bargaining process free from force or fraud and based on an equitable status quo, that is, considering the surplus net of the specific investments.

If, however, an attempt is made to reach this form of an ideal association (the 'just firm'), which eliminates all the participants' contract costs, they end up, in practice, with an organizational form that is found to be inefficient regarding governance costs. The stakeholders discover, for example, that the general assembly of all members is unable to take coherent decisions in a reasonable amount of time. In the absence of a monitoring system, once the members of the association have established fair shares of the surplus to be distributed among them, they have an incentive to act opportunistically and not to play their part. Coordination problems arise on how the joint strategy can be implemented under changing circumstances, which may alter beliefs and reciprocal expectations asymmetrically. The stakeholders consequently draw up a *second social contract* of the firm (*pactum subjections*)[14] by which they constitute, in the proper sense of the term, a governance structure for the association. It is only at this point that the association becomes a hierarchical structure.

The second social contract provides that authority should be delegated to the stakeholder most efficient in performing governance functions (the taking of residual decisions, devising coordination solutions as circumstances change, monitoring, enacting sanctions, excluding potential free riders, and so on). For this reason, it can also be seen as a contract between the stakeholders and he or she who is given control over the firm (social contract with the firm). After comparative examination of the governance costs of each stakeholder, the one with the lowest costs is selected and assigned ownership, and is therefore the one to which the right of governing the association is delegated (Hansmann, 1996). This party that is remunerated with the *residual* is authorized to delegate some discretionary decisions concerning the running of the firm to professional directors and managers, and to appoint those who are in a position of authority to run the firm. Prima facie, their authority will be effectively constituted – that is, the delegation will remain valid – as long as they comply with what I call the 'narrow fiduciary proviso': the owners are remunerated with the maximum residual revenue possible (in forms compatible with the diverse nature of the controlling stakeholder: profits, returns, discounts, improved conditions of service, improved conditions of employment, and so on) in light of the conditions obtaining in the firm's specific market.

This proviso entails that the positions of the other stakeholders change. Formerly co-equal members of the association, they are now subject in various ways to the discretionary decisions made by the stakeholder entitled to authority, and by the administrators that it has appointed. Unlike in the standard economic theory of the firm, in social contract theory the risk of the abuse of authority can be faced squarely. The second social contract is therefore conceived in a manner such that this cost of hierarchy is forestalled. Hence, under the second social contract, the stakeholders agree to submit to authority, thereby rendering it effective, if the contract contains the stipulation that the firm's new governance structure must comply with *fiduciary duties* towards all the stakeholders (owners and non-owners).

Extended Fiduciary Proviso

First, towards the non-owners:

- the firm must abstain from activities that impose negative external effects on stakeholders not party to transactions, or compensate them so that they remain neutral; and
- the firm must remunerate the stakeholders participating in the firm's transactions with payoffs (monetary or of other kinds, for example,

in terms of the quantity, quality and prices of goods, services, working conditions and so on), which, taken for granted as a fair status quo, must contain a part tied to the firm's economic performance so as to approximate fair/efficient shares of the surplus (assuming that this is positive) as envisaged by the first social contract.[15]

Second, towards the owners:

● the firm must remunerate the owners with the maximum residual compatible with fair remuneration – as defined by the first social contract – of the efficient contributions made by all the other stakeholders.

What does this hypothetical explanation yield? It yields a definition of the 'corporate interest' of the company – that is, the interest that the manager acting in the name of the company must serve – which is consistent with the contractarian model. According to this reconstruction, the manager (appointed through the second social contract) has a special fiduciary duty towards the owners (or the 'residual claimant') who have delegated authority to him or her (via the narrow fiduciary proviso). This duty applies, however, only under the constraint that the general fiduciary duties are fulfilled towards *all* the stakeholders – which is defined via the extended fiduciary proviso. One may thus construct the corporate interest by means of a hierarchical decision-making procedure, which moves from the most general conditions to the most specific ones:

● minimize the negative externalities affecting stakeholders in the broad sense (perhaps by paying suitable compensation);
● identify the feasible set of agreements compatible with the maximization of the joint surplus and its simultaneous fair distribution, as established by the impartial cooperative agreement among the stakeholders in the strict sense; and
● if more than one option is available in the above defined feasible set, choose the one that maximizes the *residual* allocated to the owner (for example, the shareholder).

Hence, the narrow corporate interest (the one usually advocated by supporters of the 'shareholder value' view) results from a series of steps, which select the admissible ways in which this interest can be satisfied – that is, those that are consistent with the various constraints imposed by the first social contract on the owner's behaviour. It should be emphasized that this concept cannot be reduced to that of value maximization for the 'residual claimant' (the owners) once constraints imposed by positive contractual obligations have been fulfilled. By recognizing that all contracts are incomplete and constantly susceptible to opportunism (even by those who run the firm), one sees that it is the entire hierarchical decision procedure that provides the basis for satisfying the corporate interest. In other words, the social contract identifies the goals or the internal (not merely external) moral constraints that channels managerial discretion. It results from satisfying, in sequence, the three requirements set out above. In summary, maximizing the value for the residual claimant under the constraint of compliance with the social contract by the firm and stakeholders, in turn, defines 'stakeholder value'.

IMPLEMENTING THE MODEL: REGULATION, SELF-REGULATION, SELF-INTEREST IN THE LONG RUN

This and the following sections address the different problems of how the normative model of CSR based on the stakeholders' social contract of the firm may be implemented through norms supported by endogenous incentives and motivations. The idea is that the normative model of multi-stakeholder corporate governance and objective function is supported by strong endogenous incentives and motivations, so that its implementation may rest largely on voluntary self-regulatory norms deliberated by companies, and on their decisions to comply effectively with extended fiduciary duties owed to their stakeholders.

Effective CSR self-regulation is, of course, only a viable option within an institutional and legal environment that does not obstruct it. Such obstruction would occur in the case of overly narrow definitions of the firm's objective function, such as that prescribing shareholder value maximization as the company's only goal, which can be found in many company laws at the European level. Whenever maximizing the joint-stakeholder value has conflicted even in the very short run with immediate shareholder value maximization, these laws have prevented the board from deciding to balance stakeholders' interests according to the social contract view, which implies a constrained maximization view (that is, constraining shareholder value maximization with the condition of the simultaneous maximization of other stakeholders' utility according to a bargaining solution). The 2006 company law reform in the UK is an example of how the corporation's goals may be enlarged by means of a general and abstract principle in order to legitimate the exercise of some balancing decision among different stakeholders, as well as giving relevance to the notion of reputation in the long run.[16] This is not at all a concrete norm prescribing a precise balancing criterion. On the contrary, it is a very general principle that enables the company board and governance structure to trade some interests off against others, at least in the short run. If complemented with an accountability requirement concerning how the board of directors will account for how it implements the balancing decisions, a regulation such as this effectively opens the door to a self-regulatory CSR standard, which more precisely specifies principles and guidelines whereby the CSR model of governance must be implemented. On being asked to account for their balancing decisions, boards would appeal to such principles or criteria in order to justify their behaviour to those stakeholders that may be disadvantaged by any particular balancing decision. This desirable complementariness between legal regulation and soft law, or social standard-based self-regulation, can be seen as very useful for the purpose of implementing the CSR social contract model and multi-stakeholder corporate governance.

Nevertheless, the thrust of my argument is that once company law has stopped obstructing self-regulation, the endogenous beliefs, motivations and preferences of economic agents (companies and stakeholders) become the essential forces driving the implementation of the CSR model of multi-stakeholder governance. To put it in game theoretical terms, the normative model is implementable *in equilibrium*. The rest of this chapter aims to give substance to this statement.

First, however, it must be said that this position should not be confused with the standard economist's view that if CSR is to emerge as equilibrium behaviour from endogenous incentives, its driving force must be enlightened self-interest in the long run. According to this view, a self-interested entrepreneur who cares only for his/her self-interest in the long run (or cares for the self-interest of the firm's owners in the long run – in other words, the shareholders) would adopt behaviour that spontaneously satisfies the company stakeholders' interests with no need to single out a principle of fairness nor to agree on any social contract principles with stakeholders in order to state explicitly that the firm owes a fiduciary duty to them. Self-interest in the long run would simply guarantee that the treatment of corporate stakeholders spontaneously simulates a behaviour that fulfils extended fiduciary duties, thus making any explicit statement of these duties superfluous. The social contract would be useless as well, since in the long run there is nothing like a conflictual 'state of nature' among the company's stakeholders. On the contrary, one would observe harmony of interest among them, so that seeking the shareholder interest in the long run would also coincide with fulfilment at any time of the stakeholders' interests. As a consequence, the only goal that must be specified as the proper constraint on managerial and entrepreneurial discretion in the management of the firm is the coherent pursuit of shareholder value in the long run. Satisfaction of the stakeholders' legitimate interests is seen as simply a side-effect of this main goal, because they are related to it through a means–ends relationship. If one strives to end the maximization of shareholder value, in the long run one will necessarily choose *as the means* those strategies that will also satisfy the other stakeholders' interests. Hence, while stakeholders are to be accounted for within the dimension of corporate means, only shareholders are recognized as sources for corporate ends.[17]

This view does not recognize any need for a norm that explicitly states a principle of fair balancing among stakeholders. Note that this norm is excluded not only from mandatory law, but also from principles of business ethics or self-regulatory standards or codes of ethics, in so far as these social norms may be seen as underhanded attempts to modify or integrate the ends or the bottom line whereby the manager must account for his/her conduct.

This 'self-interest in the long run' view is untenable. First, without the explicit statement of a CSR norm – be it worked out autonomously by the board of directors or through a social multi-stakeholder dialogue – based on the hypothetical agreement of the company stakeholders, a long-run, self-interested, corporate strategy unintentionally simulating a behaviour that pursues stakeholder value may simply not exist (or become something that the firm cannot be aware of at all). Even if it is learned that the firm was aware of such behaviour, it could nevertheless work out other behaviours in the long run that counterbalance stakeholders' claim of unfair treatment. These further behaviours would not only be preferable to the firm's owners, they would also command a certain acquiescence on the part of the stakeholders, who could be made indifferent between the prospects of giving in to the firm's opportunistic strategies or staying out of the relationship completely. I must thus conclude that the simple 'self-interest in the long run' view, translated into shareholder value in the long-run doctrine, would largely violate stakeholders' legitimate claims while allowing the abuse of ownership-based authority.

By contrast, the self-regulatory view defended here requires the putting in place of explicit norms arrived at by social dialogue and multi-stakeholder agreements – taking the form of CSR governance codes, or management standards – and their voluntary acceptance by firms, because they contain and specify the terms of the ideal and fair social contract between the firm and its stakeholders. These norms are explicitly formulated in language (written or oral), and their utterances contain the statements of extended fiduciary duties and obligations that the firm owes to its stakeholders. At the same time they are voluntarily adhered to, and as far as enforcement is concerned, they are imposed not by external legal sanction, but through endogenous social and economic sanctions and incentives. In this sense, they are self-enforceable explicit norms, put into practice essentially by means of endogenous economic and social forces such as reputation effects and conformity (Lewis, 1969; Posner 2000; Stout, 2006).

To understand why an explicit utterance of the stakeholders' social contract of the firm by means of an explicit voluntary CSR norm is so essential for the endogeneity and self-sustainability of the model's implementation, one must consider the *role* performed by explicit and voluntarily agreed norms. In this chapter I focus on one of them, the 'cognitive-constructive' role, which answers the question of how the firm works out the set of commitments that it can undertake with respect to future events it is aware of not being able to predict in any detail, and therefore what types of possible equilibrium behaviour stakeholders may expect from the firm. This answers the question about the existence of equilibria that implement the normative model through endogenous incentives to act on the part of the firm and its stakeholders. Further research is needed to address the remaining role that would make complete an implementation theory.

COGNITIVE/CONSTRUCTIVE ROLE OF A CSR NORM: FILLING THE GAPS IN THE GAME FORM

One basic idea in the domain of CSR implementation is that the incentives related to the formation of a reputation can play a key role in a firm's decision to endorse and respect the model of extended fiduciary duties owed to its stakeholders. If the firm wants to induce its stakeholders to enter into cooperative relations, it develops a reputation. Stakeholders will decide to cooperate with the firm if they trust that it will not abuse them. For a reputation to be developed, stakeholders must verify that the firm behaves according to a 'cooperative' type of behaviour and that it does not abuse them when they decide to trust it (that is, that the firm respects what is understood as the fair terms of their social contract). In essence, stakeholders must believe that the firm is an 'honest type' (that it does not abuse its authority). A firm's reputation for being a certain type increases if evidence is gathered that confirms it. A firm that wants to gain the stakeholders' cooperation must act in such a way that its behaviour becomes indistinguishable from the voluntary execution of its fiduciary duties towards its stakeholders. Otherwise, if the stakeholders observe an opportunistic behaviour, the firm's reputation will suffer a dramatic setback.

One way to illustrate the functioning of the reputation mechanism is a

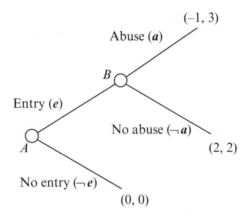

Figure 6.2   One-shot trust game in extensive form

simple interactive situation representing a transaction based on the fiduciary relation (the trust game) between a stakeholder A and a firm B (see
Figure 6.2). A stakeholder must decide whether or not to trust the firm and
enter or otherwise into an exchange relationship with it. The firm decides
whether or not to abuse the stakeholder's trust. As is well known, this
one-shot game has just one Nash equilibrium, the strategy pair (no entry,
abuse) = ($\neg e$, a).

Things change, however, when the trust game is repeatedly played
for an indefinite number of times between an infinite series of short-run
players $A_1, \ldots, A_n$ (where n goes to infinity) – each one taking part in a
single stage game – and a long-run player B taking part in every repetition of the basic stage game. Player B's strategies in the repeated game
are hence behavioural rules for choosing actions at each stage game as
a function of each history of the game until any stage at which player B
must choose. Payoff functions must rearrange accordingly. Whereas any
short-run player (A_i) is only interested in the payoff of the stage game in
which s/he takes part, the long-run player's (B) payoff is the infinite sum
of the payoffs s/he gets at each stage. A crucial assumption is that player
B is more or less far-sighted (that is, player B's discount rate δ for future
utilities is more or less close to 1).

As already mentioned, the idea that players entertain beliefs about the
possible types of the counterparty characterizes reputation games. The
long-run player is perfectly rational (from a strategic point of view) and
perfectly informed about the game. The short-run players, on the other
hand, are not perfectly informed, and hence are uncertain about the 'type'
of player B. By a 'type' is meant a commitment to choose a given action

under the different contingencies of the game, in other words, the action that player *B* chooses in each stage game. 'Type' thus reflects the idea that player *B* may be idiosyncratically committed to some rule of behaviour, even if s/he is uncertain about what it is.

The different possible types of player *B* as distinguished by A_i are the following: (1) the stage-game 'rational' type, who always chooses the dominant strategy of the stage game; (2) the type who never chooses to abuse (the honest type); (3) types who combine in different ways *abuse* and *non-abuse* randomly by means of different mixed strategies. Player *B*'s reputation is the probability assigned by each player A_i at every stage to different types of player *B*. Probabilities are updated according to the Bayes rule: at each stage, the conditional probabilities of types change as a function of the evidence produced by how the past stage games have been played by the long-run player.

Each player A_i chooses, according to the expected utility reasoning, between *e* and ¬*e*. During the first stages of the repeated game, players A_i necessarily do not trust. Eventually (say after *N* periods), however, a short-run player (say A_N+_1) may begin to trust player *B* if a series of A_i before him/her have observed ¬*a* so many times that the conditioned probability of the 'absolutely honest' type is updated to the level p^*, where the expected utility of *e* becomes higher than ¬*e*. Player *B*'s optimal choices follow from this feature of the model, and they define the equilibrium set of the repeated game. First, player *B* can decide always to choose the equilibrium strategy of the stage game, that is, always *a*, which induces A_i not to enter forever. This leads to a repeated game equilibrium, because nobody has the incentive to deviate from such choices for the entire duration of the game. Player *B* has a different strategy at his/her disposal, however. This consists of exploiting his/her awareness of the updating mechanism followed by players $A_1,. . ., A_n$. *B* can choose to simulate the behaviour of the 'absolutely honest' type until the conditioned probability reaches the critical level p^*. At this point *B* calculates whether it is better for him/her to continue playing ¬*a* – consequently over and over again inducing choices *e* from players A_i after A_N+_1 – or to defect by choosing *a*. If δ is close to 1 (that is, player *B* is not short-sighted), then the infinite sum of payoffs 2, even if discounted, will more than counterbalance a single chance of winning payoff 3 (see Fudenberg and Levine, 1989; Fudenberg, 1995).

Nevertheless, stakeholders can form their beliefs on the firm's behaviour (and, consequently, the firm can accumulate its reputation of being an 'honest' type), only if they can observe without ambiguity whether the firm has behaved according to a type. A problem with regard to this condition arises when the relations between the firm and its stakeholders take place in a setting where information or knowledge about the firm's action is incomplete. Typically, a firm and its stakeholders are involved in incomplete contract situations where a contract does not contain provisos covering unforeseen contingencies, so that there is no concrete benchmark against which claims of renegotiation can be assessed when unforeseen events occur. Because of incomplete knowledge, the stakeholders cannot verify whether the firm has behaved honestly according to the terms of the contract – in fact, the contract is mute when unforeseen events occur (Kreps, 1990a, b).

Repeated reputation games are games that firms can play with their stakeholders only in the knowledge context appropriate for the existence of the firm itself. According to the neo-institutional thesis adopted throughout this chapter, the context suited to the firm is one of incompleteness of contracts, wherein contractual commitments are badly specified or do not exist at all with reference to unforeseen states of the world. If one takes strategies that the firm will pursue and behavioural types that it will display throughout the repetition of a reputation game as coincident with contractual commitments (assuming that they are endorsed only if fair), incompleteness simply implies that *commitments* are unspecified with regard to unforeseen states. A reputation, however, is the probability that player *B* will comply with given commitments, hence neither inductive learning about compliance can work, nor can reputation be accumulated in such states.

Voluntary CSR norms – explicitly formulated through general and abstract ethical principles of fair treatment and precautionary rules of behaviour – state the commitments that a reputation mechanism takes as reference point in its workings, but that a conditional contract cannot anticipate with regard to unforeseen events.[18] In other words, norms, principles and precautionary standards of behaviour state the strategies that the firm may pursue in whatever state of the world, and they can be taken as the reference point for the formation, confirmation or refutation of the stakeholders' expectations concerning the company types. A key point in order to allow for the management of vagueness and ambiguity is to see how abstract principles and precautionary rules of behaviour may state commitments that are referred to unforeseen states of the world. In fact, their statements do not require a complete forecast of a state of the world in all its concrete details. They simply require 'fuzzy pattern recognition' of a state in terms of some abstract characteristic related to a general principle. The activation of precautionary rules of behaviour that follows is not conditional on *ex ante* complete descriptions of (unforeseen) states of the world; the rules can be activated simply by default (Sacconi, 2000, 2007b).

To illustrate, let us assume that a general principle of ethics defines as its domain of application the set of those situations that have an abstract and universalizable characteristic. In order to belong to the domain of a general principle, any given state of the world does not need to be completely and clearly described *ex ante* – which would be implausible for unforeseen states. The description of unforeseen contingencies is necessarily mute about many concrete properties that characterize the *ex ante* representation of foreseen states of the world as these properties simply do not occur in an unforeseen state (this is what makes it 'unforeseeable' in the strict sense). The situation may be very different for abstract, general and universalizable characteristics identified as relevant by a principle of ethics. In this case the description may not be simply mute, but *vague* (vagueness is the typical trade-off one may face for the comprehensiveness of a general and abstract universalizable principle). That means, however, that unforeseen states of the world will exhibit a vague but *quantifiable* membership in relation to the set identifying the domain of application of the principle (an intermediate degree between 0 and 1 in terms of a fuzzy membership function). Indeed, unforeseen states are what make the domain of a general principle or norm a 'fuzzy set' (Zimmerman, 1991).

So far so good, but what about the firm's commitments? Assume that a precautionary rule of behaviour is stated in order to pre-empt the occurrence of principle violations. This is not defined conditionally on a complete or clear *ex ante* description of any state wherein it must be conditionally implemented. On the contrary, it is defined with reference to membership in the domain of the general principle, and the commitment to carry out the rule is undertaken conditionally on just an *ex ante* 'required degree of membership' of any state, foreseen or not, of the fuzzy set that defines its application domain. The firm can undertake this commitment without knowing all the possible states *ex ante*, simply by establishing a membership threshold condition that is communicable *ex ante* to the stakeholders. This only requires assuming that whatever state (foreseen or not) may occur, both the players will be able to employ the fuzzy pattern recognition model of reasoning just illustrated. Satisfaction of the condition on the fuzzy membership threshold is shared knowledge *ex post*, because the degree of vagueness of any state in regard to the principle can be commonly understood as a matter of fact concerning the *ex post* state of group knowledge. If this were not the case, however, the *ex post* degree of vagueness to be assumed as relevant by the firm is that expressed by an impartial and non-malevolent observer who takes the point of view of every stakeholder in turn. Hence, the firm can undertake *ex ante* its commitments and be confident that *ex post* it will be able to account for them according to the stakeholders' vague judgement capacity. Note that the inference from satisfaction of the required threshold condition to implementation of the stated precautionary rule is 'default inference'. It requires one to reason according to the formula, 'even if information on the case in point x is *incomplete* and it is *no verified truth* that this state belongs to the domain of the principle P . . ., it is not *inconsistent* with the knowledge base that $x \in P$', or 'given satisfaction of the threshold condition, *normally* a situation like x is such that $x \in P$ *so that* the required rule of behaviour must be carried out.[19]

In order to avoid the consequences of incomplete information on the formation of reputation, the firm will therefore explicitly announce and subscribe to a set of CSR abstract and general principles whose contents are such to elicit stakeholder consensus, as well as to the explicit commitment of conforming with pre-established precautionary rules when they are put at risk (under a vagueness interpretation of risk), which are both known *ex ante* (before the occurrence of unforeseen events) by stakeholders. Thus, it is the CSR norm that enables the cognitive mechanism of reputation to function properly. In the absence of such a reference point, stakeholders could not develop trust, because they would not be able to check whether the firm respects its commitments.

A cognitive role is played in the working of a CSR norm as a 'gap-filling device' (Coleman, 1992) that states the types of behaviours that stakeholders can expect from the firm in situations where contracts fail, owing to the absence of conditional provisos constraining residual decisions and abuse of authority. This cognitive function is primarily constructive. The game form (Aoki, 2007a, b) is badly specified under unforeseen situations, because contingent strategies are unspecified over such states. Norms nevertheless allow by default the inference of how the 'honest type' of firm will behave under these circumstances. These 'strategies' are not defined contingently on states of the world that the parties are unable to write down in the contract or are even unable to foresee. Explicit norms complete the description of the game form by substituting default rules of behaviour for conditional strategies. These rules are based on the satisfaction of a membership condition in the domain of abstract and general ethical principles that are *ex ante* known and always *ex post* verifiable through a shared understanding of the inherent vagueness of the unforeseen contingencies. Once these norms have been stated *ex ante* in terms of precautionary standards of behaviour, it is possible to figure out how the firm is expected to behave in whatever unforeseen state that may put a general principle at risk, until a contrary proof is given that the principle does not apply to the new situation. What is involved here is not inductive learning about the probability of an already given set of possible but uncertain set of types, but the very conception of the type set itself that contributes to a (approximate) description of what may occur in the future. The role of norms is thus *constructive*: through the agreed statement of voluntary norms, firms and stakeholders are able to construct an approximate model of the game form that they will play in states of the world that they are unable to describe *ex ante* in every detail.

END REMARKS

The cognitive (and constructive) function of norms only brings us to the half-way point in the theory of the game theoretical implementation of the normative model. A well-conceived game form makes it possible to define the players' strategy combinations and the reputation equilibria wherein the firm may be described as acting in support of its reputation, so that after some time stakeholders will begin to trust it. Under the usual condition of the long-run player's far-sightedness, these equilibrium combinations include one equilibrium path such that the firm continues not to abuse the stakeholders, and the stakeholders continue to enter into the relationship with the firm. Nevertheless, in general, this will be just one of the many possible reputation equilibria of the game. Other equilibria will consist of strategy combinations including random compliance with the norm by the firm (a mixed strategy) such that the best response of stakeholders is to yield to the firm's strategy. These equilibria (see Figure 6.3, the Stackelberg equilibrium in particular) admit that a firm has been able

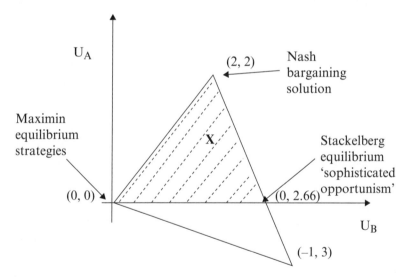

*Figure 6.3   Equilibrium set **X** of the repeated trust game*

to accumulate a reputation for mixed levels of abuse that leaves stakeholders indifferent between entering or not entering into a relationship with the firm.

In other words, when a repeated reputation game is constructively defined in terms of strategies that abide or not by the *ex ante* agreed CSR norm, it will have too many equilibrium points. This occurs for more than just the preferable equilibrium where the firm abstains from abusing stakeholders by strictly complying to the norm and cooperating with them at all times (see Figure 6.3, where the equilibrium set **X** is depicted as the dashed area). The typical game theoretical problem of *multiple equilibria* arises. Here, however, it turns out that CSR norms have three other roles to play in facilitating an equilibrium selection consistent with the normative model.

1. The *normative role*, which answers the question of what (if any) pattern of behaviour and interaction the firm and its stakeholders must select from the set of possible equilibrium patterns to carry out *ex post*, if they put themselves in the *ex ante* position enabling an agreement to be made from an impartial point of view.
2. The *motivational role*, which answers the question of what and how many equilibrium patterns of behaviour – among those that could emerge *ex post* from the interaction between firm and stakeholder – would retain their motivational force if firm and stakeholder were able to agree in an *ex ante* perspective on a CSR norm along the lines of point (1).
3. The *cognitive-predictive role* concerning how a CSR norm affects the beliefs formation process whereby a firm and its stakeholders cognitively converge on a system of mutually consistent expectations, such that they reciprocally predict from one another the execution of a given equilibrium in their *ex post* interaction (given that more than one equilibrium point still retains motivational force according to the answer to question (2)). Does the norm shape the expectation formation process so that in the end it will coincide with what the *ex ante* agreed principle would require of the firm and the stakeholder?

A detailed discussion of these further roles of a CSR social norm within a repeated trust game exceeds the limits of this chapter (see Sacconi, 2008 for more details). To conclude, it may be said nevertheless that a clear game theoretical programme for the implementation of a normative CSR model of corporate governance may be put forward in the terms of a repeated trust game, only once explicitly formulated CSR principles and rules are introduced. This makes it possible not only to make equilibrium patterns of behaviours associated with various degrees of conformity to the model recognizable, but also to allow for these norms to be used as impartial a priori selecting devices among different equilibrium paths (see Binmore, 2005). Moreover, explicit norms of CSR – in so far as they incorporate the ideal of a fair impartial *ex ante* agreement under the 'veil of ignorance' – may be taken as a basis for the *ex post* development of conformist preferences, or a 'sense of justice' (Grimalda and Sacconi, 2005; Faillo and Sacconi, 2007; Sacconi and Faillo, 2009) that reduces the feasible equilibria set to just those of perfect bilateral conformity or perfect bilateral non-conformity. Last but not least, such norms constitute the causal (and psychological) explanation of why players may subscribe to prior beliefs assigned over the different possible equilibrium points such that from these priors an *ex post* learning process may 'librate' until a unique equilibrium is predicted as the solution of the game by all its participants.[20]

NOTES

1. I am grateful to Masahiko Aoki and other participants of the Cournot Centre's conference, 'Does Company Ownership Matter?' for valuable comments. The usual disclaimers apply.
2. On the two main, somewhat alternative, understandings of the contractarian programme in contemporary political philosophy, see Rawls (1971) and Gauthier (1986).
3. To get an idea of the institutional complementarities that may be used here, see Aoki (2001).
4. This view is consistent with the EU Commission's initial definition of CSR as: 'an open governance, reconciling interests of various stakeholders in an overall approach of quality and sustainability' (*Promoting a European Framework for Corporate Social Responsibility*, Green Paper, Brussels, 18 July 2001, p. 4). Moreover, it is consistent with the way CSR is understood in many European multi-stakeholder projects of CSR management systems (see Wieland, 2003), and in particular the Q-RES Management Guidelines (see Sacconi et al., 2003). Although some authors may not subscribe to CSR as the proper term, this view is consistent with how corporate responsibilities and accountability are seen in the stakeholder approach (Freeman, 1984; Freeman and Evans, 1997; Donaldson and Preston, 1995; Clarkson, 1999; Freeman and McVea, 2002; Freeman and Velamuri, 2006).
5. On fiduciary duties, see Flannigan (1989).
6. At first glance, one might object to the idea that many stakeholders, in both the 'strict' and 'broad' senses, do not have relations with a firm such that they formally delegate authority to those who run it (for example, they do not vote). The consequence is that the fiduciary duties as defined earlier do not apply to them. In the model of the social contract as a hypothetical explanation of the origin of the firm, however – see below – all the stakeholders participate in the 'firm's second social contract'. Their trust thus constitutes the authority of the firm's owner and manager. This also explains how the latter's authority may be accepted by the other stakeholders. Moreover, the hypothetical social contract is typically used to explain how authority – that is, legitimate power – may come about at both the political and organizational levels; see, for example, Watt (1982), Raz (1985) and Green (1990). For a discussion of managerial authority, see McMahon (1989) and Sacconi (1991).

7. I have proposed in a previous book (Sacconi, 1991) a view of managerial ethics based on a similar analysis of the theory of the firm, as well as on the cooperative game theory of the firm put forward by Masahiko Aoki (1984). The idea of extended fiduciary duties based on the social contract of the firm was also given in my 1997 book (see Sacconi, 1997, 2000).

8. This contractarian view on the theory of the firm owes a great deal to both John Rawls (1971, 1993) and David Gauthier (1986); see also Binmore (1991, 1998, 2005). For the first formulation of the theory of the corporate social contract, based on the revision of the neo-institutionalist theory of the firm and including reference to the problem of the abuse of authority *vis-à-vis* stakeholders, see Sacconi (1991, 2000, 2006a, 2007a). For a formulation external to economic theory, see Dunfee and Donaldson (1995).

9. This step requires the decision maker to put him- or herself under a 'veil of ignorance' regarding his/her own identity. The aim is to put him- /herself into each of the other positions in order to discover what s/he would accept if s/he were in the shoes of each stakeholder sitting at the bargaining table. This veil of ignorance is thinner than Rawls's. Through gaining perception of each individual's point of view, the decision maker is better able to appreciate each player's preferences. The Rawlsian veil of ignorance, on the other hand, makes it impossible to learn any individual characteristics that would permit reconstruction of other individuals' life plans (Rawls, 1971). Under such a veil, the decision maker is unable to distinguish one player from another.

10. This danger is also stressed by Jean Tirole (2001), who nonetheless recognizes the relevance of the stakeholder approach to corporate governance.

11. For the theory of bargaining games, see Harsanyi (1977). Aoki uses the Nash bargaining solution in his theory of the firm, which envisages impartial governance by managers (Aoki, 1984).

12. See Brock (1979) and Sacconi (1991, 2000).

13. See Hobbes, *Leviathan* (1651 [1994], part 1, chapter 13).

14. Interestingly, Blair and Stout (1999) also adopt the analogy between the firm and the two social contracts typical of the social contract tradition.

15. Note that it is remuneration in utility that is meant here and not necessarily in money. Put in economic terms, this remuneration consists of the consumer rent, the producer rent, the worker rent, and so on, accruing to each of them from the firm's transactions. This means that some stakeholders may not want to receive monetary benefits from the firm, but rather improvements in working conditions or in purchasing power, in the quality of goods and services, of contractual conditions, and so on, to which the shares of the surplus are in any case devoted.

16. The 2006 UK company law reform, Art. 172, states: 'Duty to promote the success of the company:

    (1) A director of a company must act in the way he considers, in good faith, would be most likely to promote the success of the company for the benefit of its members as a whole, and in doing so have regard (amongst other matters) to –

    (a) the likely consequences of any decision in the long term,
    (b) the interests of the company's employees,
    (c) the need to foster the company's business relationships with suppliers, customers and others,
    (d) the impact of the company's operations on the community and the environment,
    (e) the desirability of the company maintaining a reputation for high standards of business conduct, and
    (f) the need to act fairly as between members of the company.

    (2) Where or to the extent that the purposes of the company consist of or include purposes other than the benefit of its members, subsection (1) has effect as if the reference to promoting the success of the company for the benefit of its members were to achieving those purposes'.

17. This is probably the opinion of Michael Jensen when he says, 'Indeed, it is a basic principle of enlightened value maximization that *we cannot maximize the long-term market value of an organization if we ignore or mistreat any important constituency.* We cannot create value without good relations with customers, employees, financial backers, suppliers, regulators, and communities. But having said that, we can now use the value criterion for choosing among those competing interests. I say "competing" interests because no constituency can be given full satisfaction if the firm is to flourish and survive' (Jensen, 2001, p. 17). See also Sternberg (1999).
18. This idea is closely akin to that of 'principles of a corporate culture' developed by David Kreps (1990a), with the important difference, however, that I defend universalistic corporate ethics, not the relative-to-context notion of 'culture' (see Sacconi, 2000).
19. On logic default reasoning, see Reiter (1980); on its uses in game theory, see Bacharach (1994), Sacconi (2000, 2007b) and Sacconi and Moretti (2008).
20. On 'eductive' equilibrium selection – as basically understood in this chapter – see Harsanyi and Selten (1988). On 'evolutionary' equilibrium selection mechanisms with learning through repeated plays, see Young (1998). The distinction between 'eductive' versus 'evolutionary' equilibrium selection dynamics is provided by Ken Binmore (1987).

REFERENCES

AA.VV. (1993), 'The corporate stakeholder conference', *University of Toronto Law Journal*, **62** (3), pp. 297–793.
Aoki, M. (1984), *The Cooperative Game Theory of the Firm*, Cambridge: Cambridge University Press.
Aoki, M. (2001), *Toward a Comparative Institutional Analysis*, Cambridge, MA: MIT Press.
Aoki, M. (2007a), 'Three-level approach to the rules of the societal game: generic, substantive and operational', paper presented at the conference on 'Changing Institutions (in developed countries): Economics, Politics and Welfare' Paris, 24–25 May.
Aoki, M. (2007b), 'Endogenizing institutions and institutional change', *Journal of Institutional Economics*, **3**, pp. 1–39.
Bacharach, M. (1994), 'The epistemic structure of the game', *Theory and Decisions*, **37**, pp. 7–48.
Binmore, K. (1987), 'Modeling rational players', *Economics and Philosophy*, **1** (3), pp. 9–55 and **2** (4), pp. 179–214.
Binmore, K. (1991), 'Game theory and the social contract', in R. Selten (ed.), *Game Equilibrium Models II, Methods, Morals, Markets*, Berlin: Springer Verlag.
Binmore, K. (1998), *Just Playing*, Cambridge, MA: MIT Press.
Binmore, K. (2005), *Natural Justice*, Oxford: Oxford University Press.
Blair, M. and L. Stout (1999), 'A team production theory of corporate law', *Virginia Law Review*, **85** (2), pp. 248–328.
Blair, M. and L. Stout (2006), 'Specific investment: explaining anomalies in corporate law', *Journal of Corporation Law*, **31**, pp. 719–44.
Brock, H. (1979), 'A game theoretical account of social justice', *Theory and Decision*, **11**, pp. 239–65.
Clarkson, M. (1999), *Principles of Stakeholder Management*, Toronto: Clarkson Center for Business Ethics.

Coleman, J. (1992), *Risks and Wrongs*, Cambridge: Cambridge University Press.

Donaldson, T. and L.E. Preston (1995), 'Stakeholder theory and the corporation: concepts evidence and implication', *Academy of Management Review*, **20** (1), pp. 65–91.

Dunfee, T. and T. Donaldson (1995), 'Contractarian business ethics', *Business Ethics Quarterly*, **5**, pp. 167–72.

Faillo, M. and L. Sacconi (2007), 'Norm compliance: the contribution of behavioral economics models', in A. Innocenti and P. Sbriglia (eds), *Games, Rationality and Behavior*, London: Palgrave Macmillan, pp. 101–33.

Flannigan, R. (1989), 'The fiduciary obligation', *Oxford Journal of Legal Studies*, **9**, pp. 285–94.

Freeman, R.E. (1984), *Strategic Management: A Stakeholder Approach*, Boston, MA: Pitman.

Freeman, R.E. and P. Evans (1997), 'Stakeholder management and the modern corporation: Kantian capitalism', in T.L. Beauchamp and N. Bowie (eds), *Ethical Theory and Business*, 5th edn, Englewood Cliffs, NJ: Prentice-Hall, pp. 66–76.

Freeman, R.E. and J. McVea (2002), 'A stakeholder approach to strategic management', Working Paper 01-02, Darden Graduate School of Business Administration, University of Virginia.

Freeman, R.E. and S. Ramakrishna Velamuri (2006), 'A new approach to CSR company stakeholder responsibility', in A. Kakabadse and M. Morsing (eds), *Corporate Social Responsibility Reconciling Aspiration And Application*, London: Palgrave Macmillan, pp. 9–23.

Fudenberg, D. (1995), 'Explaining cooperation and commitment in repeated games', in J.J. Laffont (ed.), *Advances in Economic Theory, 6th World Congress*, Cambridge: Cambridge University Press, pp. 89–131.

Fudenberg, D. and D. Levine (1989), 'Reputation and equilibrium selection in games with a patient player', *Econometrica*, **57**, pp. 759–78.

Gauthier, D. (1986), *Morals by Agreement*, Oxford: Clarendon Press.

Green, L. (1990), *The Authority of the State*, Oxford: Clarendon Press.

Grimalda, G. and L. Sacconi (2005), 'The constitution of the not-for-profit organisation: reciprocal conformity to morality', *Constitutional Political Economy*, **16** (3), pp. 249–76.

Grossman, S. and O. Hart (1986), 'The costs and benefits of ownership: a theory of vertical and lateral integration', *Journal of Political Economy*, **94**, pp. 691–719.

Hansmann, H. (1996), *The Ownership of the Enterprise*, Cambridge, MA: Harvard University Press.

Hare, R.M. (1981), *Moral Thinking*, Oxford: Clarendon Press.

Harsanyi, J.C. (1977), *Rational Behaviour and Bargaining Equilibrium in Games and Social Situations*, Cambridge: Cambridge University Press.

Harsanyi, J.C and R. Selten (1988), *A General Theory of Equilibrium Selection*, Cambridge, MA: MIT Press.

Hart, O. (1995), *Firms, Contracts and Financial Structure*, Oxford: Clarendon Press.

Hart, O. and J. Moore (1990), 'Property rights and the nature of the firm', *Journal of Political Economy*, **98**, pp. 1119–58.

Hobbes, T. (1994), *Leviathan*, English edition with selected variants from the Latin edition of 1668, Edwin Curley (ed.), Indianapolis, IN: Hackett.

Jensen, M.C. (2001), 'Value maximization, stakeholder theory, and the corporate objective function', *Journal of Applied Corporate Finance*, **14** (3), pp. 8–21.

Kalai, E. and M. Smorodinsky (1975), 'Other solutions to Nash's bargaining problem', *Econometrica*, **43** (3), pp. 880–95.

Kreps, D. (1990a), 'Corporate culture and economic theory', in J. Alt and K. Shepsle (eds), *Perspectives on Positive Political Economy*, Cambridge: Cambridge University Press, pp. 90–143.

Kreps, D. (1990b), *Games and Economic Modelling*, Oxford: Oxford University Press.

Lewis, D. (1969), *Convention. A Philosophical Study*, Cambridge, MA: Harvard University Press.

McMahon, C. (1989), 'Managerial authority', *Ethics*, **100**, pp. 33–53.

Meese, A.L. (2002), 'The team production theory of corporate law: a critical assessment', *William and Mary Law Review*, **43**, 1629–39.

Nash, J. (1950), 'The bargaining problem', *Econometrica*, **18**, pp. 155–62.

Posner, E.A. (2000), *Law and Social Norms*, Cambridge, MA: Harvard University Press.

Rajan, R. and L. Zingales (2000), 'The governance of the new enterprise', in X. Vives (ed.), *Corporate Governance, Theoretical and Empirical Perspectives*, Cambridge: Cambridge University Press, pp. 201–26.

Rawls, J. (1971), *A Theory of Justice*, Oxford: Oxford University Press.

Rawls, J. (1993), *Political Liberalism*, New York: Columbia University Press.

Raz, J. (1985), 'Authority and justification', *Philosophy and Public Affairs*, **14** (1), pp. 3–29.

Reiter, R. (1980), 'A logic for default reasoning', *Artificial Intelligence*, **13**, pp. 81–132.

Sacconi, L. (1991), *Etica degli affari, individui, imprese e mercati nella prospettiva dell'etica razionale*, Milan: Il Saggiatore.

Sacconi, L. (1997), *Economia, etica, organizzazione*, Bari: Laterza.

Sacconi, L. (2000), *The Social Contract of the Firm. Economics, Ethics and Organisation*, Berlin: Springer Verlag.

Sacconi, L. (2006a), 'CSR as a model of extended corporate governance, an explanation based on the economic theory of social contract, reputation and reciprocal conformism', in F. Cafaggi (ed.) *Reframing Self-Regulation in European Private Law*, The Hague/London/Boston: Kluwer Law International, pp. 289–346.

Sacconi, L. (2006b), 'A social contract account for CSR as an extended model of corporate governance (Part I): Rational bargaining and justification', *Journal of Business Ethics*, **68** (3) pp. 259–81.

Sacconi, L. (2007a), 'A social contract account for CSR as an extended model of corporate governance (Part II): Compliance, reputation and reciprocity', *Journal of Business Ethics*, **75** (1), pp. 77–96.

Sacconi, L. (2007b), 'Incomplete contracts and corporate ethics: a game theoretical model under fuzzy information', in F. Cafaggi, A. Nicita and U. Pagano (eds), *Legal Orderings and Economic Institutions*, London: Routledge, pp. 310–50.

Sacconi, L. (2008), 'CSR as contractarian model of multi-stakeholder corporate governance and the game-theory of its implementation', Department of Economics Working Paper 18, University of Trento.

Sacconi, L. and S. Moretti (2008), 'A fuzzy logic and default reasoning model of social norms and equilibrium selection in games under unforeseen contingencies',

International Journal of Uncertainty, Fuzziness and Knowledge-Based Systems, **16** (1), pp. 59–81.

Sacconi, L. and M. Faillo (2009), 'Conformity, reciprocity and the sense of justice: how social contract-based preferences and beliefs explain norm compliance: the experimental evidence', *Constitutional Political Economy*, forthcoming.

Sacconi, L., S. DeColle and E. Baldin (2003), 'The Q-RES project: the quality of social and ethical responsibility of corporations', in Wieland (ed.), pp. 60–117.

Sternberg, E. (1999), 'The stakeholder concept: a mistake doctrine, foundation for business responsibility', Issue Paper 4, November, available at: http://papers.ssrn.com/sol3/papers.cfm?abstract_id=263144.

Stout, L. (2006), 'Social norms and other-regarding preferences', in J.N. Drobak (ed.), *Norms and the Law*, Cambridge: Cambridge University Press, pp. 13–34.

Tirole, J. (2001), 'Corporate governance', *Econometrica*, **69** (1), pp. 1–35.

Watt, E.D. (1982), *Authority*, London: Croom Helm.

Wieland, J. (ed.) (2003), *Standards and Audits for Ethics Management Systems: The European Perspective*, Berlin: Springer Verlag.

Williamson, O. (1975), *Market and Hierarchies*, New York: Free Press.

Williamson, O. (1986), *The Economic Institutions of Capitalism*, New York: Free Press.

Young, H.P. (1998), *Industrial Strategy and Social Structure: An Evolutionary Theory of Institutions*, Princeton, NJ: Princeton University Press.

Zimmerman, H.J. (1991), *Fuzzy Set Theory and Its Applications*, 2nd rev. edn, Dordrecht and Boston, MA: Kluwer Academic Press.

7. Round table discussion: Shareholder rights in European corporations: impact on economic performance

Margaret Blair, Jean-Paul Fitoussi, Gregory Jackson and Robert M. Solow

Robert Solow (MIT)   What are the effects of new forms of shareholder participation in companies in Europe, and in particular their impact on growth? I think that 'growth' has become too much of a buzz-word in discussions like this, and I would rather think that the subject is not the influence of new forms of shareholder participation on growth, but on economic performance – however one cares to define that. I would invite everybody not to be too narrowly focused on proportional rates of growth, but to think about such things as the level of output, the ability to exploit capacity to produce, the ability to generate an equitable distribution of income, and so on.

We have three participants in the discussion: I'm going to ask Margaret Blair to be the first speaker. She is at the Vanderbilt University Law School – that's her permanent base. For Europeans, Vanderbilt is in Nashville, Tennessee – centre of the cult of Elvis Presley and home to the Grand Ole Opry – institutions with which you are probably not acquainted, and with which I think you will survive not being so well acquainted. Margaret Blair is, I think, on the other side of the Atlantic, in North America, the pioneer in challenging sole attention to the shareholder benefit model of the corporation, in favour of a sort of team model, recognizing the business enterprise as a team involved in production and marketing.

After that I shall call on Gregory Jackson, who is at King's College London, and whose work – much of it at least – on the effect of corporation governance on relations with employees has been referred to throughout this book. Then, third, I shall call on Jean-Paul Fitoussi, who is an old friend of mine, and an important all-round economist and chairman of the French Observatoire des Conjonctures Économiques, which is a research institution and think-tank. I shall ask him to be the concluding speaker.

Margaret Blair (Vanderbilt University)   When I began to think about it and to engage in the issue of understanding corporate governance – thinking about who should play what role and what the incentive structure should be like, what the institutional arrangements should be like – I was struck from the beginning that the agency theory model had gained an enormous amount of importance in directing and framing discussions in the US, particularly those taking place not only among economists, but also among finance theorists and legal scholars. I felt that there was something troubling about that model, and that was that the agency model is an asymmetric model: it starts from the premise that the problem is defined as how the principal is going to get the agent to do what the principal wants the agent to do. That model was very smoothly applied to the corporate governance problem by saying that the central problem of corporate governance is that of getting the management to do what the shareholders want them to do. Notice how several things happened in that transposition, in that we substituted the shareholders for the principal in that relationship, and in so doing we assumed some things that are not consistent with corporate law about what it is that shareholders do and what their role is. We were told that shareholders were the owners and the bearers of the residual risk, which is why they were the principal in the relationship. We were told a variety of different things about that, but in setting up that model, we asked, 'how did corporate governance have to work, so that managers would do what shareholders wanted?'. No one ever asked whether shareholders would be required to do what managers wanted. The assumption was somehow that managers and other employees could be protected by complete contracts. The problem was therefore simply getting all those people who work under contract to do what the shareholders wanted.

I found this very troubling, and I began to think about a team production style of model, which interestingly has its roots in the way Ronald Coase, Adolf Berle and Gardiner Means, and Armen Alchian and Harold Demsetz first described the problem. That is the notion that there is a group of parties that come together, and each of them brings a different kind of input, and that input may be difficult to measure and difficult to contract about. So the parties look for an institutional arrangement that will help them all to work together to create an economic surplus. The question is then how to achieve that. There have never been many good solutions to that problem; they all bring their own problems. Nevertheless, there has been a variety of solutions that have been put out there. Oliver Hart, for instance, suggested that the parties who come together would allocate control rights to the party who brought the most important team-specific inputs to the problem – so that party would have the control rights.

The solution that I found the most intriguing argues that a solution to the problem would be for all of the team members to delegate an important control right to an outside third party, which would then be charged with making one important decision. That would be to decide which team, or which coalition of participants, should be awarded the operating rights, and to award them to the team that could produce the largest surplus. The role of the third party – in being delegated that important control right – is to prevent the other participants in the team – who no longer have that control right – from selling the assets out from under each other. So no party who is a member of the team, in terms of bringing some team-specific assets to the table, is allowed to sell control rights over team-specific assets; that right is delegated to a third party. I looked at that argument, and I thought, 'It sounds to me like what a board of directors does'.

I then began to look at corporate law, and I started to work with Lynn Stout, who is a corporate law scholar (unlike myself, a mere economist), and she began to explain to me all the ways in which corporate law works in that way. Corporate law in the US delegates incredible power, almost all powers over the operation of the corporation, to the board of directors. Now, the board of directors can delegate to internal management – and they usually do – but the statutory power lies with the board of directors. Shareholders have extremely limited power. They can basically vote up or down on a board of directors nominated by the existing board; they get the possibility of veto rights for certain transformative transactions, and they get a claim on any distributions made – a *pro rata* claim – but they don't get to control the choice over whether to make those distributions. So the way in which corporate law operates is that shareholders who put money into the firm in effect accept a very important constraint: they cannot get their money back out at their own discretion. If they want out, they have to find another party to buy their shares from them, and the capital remains locked in the enterprise. This is really important for preserving and protecting the interests of the non-shareholder participants in the enterprise, that the shareholders' capital is stuck inside the firm until and unless the board of directors decides to pay it out. So that was what got me interested in the team production idea.

I sat down the other night and thought: we've got the team production idea, let's set up a contest here, a horse race if you will, between the shareholder-primacy/shareholder-control story of what corporate governance ought to be about and the team production story. I came up with a total of six reasons why shareholder primacy and/or shareholder control are *not* likely to be consistent with maximizing total social wealth. The first is that shareholders – and this isn't necessarily part of team production theory, but it's a standard argument – don't have the day-to-day operating knowledge about what's going on inside the corporation; they're too diffuse. It's very costly for them to make decisions, and to put the decision-making authority in the hands of shareholders is to take it away from the parties who know best what's going on. Second, there's the problem of inter-shareholder opportunism. Minority shareholders need to be protected from oppression by the majority and controlling shareholders, and also majority shareholders need to be protected against hold-up by the minority. So shareholders might not necessarily have the same interests, and they need to be protected from each other. That suggests putting decision-making rights into the hands of someone other than the shareholders. Third, there's the problem of inter-stakeholder opportunism. Shareholders are not the only parties who make investments that are at risk in the enterprise, contrary to the standard principal–agent story, which is that shareholders bear the residual risk, and so they should have the residual control rights. That is simply not true. Any party that contributes a firm-specific kind of input has something at risk, and that party needs to be protected from the shareholders and from other stakeholders. The fourth idea is the one I just mentioned, that yielding control to a third party, such as a board of directors which does not itself have to make extensive firm-specific investments, serves as a mechanism by which all of the team members can credibly commit to each other – that they aren't going to pull the plug on the enterprise prematurely as a way to hold up and grab more of the surplus rents.

Fifth, going back to the question of who's bearing the risk, it is now very clear, seeing some of the things that have been going on with hedge funds, that shareholders not only don't bear all the risk, but that they can benefit (as we know from options theory) by pushing risk off onto other participants. Moreover, it appears that with the kind of capital structuring opportunities now available on the market, shareholders can hedge away their entire risk, which means that they are in a position to be able to completely separate the risk-bearing from the control rights. Other stakeholders cannot do that, or rarely. Other stakeholders have investment risks, such as human capital, that are specific and not fungible. There is not a security that they can buy or sell in the market in order to hedge their risk, whereas the shareholders' only claim is a financial claim. Money is fungible, so they can go into the market and buy and sell securities and completely hedge their risk. And sixth is a point that Christophe Clerc makes, that giving shareholders control means taking control away from parties that are accountable and giving it to parties that aren't accountable. So giving control to shareholders strikes me as very troubling.

Those are theoretical reasons. Do we have empirical reasons to believe that shareholder primacy maximizes social value? The answer is very little, if any. There is very little evidence that when shareholder activists begin to get involved, they actually create value – even for other shareholders, let alone value in the sense of total social value. And another empirical observation: the attempt to align directors' and managers' interests with those of shareholders through what is an extensive practice in the US, and is now moving overseas, of compensating executives and directors with stock options, does not appear to have had the effect of preventing executive malfeasance (as we have seen in the case of Enron, WorldCom and the banking crisis that precipitated a world-wide recession in 2008–2009). Neither has it served to rein in executive compensation generally. In fact, it appears to have created a mechanism by which executives can capture more of the rents and increase their total compensation substantially.

On the other side of the scales, it seems to me that there's really only one powerful argument in favour of shareholder primacy. That is that the share price provides a convenient metric, which is readily available at all times, by which to measure and evaluate executive performance. 'What have they done for the share price?' We look at the markets, and we have reason to believe that the markets are reasonably efficient, and that markets at least reflect the value that shareholders can capture, if not total social value. So because we have a simple metric, it becomes easier to create compensation systems and evaluation systems to try to get managers to focus on their version of wealth creation, which then becomes just share value maximization. Of course, as we've already said, share value maximization may not be wealth creating; it could be wealth diminishing in some circumstances. So that's one set of responses. What I find really delightful about Lorenzo Sacconi's contribution is that it appears that he may have come up with a response to that particular argument – that we need a metric that produces a unique solution. I think Lorenzo and others who are interested in this problem have a lot more work to do to be able to answer the question about how to implement it. Clearly, it is easy to say that there is a nice, unique solution in game theory; it's harder to say how individuals operating with each other in the real world will arrive at that particular solution. That's a reasonable direction to go in for future research: to think about how the parties that participate together can, if possible, implement the solution that Lorenzo Sacconi has recommended.

Another problem that we need to look at with respect to that particular structure, and that we need to solve before the team production model will be widely accepted as a substitute for the agency model, is what to do when the external environment changes. Lorenzo Sacconi looks at what constrains the participants to choose an equilibrium that doesn't produce negative externalities on the parties who are not part of the decision-making process. In addition to that, and I think that's a real problem, his answer is to appeal to certain norms and certain ways of getting managers and board members to internalize the broader social interest, so that they won't form a corporation in the first place if it's not expected that there are some net rents to be created. This is because none of the voluntary partici-pants in the firm has an incentive to participate in the firm if it's not creat-ing rents. If there's no surplus being generated, then why do it? I thought that that was a good answer, as far as it went, but it leaves open the ques-tion of what happens if the environment changes, so that the solution they thought they had agreed upon when they formed the corporation is no longer the best or a good solution, or even a potential solution. One of the things that we don't understand very well is how institutions can and do evolve in response to changes in the external environment that undermine the validity, or the 'social acceptance', if you will, of the solution that had been reached by the previous participants in the firm.

I have an idea about beginning to think about this that I want to toss out, because I have this tremendous opportunity to put this on the table before one of the world's most renowned macroeconomists. (I took inter-mediate macro theory from Professor Solow in 1983; that was my intro-duction to macroeconomic theory and some of the important work that he has done.) In thinking about institutional change, there is a problem of trying to do these empirical studies about whether corporate governance affects human resources management (HRM) or whether HRM affects corporate governance, or corporate governance affects value creation, or corporate governance affects HRM, which in turn affects value creation. The question is: how long does it take, given a change in the environment, for institutions to move to a new equilibrium? They may be out of equilib-rium for a very long time, I suspect, and I think that we need to look at it in terms of decades rather than years. Annual data helps, and 20 years of annual data is better than three, but, nonetheless, trying to get some sense of how long it takes institutions society-wide – rather than a single institu-tion, a single corporation, for example – to respond, must be approached in terms of decades, and here's what makes me think that.

I was looking at what it was about the 1980s that caused the market upheavals we saw in the form of leveraged buyouts and hostile buyouts, which forced us to rethink what we thought we knew about corporate law and corporate governance. What is it that may be going on in the economy now would be a similar question. I had what I thought was a reasonable answer to what was going on in the 1980s, but I don't have a very good answer for what's going on now and why we're seeing the resurgence of private equity buyouts of various sorts. What I did earlier was to take a look at the macroeconomic data on how total output is divided between labour and capital. If you do that (at least for the US), you see that the share of capital was high in the 1950s and 1960s, but it seemed to peak some time around 1968, and then it started falling, and it fell and fell and fell, until about 1982, and beginning in about 1983 it turned back up. I haven't looked at it in about the last 18 months to two years, but when I did look at it – and I don't have any reason to believe that it has collapsed since then – the share of output going to capital was finally above the levels that it had reached in the late 1960s, for the first time. So, what happened in the 1980s, I suspect, was a massive change in the underlying institutions, so that they could focus on the return to capital for a change. The returns to capital had been declining for a very long period of time by the early 1980s.

What we saw in response was the institutional argument that we need to give shareholders control 'because that's the right thing to do', not because shareholders' returns had been so dismal for a long period of time that we need to make some adjustments. The argument was that managers are bad, managers are misusing resources, and in order to correct that, we need to give a lot more power to shareholders. That began to happen over the course of the 1980s. As I mentioned, we saw the share of total output going to shareholders rising, with a fairly dramatic change between 1982 and 1990, but continuing to go up in the 1990s and, as far as I know, in the twenty-first century. That suggests to me that institutional change was very slow, and that it took several decades to get the complete adjustment.

I don't know whether we now have in place something that will continue to produce more and more returns to capital and lower returns to labour, or whether we are now ripe for a reversal of that. But the fact that private equity firms have been able to raise capital – not only in the US but around the world – and to begin to go in and force changes in corporations that go in the direction of increasing returns to shareholders (sometimes at the expense of returns to workers, of wages or working conditions or other ways in which workers can capture the wealth created), suggests to me that the cycle hasn't run its course and that we're still observing institutional changes that are moving in the direction of rewarding capital. So is this crazy, or is it a reasonable framework to look at this in terms of the share of output going to labour versus capital over an extended period of time? I don't have a conclusion, just those thoughts and questions to leave you with, that I hope over time those of us who are in this business can begin to pursue and take apart.

Gregory Jackson (then at King's College London)[1] I have some empirical and comparative observations to make. This round table is about European companies and shareholder protection. I'm going to look at the legal protection of shareholders from a cross-national comparative perspective and talk about economic growth, mergers and acquisitions (M&A) and employment, and give some critical reflections on the state of play in this research area.

In Europe, there's a lot of concern about minority protection for share-holders and the idea that the high level of blockholding in Europe makes it important to enhance the legal rights of shareholders, particularly minor-ity shareholders. If you look at the policy debate, the expected impact of that might be to de-concentrate ownership, improve the allocation of risk in financial markets, solve agency problems by giving shareholders more leverage to influence companies and is even sometimes hypothesized to improve economic growth rates in Europe through more investment. That said, it's not particularly clear in the literature how shareholder rights impact growth, how they impact markets such as M&A, or particu-larly how they impact employment issues. A first issue involves measur-ing investor protection, which relates to Simon Deakin's research with Matthias Siems and other colleagues at Cambridge.[2] It is worth briefly reviewing several figures from their paper. You are probably familiar with the La Porta index of shareholder rights around the world for major OECD countries. If you look at 1990, the average score on this index was 3 out of 6; in 2000 it was something like 3.7 out of 6. So over the last decade, the trend has been towards a modest increase in shareholder protection around the world. But this particular measure has been criticized for not being very accurate, countries put in the wrong places, and so on. More recently, the leximetrics approach from Cambridge has given us a differ-ent picture. The interesting thing is that it shows, over the last 10 years, a very strong convergence in the sense of a general trend towards increasing shareholder protection (see Figure 7.1). It also gives a different picture of where countries fall relative to the La Porta index.

We see here that France may be surprisingly high on shareholder protection. Compared to the La Porta index for countries like Japan or Germany, the differences across what we usually think of as high share-holder-protection countries and low shareholder-protection countries are not that big on aggregate according to this more comprehensive measure. If you read the very good paper by Matthias Siems,[3] he says that although the aggregate scores that are similar, the 'styles' (though he doesn't use that word) of how shareholders are protected and what protections they get are different across countries. For me as a comparative sociologist, not a lawyer, the interesting point is that when we compare countries in terms of legal protection of shareholders, the question is perhaps no longer 'do countries protect shareholders', but *how* do they do it.

Now, if we look at the impact in terms of growth based on aggregate country-level evidence – linking shareholder protection on aggregate

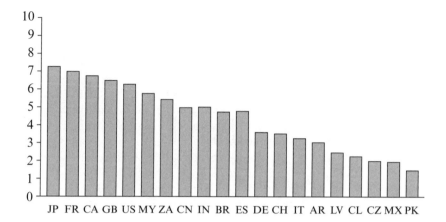

Notes: JP – Japan; FR-France; CA – Canada; GB – United Kingdom; US – United States; MY – Malaysia; ZA – South Africa; CN – China; IN – India; BR – Brazil; ES – Spain; DE – Germany; CH – Switzerland; IT – Italy; AR – Argentina; LV – Latvia; CL – Chile; CZ – Czech Republic; MX – Mexico; PK – Pakistan.

Source: Siems (2008).

Figure 7.1   Shareholder protection aggregate, 2005

with growth on aggregate – it's a tricky business. It is hard to find much evidence of direct links at that level of analysis in the literature. More evidence exists regarding the impact of shareholder rights on other things, like ownership dispersion, stock market activity or M&A activity. It's also well known, although I wouldn't say it's a causal link, that protection for shareholders and protection for employees have an inverse relationship.

So if we look at what would happen if we increase shareholder rights in Europe, it raises a whole other set of interesting questions about stock market activity or M&A activity. There is no correlation between countries that have high aggregate levels of M&A activity and growth as far as I can determine from the studies. But high M&A activity has a strong negative correlation with, say, the average tenure of employees or the rates of corporate downsizing, and a positive correlation with the Gini coefficient. So countries that have lots of M&A activity, for whatever reason, seem to have a more unequal distribution of incomes, on aggregate. So we need to look at inequality, as well as growth.

From the perspective of comparative institutional analysis, an interesting question is: how are shareholder rights related to the other institutional features of different national economies? Some papers have looked at this. We have already had a critique of the distinction between

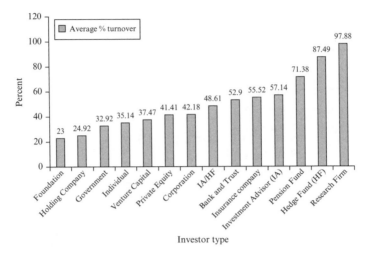

Figure 7.2   Percentage of annual turnover of equity portfolio

coordinated-market economies and liberal-market economies, the argument being that shareholder rights can produce growth if they complement
the other types of institutions in the economy. The idea is that if you have
two types of economies, then you should find growth in a U-shaped relationship; if you have a pure liberal or pure coordinated market economy,
you should find higher growth than if you have a 'mix-and-match'
approach to institutional design. Again here, the evidence is patchy, and
it becomes surprisingly hard to draw general conclusions. It's an interesting approach, nonetheless, to look at combinations or configurations of
institutions rather than seeing shareholder protection in isolation.

The other more micro-level issue emerges when shareholder rights
concern the different types of shareholders themselves. Shareholder structure is mostly talked about in terms of the concentration of share ownership, so that we look at the relative protection of blockholders versus
minority shareholders. Here are some data that I calculated on investors
registered in the UK in 2006 as part of an ESRC (UK Economic and
Social Research Council) project (see Figure 7.2). The aim was to look
more closely at the issue of the strategies of investors, and the issue of
short-termism.

If you look at the data for hedge funds or pension funds, they have
very high rates of turnover compared to private equity, or venture capital,
which are potentially more 'long term'. I don't think you could describe a
40 per cent turnover rate for private equity as 'long term', but it is longer
term than hedge funds and pension funds. In our ESRC project, we

Table 7.1 *Comparison of equity portfolio characteristics of 10 largest UK investors, by type*

	Number of stocks in equity portfolio	Largest holding as a % of portfolio	Largest purchase as a % of largest holding	Largest sale (%)
Hedge funds	302	15	27	−47
Pension funds	214	16	20	−19
Private equity	8.7	63	10	−46

Source: Own calculations, Thomson BankerOne Ownership.

compared portfolio characteristics of UK hedge funds, pension funds and private equity funds. Here we see big differences in their styles of investment and the numbers of stocks held, and the portfolio of the typical size of the larger size of holding is much higher for the private equity funds (see Table 7.1). It is also interesting to look at the size of chunks with which the investors buy in and exit out, and how quickly they do so. The largest sale of a hedge fund was 47 per cent of its holding, while the largest sale of a pension fund was 19 per cent. This suggests that hedge funds may be going out much more quickly than pension funds.

These types of differences raise the following question: when you protect shareholders, who are you protecting, and what sorts of styles or strategies for creating and realizing value are important? This is starting to be looked at in Europe because of the debate over hedge funds and private equity, but there's plenty more research to do.

Now moving on to mergers and acquisitions, the comparative literature again suggests that there are some countries where the market for corporate control is very active, and there are some, in continental Europe or Japan, where it's not very active. In Figure 7.3, we look at how these M&A markets are evolving: the lines show the value of M&A deals over GDP, comparing the early 1990s with the more recent period. In France, Germany and Japan, the level of M&A is going up dramatically – in Japan from an extremely low level – so there's a fivefold increase from the baseline.

The UK seems to have an almost hyperactive market: it is nearly twice as high as the levels of deal activity that you find in the US. What does this general increase in activity mean for the role of shareholders or corporate governance? Takeovers are a very interesting topic, because it's an area where the two shareholder-oriented models of the US and UK actually differ in their approach to the legal regulation of takeovers and the role

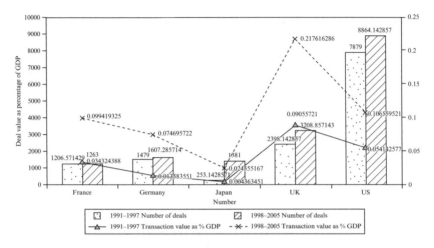

*Figure 7.3   Volume of M&A 1991–97 versus 1998–2005, number of deals
            and deal value as percentage of GDP*

of shareholders in deciding the outcomes of takeovers. For example, the
idea of equal treatment of shareholders during a bidding period is crucial
in the UK, and has been transplanted to Germany and France through
European measures. However, as Margaret Blair pointed out, in the US
quite a few rights are vested within the board itself. It's the board that represents shareholders' interests initially in the case of a takeover, and maybe
not surprisingly, Japan has followed this approach. The main knock-on to
that is that you have, in different shapes and sizes, something like 'poison
pill' defences in the US and Japan, but not so in Europe – although I do
understand that in France some firms have adapted quasi-poison pills in
some fashion, so please help me to understand this point!

So there's a fundamental difference. If you think of the UK and US as
both being countries where shareholder protection is high, the conception
of how shareholders should be protected in the event of a takeover is still
very different and leads to interesting differences in takeover activity. I'll
run quickly through some data points. Looking at the increasing M&A
activity in France, Germany and Japan, we find that M&A activity in these
countries is very different from the US and the UK (see Table 7.2). The
most obvious point is that most deals in the UK/US are mergers – companies merge together – whereas in Europe and Japan it's more common just
to acquire an ownership stake. So it's not a merger, but an acquisition of a
stake where the target company remains legally independent.

Next, the percentage of ownership the buyer has before a deal is rather
high in France, Germany and Japan; in the US and UK it might creep up

Table 7.2   Mergers and acquisitions of listed firms, by form of transaction, 1991–2005

	France	Germany	Japan	UK	USA
Acquisition of majority interest (%)	23	30	13	6	6
Acquisition of partial interest (%)	52	55	68	46	45
Acquisition of remaining interest (%)	17	8	7	3	3
Merger (%)	8	7	12	45	45
Number of transactions	2,000	1,110	2,256	2,715	13,398

to about 5 per cent, but not exceed that. Now, looking at what happens during a deal, as I just said, in France, Germany and Japan you might acquire 30 or 40 per cent of the target company; in the US and UK you acquire majority ownership; you take it over properly. So you can think of M&A markets as being much more 'arm's length' or distant and market-like in the US and UK, so that buyer and target go from having no prior business relationship to one of complete control. In Japan, a pre-existing social and business relationship exists – maybe as a group company, or through a relationship with a main bank – and that continues in a different way after the acquisition. Not surprisingly, the degree of hostility of takeovers is different.

In the 1990–2005 period, the number of hostile deals was still very small in France, Germany and Japan, compared to the UK/US. (The success ratio of hostile deals is about twice as high in the UK as in the US – which reflects the differences mentioned before regarding the role of the board and defensive measures.) You might be tempted to conclude: 'Well yes, but the Japanese market, the French market and the German market are not very open. They're not real markets for corporate control in the sense that you can buy and sell any type of company you like'. Most agency theorists would also infer that the markets serve no real disciplinary function. However, if I can draw your attention to the Japanese data, we calculated for two periods the percentage of companies with a negative price-to-book ratio (see Table 7.2) or negative return on assets (ROA) (see Table 7.3), and the likelihood that those would be taken over in a given year. In Japan, 20 per cent of poorly performing firms were taken over in the 2000–05 period. This rate is much higher than the US or even the UK. So one provocative conclusion is this: it may be hard to infer the economic function of the takeover market as a whole based on the style of transaction. What you often find in Japan is that the main bank, rather than rescuing companies, uses a more market-based mechanism to promote mergers to support or also to reform poorly performing companies. I don't yet have data on

Table 7.3 *Proportion of firms with low price–book ratios (less than 1), targeted in M&A (%)*

	1991–1999	2000–05
France	4	8
Germany	2	2
Japan	1	20
UK	7	8
USA	25	6

Table 7.4 *Proportion of firms with negative return on assets, targeted in M&A (%)*

	1991–99	2000–05
France	22	13
Germany	13	10
Japan	5	21
UK	18	11
USA	32	10

whether this approach is successful in terms of post-merger performance, but several Japanese studies point in this direction. Again, this topic would be an interesting area of further investigation.

My last topic area is more directly to do with employment. This is an area I've been working on for quite a while, so I very much appreciate the contribution on the UK–French comparison by Simon Deakin and Antoine Rebérioux [see Chapter 5]. Broadly speaking, in countries where shareholders are powerful, labour is weak. More recent research tries to break this down by looking at the mechanisms that link shareholder influence or shareholder power and labour. If you imagine different features of corporate governance patterns, like changes in ownership, foreign investment, giving shareholders legal rights or information disclosure, putting outsiders on the board, giving stock options or hostile takeovers: all of these different mechanisms of shareholder rights or shareholder power may have different impacts on the firm, and they may have different impacts in different countries.

In the case of Japan, we have detailed company-level data on some of this, and so we can start to differentiate some of these effects. For example, foreign institutional ownership has little direct effect on downsizing. It did for a while in the early 1990s, and there's a nice paper by Christine

Ahmadjian and Gregory Robbins (2005)[4] showing that this effect disappears over time. After a few leading companies were pressured to downsize by their shareholders, it gradually became more legitimate for Japanese firms to restructure, making the direct effect of shareholder pressure on companies disappear. What you do see is bigger effects where 'shareholder value' enters the board. Having outside directors, for example, has a large influence on choosing human resource management practices. The largest influence is in firms paying executives with stock options, which only about a third of Japanese companies do. So management plays a big role in mediating shareholder influence. If we look at who gets what in Japan, there's an interesting observation to be made. In my paper with Masahiko Aoki[5] we presented a somewhat optimistic view about employment in Japan. It is certainly right to say that the lifetime employment norm has continued and firms care about human assets, but other changes are going on under the surface. If you look at value added in the corporate sector during the different periods of growth and recession, in the 1980s or early 1990s, we see that it's growing each year by a certain percentage. The data show that from the 1980s to 1997, there is a positive-sum relationship, that employees, managers, shareholders, the government in the form of tax, and the firm are each getting a piece of the pie. Only the banks lose out, as interest payments decline. When Japan went into recession from 1997 to 2001, value added from the large corporate sector declined, but labour was not affected by that too much, plus or minus zero. So, Japanese companies were caring about their employees, directors were taking a bigger cut, banks took a big cut, shareholders stayed about even and tax payments to government went down because companies were not making much profit. But after 2001, the corporate sector was rebounding. Here the labour share continued to go down, so labour was not benefiting from this growth. Directors' salaries have been going up, and the share going to dividends has rapidly increased at nearly 35 per cent per year, although starting from a very, very low level. So I think that we can say that underlying this stability among core workers, there is a changing distribution of incomes in Japan, which Masahiko Aoki has alluded to, at least briefly.

Now, my final point is that it's a very interesting area of study to look at the impact of finance on employment, but if you look at the UK, the question arises, 'Why isn't there much political attention to this in the UK?'. One reason must be that in the UK, the financial sector *is* the industry: it almost doesn't make much sense to look at the impact of finance on industry. In the UK in 1978, manufacturing accounted for 26 per cent of jobs and the financial and business services sector accounted for 10 per cent; in 2007 manufacturing was 10 per cent and financial and business services accounted for 20 per cent of jobs, so the net gain and net loss in the two sectors was almost one-to-one. Equally, the financial sector has risen to 33 per cent of gross value added of the UK economy, so this is twice as big as any other sector. But even in the era of financialization, can finance simply replace industry?

Jean-Paul Fitoussi (OFCE – Observatoire Français des Conjonctures Économiques de l'Institut d'Études Politiques)   I can say, from the outset, that for the board, in France, or in any European country, if there is a reference model, it is the US model. What we mean by the US model is a kind of stereotyped, idealized model, and I am sure that this model has nothing to do with the American way of managing firms, but it is the reference model of all the big companies operating in Europe. This rhetoric accomplishes many purposes. One of them is, through the search for shareholder value, to make the board of directors happy and especially the CEO. Now, I'm sorry to be frank, but when I come back to the problem and its complexity, I do not believe in the concept of model. I do not believe that there exists a US model, a Japanese model, a German model or a French model. What I know through studies that have been done in other fields is that each country is specific. Each country has a set of institutions, which can be more or less coherent, and which can lead to different performances according to its coherence, but not a different performance according to the fact that it is different from another country's model.

For example, if we look at the labour market institution, there is no relationship, although hundreds of studies have been done, between the institution and economic performance. What I have seen in the contributions for this conference is that there is no relation between financial institutions and macroeconomic performance – that is, between shareholder rights in companies and economic performance. In other words we don't know what the best way to organize the institution is. The problem is very complex; it has been put very clearly by Jean Tirole and Jean-Jacques Laffont.[6] If we take a stakeholder point of view, the objective function is so complex that freedom of management is extraordinarily large, and the rent that management can capture from this 'stakeholder' organization of companies is extremely high.

Second, when we don't take into account the stakeholders – when we take the simple model of maximizing value to the shareholders – there is no one clear intertemporal profit maximization function that may lead to the same result, and the freedom of management is very wide when it has to maximize an intertemporal profit function. The problem is always, in all boards, the decision about the time horizon, the trade-off between short term and long term. It is not put that way, but it amounts to that. You can always argue that what looks like a bad decision is a very good decision in the long run, and you can always argue that the very bad policy of distributing dividends is very good for the future financing of the firm. There is clearly, on the board, before the annual assembly, always a trade-off between dividends and investment, at least from what I have seen. So here also, there is no clear objective function which can lead to the optimum management of a firm. This may explain why it is so difficult to identify a performing model of governance: if the objective function that governance has to maximize is so unclear from the outset, it will depend on whether stakeholders are taken into account or not. There are many new studies by a team in Princeton, which show that family management is better adapted to globalization than shareholder management.

Now, to return to the problem of how to take into account the conflicting interests of all the persons who have a stake in the company, including the shareholders. In trying to answer this question, I usually use the Akerlof model[7] – the theory of social custom – of which unemployment may be a consequence. Let us start from a kind of augmented Akerlof model, where the enterprise wants to be rich *and* famous. Akerlof would say that the 'and famous' is non-redundant. So here we have two objectives. They may hide behind this second objective the fact that they want to gain a supplementary market share or, as in the original Akerlof theory, that they want to be attractive to competent workers. They have to gain a reputation *vis-à-vis* competent workers, so the reputation element of the objective function also participates in increasing profit, in increasing shareholder value, and so on. So, let us assume that firms are very greedy: they want to increase both their attractivity for human capital and their market share. If one firm begins, the other firms will follow suit, otherwise they will lose market share.

Let us imagine a system, and I come to the social contract theory of Lorenzo Sacconi [see Chapter 6], where all firms are pursuing their own interest to gain market share and attract the more competent workers through this game of reputation. Then at the end of the game, we are left with a situation where reputation will play an independent role. So this is a kind of social contract where if we start at the outset with reputation as a game, we end with reputation as a real independent variable, which may substitute for the representation of a stakeholder on the board. That is telling us that everything is in a state of flux: we have not identified the best form of governance; we know that each model is specific; we know that reputation is playing an increasing role for attracting human capital and also for increasing concern about the environment. We also know that we now have rating agencies for the social climate in firms, which may give some quantification to this variable of reputation, so let us hope that in the end reputation *will* become an independent variable.

Solow   Before I open up the discussion among the people on the plat-
form, I would like to make two remarks of my own at this point. One is a
response to the question that Margaret Blair asked about whether, from
the particular course of the capital share in American industry, anything
could be deduced about the pace of institutional change in the US. I
think that would be very difficult. First, I have no doubt that Margaret's
intuition is right, and that institutional change is very slow, because, in this
respect, there are a lot of commitments that have been made – explicit or
implicit, contractual or non-contractual – and when there is a change in
external circumstances, those have to expire and be renegotiated, and that
takes a long time.

However, I don't think that looking at the behaviour of capital share is
a very good way to do that for several reasons. First, I think that the factor
'shares' is a statistic that gets more attention than it deserves. I would much
rather look at the rate of return on capital and ask how that has moved.
Second, in interpreting movements in the rate of return – and over the last
few years, up until *very* recently, profitability has been extraordinarily high
in American industry – one has to distinguish changes which have their
base in changes in technology, changes in the nature of markets, things of
that sort, from purely institutional changes, from those mechanisms that
have been established in firms for allocating the total rents amongst the
various participants. That's a very difficult thing to do. I think that there
is some reason to believe that the increase in profitability in US industry
reflects in part, not necessarily completely, a change in the determinants
of the productivity of labour and capital in US industry. That's a research
task that hasn't yet been accomplished.

The second remark I would like to make relates to shareholder primacy
or shareholder orientation. Jean-Louis Beffa and Xavier Ragot [see
Chapter 3] point out that shareholders are not all alike. They classify them
as 'passive shareholders', 'active shareholders' and 'activist shareholders':
activist shareholders being shareholders who have essentially no commitment to the enterprise at all, but who will take daily profits if they can get
them. I don't know if anyone rises to the defence of activist shareholders
– I'm not about to do that now – but if there is general agreement that
activist shareholders – very short-term profit-takers, 'in-and-outers' – are
a nuisance to the conduct of productive enterprise, then some things follow
from that. If there is nothing, or very little, good to be said about activist
shareholders, then they are a negative externality, and we've learned that
one way to treat negative externalities is to tax them.

Long ago, well, fairly long ago, the US tax code made a distinction
between short-term and long-term capital gains. The cut-off point was
six months during most of that time, and short-term gains were taxed as

ordinary income, whereas long-term capital gains were taxed at about half of that rate. In those days, tax rates were higher than they are now, so half of a high tax rate was still a high tax rate, but that distinction has been lost as part of a general lowering of tax rates. But it would be possible, if there were general agreement about the nuisance value of the activist shareholder, to have a sort of Tobin tax applied to stop transactions, equity transactions, and simply make transactions costly. It would generate revenue and discourage rapid turnover of shares. That seems to me a perfectly reasonable thing to do. Before one does that, one has to have agreement that the activist shareholder is fundamentally a nuisance rather than performing any redeeming social value in economies like ours.

I do think that in talking about shareholder primacy, one needs to realize that shareholders are different amongst themselves, not only in their degree of passiveness, activeness or activism, but in their time preferences: we speak of providing a return to shareholders, but what the corporation provides is an uncertain time profile for returns to shareholders. Now, the stock market is supposed to sum all that up in a single number, but if you believe *that*, you can believe anything. There is a real problem here in thinking of the shareholders: they should be thought of as non-homogeneous, as a heterogeneous group of people.

Blair   I agree that in principle rate of return is the right metric for measuring how well off capital is and how much of the rents it is capturing, but rate of return is so complicated by the fact that we don't know how to measure capital independently of the rate of return on capital. So, to the extent that capital value represents the discounted present value of a future stream of returns, we apply this discount factor, which means applying a rate of return that we are going to use, and *voilà* we get the value of capital. So we don't have a way to value capital independently. I don't know how it's done in the national accounts, but I don't think they make that kind of adjustment; they just treat investment capital at its cost of having been made. That wouldn't be too bad if most investments in capital were investments in physical capital that get measured in the national accounts.

Our economy has shifted dramatically towards the importance of non-physical assets, in terms of the source of value creation, but we don't measure the investments in human capital; we don't measure the creation of patents, at least not in the US; we don't measure R&D as assets, as contributions to assets, so we're missing a lot. The last time I looked at this – it jumps around, obviously, depending on the stock market, which is another reason why this is hard to do, because stock market valuations change so much – the total value as estimated by the financial markets of equity capital in the US was something like three times the book value of assets. So you've got this huge discrepancy between what the financial markets think the capital value is and what companies have recorded as the amount they have spent on capital, adjusted for depreciation. So I despair of using rate of return on capital for that particular reason. Far be it from me to argue with Bob about macroeconomic statistics: I'm going to lose that battle, so I'm not going to go there!

Jackson   If you look across countries again, you can have the same rate of return on capital growth with different underlying distributions, and that relates to the point just made, about how the stock market values capital. So if the stock market values one company at twice the level of another, the company must produce twice as much real profit in absolute terms to produce that same rate of return. Although investors within a particular economy may have the same rate of return, if you look at the underlying way it affects the firm, there's a kind of 'inflation' of assets (though not in the technical sense of 'inflation'). Since the market places a higher value, the behaviour of companies must be different to sustain that rate of return for investors. I think that's an interesting point in this macro discussion about shareholder rights increasing the level of activity in stock markets.

Fitoussi   It is difficult to have a clear interpretation of the wage share. What seems to be clear, however, is that almost everywhere the wage share decreased in the 1980s, but not so much in the 1990s. The decrease in the 1980s was more or less related to the jump in the real interest rate, which characterized the end of the 1970s and the beginning of the 1980s. So it's very difficult to make sense of the level of the wage share now, as the real interest rate is much lower than it was at the beginning of the 1980s.

Solow   I have a particular question I wanted to put to you, Gregory. What does account for the extraordinary level of M&A activity in the UK? That was the biggest single difference that I could see between any pair of numbers, and I was thinking that there must be some kind of hypothesis about that.

Jackson   A large proportion of the increase is cross-border, particularly within Europe, so the UK companies have been very successful in acquiring other companies. There are other reasons to explain the general takeover wave. A lot of it is in communications, in growing sectors, in sectors that have been deregulated. So, there are a lot of opportunities there for M&A, but it is less clear as to why UK companies are so active in doing it or so successful in doing it. One factor is the use of shares as acquisition currency, which gives UK companies an advantage, as they have historically higher rates of valuation. If you look at the case of Mannesmann and Vodaphone, it's clear that Vodaphone was a small company that took over this German giant by leveraging the institutional characteristic of higher market valuations.

Solow We're all aware of the famous Tobin–Brainard 'Q', the ratio of the stock market value of a company to the replacement cost of its assets: are you saying that the average 'Q' is higher in the UK than elsewhere in Europe?

Jackson Yes.

Solow Well, that explains one mystery by another, but it's interesting.

Jean-Louis Beffa (Saint-Gobain) [from the floor]   As someone with experience in this, I would say that it's easy to buy a UK company; it's more difficult to buy a company in other countries. The UK's for sale! The role of the chairman in the UK – I mean the non-executive chairman – is to sell the company. That's why you go to the UK. UK companies, on the other hand, are strong in acquiring companies from elsewhere. But UK companies are very easy to buy, and there's nothing political about it. At Saint-Gobain, we acquired British Plasterboard (BPB), which was a big name in the UK. That would have been a shock in other countries. Pilkington, the founder of the glass business, was acquired by a Japanese company with no reaction. The UK cares only about the City, nothing else.

Solow That's interesting, because from that point of view, the high valuation of UK companies relative to the replacement cost of assets is a demand-side phenomenon: if they are all for sale and if there are many people after them, that may drive up the market value. So it would be interesting to break down that measure of M&A activity as to the inbound and outbound sides of it: how many of the acquisitions taking place in London are of non-UK companies by UK companies, and how many are of UK companies by non-UK companies.

Jackson Certainly both, and I think that our points don't contradict each other: I have just emphasized the outgoing rather than the incoming side.

Robert Boyer (EHESS – École des Hautes Études en Sciences Sociales) [from the floor]   There seem to exist three hypotheses. The first is that shareholder value is the one best way. The second is the Hayekian model presented by Xavier Ragot: everyone should select their governance according to their activity. The third is Deakin and Rebérioux's [see Chapter 5] that national regulation plays some role in governing the impact on growth. So what are the feelings of the panellists, because you have tried to find a determinist or totally neutral adaptation? Is ownership distribution so important after all, and if it is, why? Is it at the macro level, at the level of the sectoral distribution of firms or in terms of specialization or management?

Solow Do the people sitting here have any opinion as to whether ownership matters? Is it in fact totally neutral? The world is a store. You can buy what you like, and it doesn't really matter very much? And if ownership matters, then the question is what does it matter for?

Blair What I suspect may be the case is that ownership structure may mean different things in different countries. That's one of the things that has come out of the research we have seen. So ownership structure may mean different things. But in terms of what may matter for changing institutions or in the way we think about how resources should be managed or who should get the rents, it may be that changes in ownership and turnover matter, so that it matters when there's a lot of buying and selling, because the buying and selling activity can drive the price up or down, and it may deliver a message of various types to management. Now, if ownership structure were completely stable, then it might not matter what it was. But when it is unstable, so that there is this turnover, the turnover then has the effect of creating market signals that over time certain institutions may react to.

Jackson The argument is about strategic 'fit'. I like your second proposition. In the case of Japan, for example, one may ask how you get the compatibility, or complementarity, between a market-oriented ownership structure and long-term employment, which you wouldn't expect. I think that's very precarious. If you look at the fine-grain answer in the Japanese case, corporate governance has become more market oriented, but there is some selection or adaptation or management of that process. So you have a lot of information disclosure to shareholders, and you have a lot of trading and valuation by foreign investors, but you don't have hostile takeovers. Japanese firms now use the market to M&A, but you don't have a lot of outsiders on the board. In our paper,[8] we call this a hybrid model, not just in the sense of mixing shareholder and stakeholder models, but also in the sense of selective adaptation or management of the relation to the capital market, which has a different style from what a US company would do. So I think companies are trying to find a strategic fit, or, in a way, to make ownership less relevant to what goes on inside the company than it might be under different circumstances. But I'm not sure that rules out your third possibility.

Fitoussi   I think that ownership matters – for the owner, of course! But we know that we have failure and success, whatever type of ownership we are contemplating, whether public or private. Some public firms have been very successful, others not. And some private firms, running utilities, for example, have been a failure, in the UK as in the US. On your third point, of course, ownership is relative. It is relative to the institutional world in which it is applied. I am trying to say that what is important is the coherence with the whole institutional set-up in which ownership is considered. Ownership alone is not a strong concept, except for the owner.

Solow   I said at the beginning that these are not issues I have thought much about, so my answer to Robert's question comes from what I've learned from the foregoing contributions: that ownership, or various aspects of who owns companies, turns out to be correlated with some institutional facts in a given economy. For instance, much of the emphasis in the contributions has been on correlations between the nature and structure of ownership and human resource management in companies. Interestingly, it is not training particularly, as I understand it, but other aspects of HRM. Now the management of human resources clearly matters. So if the correlation between ownership structure and these other institutional facts has anything causal about it, then ownership matters. If it doesn't have anything causal about it, then it's really up in the air, and one needs to know what the causal structure is.

Then there are of course – what Jean-Louis Beffa was describing – issues of national interest or national 'pride', that seem to turn on ownership. The example that comes to mind is probably a totally nonsensical one. You remember the enormous fuss that the American press made over the acquisition by a large Abu Dhabi corporation of rights to manage several large American ports. This was phrased in the newspapers, of course, as a matter of security against terrorism. That's no surprise, since *everything* in the American press is phrased in terms of security against terrorism, but suppose it were true. Suppose there was something to that, then that's a case in which ownership matters. It may matter to France or the US, Germany or the UK, that they are nations in which first-class civilian aircraft are produced. Why should it matter? Well, that's a deep question, and I'm not sure how to go about thinking about that. I have had years of training which lead me not to think about things like that.

Make-or-buy decisions are pure cost margin decisions, rather than any-thing else. But maybe on a national scale that is simply not true, and there are other factors at play, of which some are, so to speak, realistic, others are fantastic, and it's very hard to know which is which.

Questions from the floor I was wondering why we shouldn't also take into account the demand side of the equation, because Margaret Blair was alluding to the redistribution of rents. In fact, you can only redistribute if you have market power, so looking at competition in goods markets might be one of the constraining influences on whether one has the possibility to redistribute. A substitute for the market for corporate control in the German case has been, or at least we have pretended that it has been, a high level of competition in the goods markets, so we might wonder about the other part of the equation as well. If you have a very inelastic demand, if you have a very low level of competition, it is of course for Jean-Louis Beffa to produce a decent margin.

Solow It seems to me that the intensity of competition matters for the amount of rents, but it's not clear to me why the intensity of competition should matter as to how much of the aggregate rent associated with an enterprise gets allocated to skilled labour, unskilled labour, management, owners of capital . . . to all that. One would almost think that it might be more a matter of competition in factor markets than in product markets. I have no doubt – well that's not true, I have doubts about everything – but I don't have very much doubt that some part of the fall in the wage share in recent years has been a function of the entry into the world market of enormous pools of low-wage, unskilled and semi-skilled labour. And in just the way that the discovery of an enormous, cheap deposit of copper would depress the profits of owners of existing deposits of copper, so I should think the appearance of a large pool of low-wage, unskilled or semi-skilled labour cannot be good, at least, can only be bad, for those people who already own semi-skilled or unskilled labour, that is, many of the workers themselves. So I think that's both the supply- and the demand side answer to the question.

Blair My hunch is that that's right. I think it explains a lot about what was going on in the 1980s in the US, in the sense that in the 1970s, the return on capital was really low; real interest rates were very low. That meant that the opportunity cost for capital to be invested in corporate equities was low, and so capital investors put up with low returns on equi-ties. We saw that turn around very dramatically in the early 1980s when our central banker at the time, Paul Volcker, said he was going to drive inflation out of the market. He did so by dramatically manipulating the tools that he had available to drive up real interest rates – and real interest rates were quite high in the 1980s – which suddenly, dramatically increased the opportunity cost for financial investors to leave their investments in corporate equity when they could get 16 per cent, 14 per cent real return on government bonds. What happened then was that the financial institutions decided, 'maybe we'll go along with these so-called raiders who want to issue junk bonds that promise to pay 16, 17 or 18 per cent. We'll sell them our equity, and let them finance their purchase by buying their junk bonds, because we need a higher rate of return if we're going to keep our money invested and not pull it all out and put it in government bonds'.

I think that drove a significant amount of the restructuring that took place in the 1980s, which laid the groundwork for a kind of institutional change in which we shifted our views about what was the right way to run corporations. We shifted from an attitude that corporate managers were supposed to build institutions for the long run, to an approach that said the corporate managers' job was to get the highest price they could for shareholders as quickly as they could. That was accepted not just as a normative goal tied to the conditions of the market, but as a general rule, that we should always try to get the highest price for shareholders. And so we had a massive institutional shift that I think is now playing itself out in other parts of the world. So by the 1990s and in the first years of the twenty-first century, the impact of the tremendous increase in the availability of low-wage labour (which is now reducing), is once again giving capital a chance, even with low nominal rates of return, to capture more of the total share of output. So the institutions that were put in place to respond to one supply and demand situation, in the 1980s, are being carried over into the current environment and being applied to corporations around the world.

Fitoussi   The intensity of competition in the products market may play a role, because the problem of ill management in such a setting, the conse-quence of ill management, can be the death of the firm. So there is a strong incentive when there is very intense competition to distribute the rent in a way that is not bad for the firms – maybe.

Xavier Ragot (CNRS – French National Centre for Scientific Research) [from the floor]   One of our hypotheses in linking this corporate govern-ance issue with growth in the long run, is that there are actors with different discount factors, who can have different powers in investment decisions. These differences are amongst shareholders, and between sharehold-ers and other stakeholders. Perhaps the main point we should focus on (although this means disregarding a little bit the risk-aversion issue, which all finance is about) is, in the first order, the discount factor of various agents. What could be beneficial at the social level would be to tax, as you said, the people with the shortest discount factor, but maybe also to try to increase at the margin the power of the agent who is the most patient, which may vary from country to country. This affects the investment in implicit contracts with employees, innovation decisions, diversification of the firm: all those decisions of the firm. What we must then determine is who this marginal player is, whose power we could increase to improve the investment decision of the firm. It may be that in France some types of wage-earners could intervene more in the firm's investment decisions.

Solow That's an interesting set of questions. My late colleague Franco Modigliani had a notion about how to look at the yield curve, at the pattern of interest rates of different maturities at a given level of risk. His thought was that there are various kinds of lenders and borrowers who have, as Xavier put it, different discount rates. Modigliani used to say that their 'natural habitat' is credits or loans of different maturities, so that there was an intrinsic demand and supply for assets of a given maturity. How he could reconcile that with the arbitrage possibilities along the yield was never very clear to me. I do think that this is another way to put the issue that Xavier and Jean-Louis have raised, and that has come up occasionally in the course of this discussion, that there are agents in the market – potential owners or actual owners – who have different time preference rates, and somehow the credit market has the task of reconciling them. There is a normal way that the market could do that. If you have someone with a very high discount rate – and who therefore prefers short-term assets – then provide a lot of short-term assets, satisfy that demand until the further demand diminishes, so that at the margin you could produce some sort of equilibrium yield. But that's a very complicated set of operations, and I don't know if it can be done.

Beffa [from the floor] I would like to comment on that and qualify what I said about the UK. I said it's easy to buy in the UK, but I should have added that it's never cheap in the short term. This is also related to the structure of the UK firm: there is a diversified group of shareholders whose relationship with the company is not strong, compared, for example, to block shareholders in Germany, where the relationship is very strong. So it's easy. But then you have to justify, in the longer term, that you have made no mistake in buying the company at a price which always appears high in the short term (or the UK investors will not sell). So it's more doable because of the dispersion of capital, but it's not cheap, so you must be sure of your long term. What I'm saying is that most of the UK shareholders have a discount rate that is different from those in other countries: they are short term; they want to have the money quickly, and so they have a higher discount rate. You asked a question Bob, which I thought was very interesting in terms of what I have seen in our company: does a change in structure, and especially a rise in the demand and strength of shareholders, change something in the strategy of the company, or is it other factors? I would say, from our own experience, and because the growth rate is now generated more by the emerging countries, that in the industrialized countries, the influence of the shareholders incites you to underinvest, or to be prepared to underinvest, because you are not sanctioned for underinvesting, but for investing a bit too quickly. So in my view, the economic impact is that you are much more prudent in investing, and this is partially the reason why today there are somewhat more shortages than in the past. It is because you are pushed not to make mistakes, and you are followed by very specialized analysts who will criticize you greatly if you overinvest. So, there is an impact, but the impact is on the rate of investment in industrialized countries.

Solow That's a very interesting argument, related to the Tversky–Kahneman notion of loss aversion, that there is a fundamental dislike of loss – not simply to be offset in an expected value sense – in that if you underinvest, you have missed profit opportunities. But no one, or hardly anyone, will later on say, 'You know, you should have made that investment some years ago, because look at the profits you are forgoing'. Whereas if you overinvest, you incur actual losses, and then the hyenas gather and *that* they remember. I think there's a lot to that argument, and there have been experiments, not in that actual context, but in hypothetical conditions, by researchers in behavioural economics – by Daniel Kahneman and Amos Tversky[9] in the first instance – and it does create a rather difficult problem in evaluating income streams, because simple present-value calculations at a given rate of interest are not the right things to do if pluses and minuses count differently.

Question from the floor I would like to return to a point raised by Jean-Paul Fitoussi and Margaret Blair about the difficulty of getting the right objective function for the firm. Now, Lorenzo Sacconi seemed to have provided a way of calculating an objective function that takes into account all stakeholders, even the outside, third-party ones who experience external effects. But then there's that interesting question raised by Margaret Blair, about how you ensure that the solution is adhered to, and what happens if the environment changes. As I see it, a possible way of incorporating those points would be to allow the game to be repeated, so that deviants could be punished, and also to allow for utilities to change, whenever the environment changes. But if the environment changes – not deterministically but in a somewhat unpredictable manner – then maybe we should also account for the fact that utilities can change stochastically. In that case, it's like a repeated game, allowing for changes in utilities, but also allowing for that stochastic change in utilities. I would think that is a way to go about it. My background is in evolutionary games, and I think that would be a good framework for this.

Blair   I like the idea in principle, although I'm not familiar or comfortable enough with that particular approach to modelling to know for sure how this works. But the problem is, once you have sunk investment, you can't really start the game over from the beginning. You have to start from where you are, and if you allow the game to be 'repeated', it isn't really repeated. It starts over from a new place, and that opens up all the opportunities for opportunism that created the problem in the first place. So I don't know how you'd get around that in your approach to modelling. That's my gut reaction to this.

Solow   I don't see how the repeated game idea can be applied, can be made real in these circumstances, which is what Margaret was saying. I would go along with Margaret Blair on this: if only economic life were a repeated game, then the theory would be a little different. The trouble is, it's not. I don't see how one could have a virtual repeated game.

Fitoussi   You can have that, once the investment is done: you have a repeated game amongst the stakeholders.

Solow   But this was Margaret's point: it's not quite repeated, because the second time around, the initial conditions are different, in that something has already happened, in the real world.

Lorenzo Sacconi (University of Trento) [from the floor]   The fact that the environment changes is the basis of this kind of thinking, because why should the contract be incomplete? It is because some events are unforseeable and this is because the environment changes. If everything is stable, we should more or less know it. So in a sense, contracts connecting stakeholders to the firm are incomplete, because the environment may change. So I think that the cooperative bargaining solution to the relationship between the different stakeholders should provide not exactly a complete contract that will be applicable in the presence of new states of the world, but exactly constitutional principles that are typically the general and abstract principles that provide for something that can be saved, even if the environment changes. So there is a general principle, for example, for distributing the rent, but not *exactly* distributing the rent between the different stakeholders. The normative model must be used as a gut feeling for the incompleteness of contracts that is due to the changing environment. Of course, if the changes are so strong that the players are not the same in the second round, this may be a change too great to be captured by a stable abstract general principle.

For clarity's sake, remember how David Kreps[10] attempted to explain corporate culture in terms of general principles that are able to make possible reputation games in the situation in which there are unforeseen contingencies. This is exactly the same problem. The 'Aoki-like' model of the cooperative firm with different kinds of stakeholders should provide a principle for regulating conflicts among the different stakeholders that can be used when we discover changes in the environment that make concrete contracts incomplete. In this sense, I agree with the suggestion that the game can be repeated, because the real-life game is repeated, and the principle says in every new situation how to define the commitment that is used in order to accumulate repetition. So you will accumulate repetition if you comply with the general principle as it is specified in the new situation. This is more or less the idea of repeating the game in this context.

Solow   There is a question about incomplete contracts that has puzzled me, so let me ask the people here who know about this sort of thing. Is it possible to imagine something intermediate, between incomplete contract and complete contract: namely an incomplete contract with a specified arbitration mechanism for cases that are not covered, the unforeseen, unforeseeable cases?

From the floor   That's corporate law, and the board of directors!

Solow   Yes, but the board of directors is only one party, so to speak, to this arrangement, and there are other stakeholders . . ., but I suppose it could be taken that way.

Blair   That's the concept I talked about in my team production work. The board of directors doesn't necessarily have to be a part of the team. There may be board members who are senior executives in the company or major shareholders who are part of the team. But one of the stylized facts I have seized upon (and I don't actually know how applicable it is) is that in a lot of venture-capital type organizations – and I got this from a study I saw on the pharmaceutical/biotech kinds of enterprises – the typical structure of the board was not what you would imagine if you think of the agency theory as the right way to understand corporate governance. In that case, I think you would predict that the venture capitalist would control most of the seats on the board, if not all the seats on the board, because the venture capitalist is the one who put up the capital, whereas the entrepreneur or the person who came up with the idea are recognized as being protected by contract. In fact, what you see on the boards of these types of companies is the following: a typical size is seven; two of the members of the board will be taken from the senior management of the firm, two will be from the venture capitalists and three will be recognized outsiders who know something about the industry, sometimes academic scholars who have pushed that technology to the forefront. So in effect, the deciding vote is put in the hands of a neutral party, who doesn't have any particular reason to be aligned with either of the others, and that's conceptually what I think the board of directors is about, placing the decision making in an institution which is by structure designed to be neutral.

Beffa [from the floor]   What new instructions should we give to management? In management, we know two things. First, decisions have to be approved by the board of directors and sometimes by the assembly of shareholders. Second, we have an accounting system where we pay taxes. We pay a local tax to the town, which is a stakeholder around us, and to the government, which provides skilled employees. If we want to have a discussion with our employees, we give a bonus if the results are good. We allow them to be shareholders at a discount. Practically speaking, in the model of Lorenzo Sacconi, what do you change in the way that you are controlled by the board of directors? And second, do you change the accounting system where the job of the CEO is to get a net profit? What do you change in the new design of stakeholder negotiations or new contracts?

Blair   The CEO gets his position by delegated power from the board, at least that's the statutory arrangement in the United States, and in the US the shareholders have very little direct influence over that, with respect to their position *qua* shareholders. Now if the shareholder also happens to be in senior management, or happens to sit on the board, or holds six out of eight seats on the board, then obviously that shareholder has special influence. But the statutory arrangement is that the board is meant to be the decision maker, not the shareholders, and my argument is that that is simply a description of how corporate law works. It is not intended to suggest that the board should make one decision or another. I'm inclined to agree in a sense with Bob Solow's idea that to the extent that other parties are protected by their contracts, the contracts have to be satisfied. And it's only in the space in which there is surplus that is generated that isn't already contracted away that the management has the discretion, overseen by the board, to award some of that to research institutes and universities, to improvements in the healthcare plan for retirees, to increases in their recruiting budget, or to make some of that go into higher dividends or share buybacks. They make the decision about what to do with that surplus. That's their function, and I'm not arguing that that changes anything. I'm just saying that's the way it works. The description by the finance theorists that the board of directors is the agent of the shareholders is not accurate. It's not justified economically, and it's not an accurate description of the way the law works and the way the board institution works.

Solow   Jean-Louis, I would have thought that governments decide for you what the accounting system must be like, and insist on ordering and on rules that you are not allowed to violate without being punished if you're found out. And that's precisely the response to the possibility of choosing an accounting system which is to the benefit of one of the stakeholders. That is forbidden.

Question from the floor   Professor Sacconi suggested earlier that the level of effort by the owners of human capital in an economy is related to total macroeconomic output. Then he said that a sense of trust in the fundamental fairness of the decisions when circumstances change is correlated with effort: that if you do something to undermine the trust that people will be treated fairly when circumstances change, you therefore threaten the productivity of a national economy or a large corporation. So he was throwing up a flag, it seems to me. If that's correct – that rebuilding trust after it's been destroyed is an extraordinarily difficult, if not impossible, enterprise – then you would want to be alert to changes that threaten trust, and the growth in shareholder power may be doing that. So I ask the panel: how would we know in advance that we were threatening the trust on which effort is based? And do you see any indication that the growing returns to financial capital today in the developed world, in France, in the US, might be nearing that fatal mark?

Solow   A few years ago in a cartoon in the New Yorker magazine, there was a man sitting behind a desk who was obviously a potential employer, and a man standing in front of the desk who was obviously a potential

employee, and the man behind the desk was saying, 'We offer no loyalty
to our employees, but of course we don't expect any from them'. And the
natural answer to that question, from an economist who does the kind of
work I do, is that one of the jobs of the price and wage system is to diminish
the dependence on trust. For instance, there is a whole body of model building which goes along the following lines: 'It is impossible for the employer
to monitor completely the amount of effort that each employee is putting
out. On the other hand, the employer can do some monitoring. So there is
some probability that an employee who doesn't do a full day's job will be
found out. And in order for that mechanism to work, the firm has to pay a
wage higher than the market wage normally available, so that there is a cost
to the employee of being found out'. You can calculate that kind of thing. It
has a macroeconomic effect on the volume of employment if it's an accurate
representation of what happens. So – but this is just a personal preference –
I have a distaste for making too much depend on unmeasurable quantities
in one's thinking. But I also think the economic system has the same aversion that I do and tries to find mechanisms which substitute for things like
trust. And I've just given you an example of such a mechanism.

Masahiko Aoki (Stanford University) [from the floor]   I'd like to respond
to the question on the reputation game a little bit. In the first stage, from
a state of ignorance, people put themselves in different positions and so
forth, and some kind of cooperative game solution, a best solution, comes
out. Then the question is how it can be implemented. If a game of real
life is played only once, then the problem of opportunities, opportunistic behaviour, and so forth, comes in, so the best thing you can do is a
second-best solution. And then the solution proposed by many people
is a reputation game. People might have some altruism or other capacity
to empathize with other people, and these are things that experimental
economics has resolved.

   If we consider only the transaction in the economic domain, then, as
you say, the environment changes, and people are rather quick to exploit
this kind of situation – that is, if you are confined solely to the domain of
economic exchange, particularly transactions that are not repeated. But I
think we are actually facing not only a domain of economic exchange, but
a domain of social exchange and a domain of political exchange. So how
these games in other domains also affect the transaction in the economic
domain is probably an important question. For Paul Samuelson in 1948,
in the *Foundations of Economic Analysis*, trust, norms and all these kinds
of things are determined outside of economics, and should be treated as
given. Then recently Avner Greif and Michihiro Kandori and others have
tried to explain the norms more endogenously in the economic domain: if

somebody defaults on the contract, then others stop contracting with that person, thus excluding that person from this domain.

When I look, however, at, say, the commons domain where it is very difficult to exclude 'sharks', the question of how the deviant behaviour is restrained cannot be explained by economic games alone. People are also engaged in the social domain, particularly people who use the same commons repeatedly. In social interactions, if you do wrong things, people criticize you and say bad things, affecting your emotional payoff. This game is a bit different from the economic exchange where people try to make exchanges in order to satisfy their own materialistic needs. In a social exchange domain, they try to affect the emotional consequences of other people. If I have some kind of social message from some of you, then I have to return something to you, and so forth.

In the same way, politically, the government decides the tax, for example, and if the people think that the tax scheme is bad, they will try to influence the government, so the government loses support and the tax code changes. But these changes take time compared to changes in economic exchanges, so I think that for the social sciences it may be better to broaden the perspective a bit: the social exchange domain, the political exchange domain and the economic exchange domain all interact. This is an issue to be discussed. I think that even the social and political exchanges can be analysed within the framework of a game. I also think that the social interaction is different from a physical phenomenon, in the sense that people have to form some kind of expectations about how the other people will react. On the basis of these expectations, people will try to do the best thing. In that way, politics, sociological interactions and economic exchanges all accompany each other in a game framework. Although the rules of the game, the set of instruments, are different, and payoff functions may be different, I think this is probably the way to properly approach how the game of real life is going to be played.

NOTES

1. Gregory Jackson was at King's College London at the time of the conference, 'Does Company Ownership Matter?', 29–30 November 2007. He is now Professor of Business and Society at the University of Bath.
2. Deakin, S., P. Lele and M. Siems (2007), 'The evolution of labour law: calibrating and comparing regulatory regimes', *International Labour Review*, **146**, pp. 133–62.
3. Siems, M. (2008), 'Shareholder protection around the world ("Leximetric II")', *Delaware Journal of Corporate Law*, **33**, pp. 111–47.
4. Ahmadjian, C.L. and G.E. Robbins (2005), 'A clash of capitalisms: foreign shareholders and corporate restructuring in 1990s Japan', *American Sociological Review*, **70**, pp. 451–71.

5. Aoki, M. and G. Jackson (2008), 'Understanding an emergent diversity of corporate governance and organizational architecture: an essentiality-based analysis', *Industrial and Corporate Change*, **17** (1), pp. 1–27.
6. Laffont, J.J. and J. Tirole (1993), *A Theory of Incentives in Procurement and Regulation*, Cambridge, MA: MIT Press.
7. Akerlof, G. (1970), 'The market for "lemons": quality uncertainty and the market mechanism', *Quarterly Journal of Economics*, **84** (3), pp. 488–500.
8. Aoki and Jackson (2008); see note 5.
9. Kahneman, D. and A. Tversky (1979), 'Prospect theory: an analysis of decision under risk', *Econometrica*, **47** (2), pp. 263–92.
10. Kreps, D. (1990), 'Corporate culture and economic theory', in J. Alt and K. Shepsle (eds), *Perspectives on Positive Political Economy*, Cambridge: Cambridge University Press.

Index